To alicia:

For the GateKeepers
in the Kingdom!

Be Blessed as you
read these stories

See p. 243

THE CALL
TO MISSIONS

LIVING THE BOOK OF ACTS

a book by Brad Guice

foreword by David Wilkerson

large family, living in one room roadside shanty
Mumbai / India

THE CALL
TO MISSIONS

over 60 testimonies of missionaries
from around the world

photography and book by
Brad Guice

foreword by
David Wilkerson

LIVING THE BOOK OF ACTS

Editorial and book design by Brad Guice with Lou Morales, designer and missionary
Original design consultations and design layout ideas with 3rd Edge - www.3rdedge.com
Frankie Gonzalez and Nick Schmitz, designers.

Cover Photo: shot in a rural mountain village near Medellin, Colombia. The majority of the photographs in this book were taken with a handheld Hasselblad 500C/M medium square format camera, while using a 60mm or 80mm Zeiss Distagon lens. The film used was Kodak B/W Professional Tri-X 320, in 220 roll film size.

Some of the names of people in the testimonies were changed for their protection. Several of the testimonies were transcribed and edited from tape recorded interviews. All testimonies used with permission of the contributors.

Some paper and textured backgrounds in this book purchased through stock photo agencies
All other photography contained in this book by © Brad Guice - All Rights Reserved

For Worldwide Distribution
Printed in China

ISBN 978-1-58169-379-9

Evergreen Press, P.O. Box 191540, Mobile, AL 36619
800-367-8203
christian-publishing.net and evergreenpress.com

I personally stand by all the testimonies in this book as being true. I know almost all of the contributors personally and was a witness to most of these testimonies and miracles. God has greatly used the contributors of this book to advance His kingdom through their lives and ministries. I honor all of these individuals for their selfless servanthood to our Lord and Savior, Jesus Christ.

Unfortunately individuals are able to backslide in their walks with God and even take on different doctrines. Inasmuch as these testimonies are true, if a contributor takes a course with his life and ministry that is not acceptable by normal biblical standards, their actions should not in any way affect or be a stain or blemish of any kind on the other contributing ministries or individuals that generously contributed to this book, or to this book in general.

Sincerely - Brad Guice

God—May You be gloried through this book!

Dedication

to all missionaries
Thank you for unselfishly
laying down your lives for the sake of "The Call"

to all those about to be called
This book was birthed of the Holy Spirit for you.
I'm excited for you. May God use you
tremendously for His glory.

to my wife
Lisa
Without you, this book wouldn't have been possible.
Thank you for all your support and lifting up my arms
throughout this entire project.

to my children
Phoebe and Parker
I leave this book as a legacy of my own love for Jesus Christ to you.
In these pages you will see God's heart for the world.
You will experience His love, grace, faithfulness, and power.
Always believe in Him, trust Him, and serve Him.

Table of Contents

Romanian Shepherd
Ocna Mureš

Foreword

Dearly Beloved:

Brad Guice is an anointed servant of God with a unique calling: he is a missionary photojournalist.

When I consider the gifts Brad has brought to the kingdom of God, I am simply amazed. It's not just that Brad's photographs are stunning. It is the clear and powerful message they speak. The photos and messages simply cannot be ignored. There is nothing typical in these pages.

First, Brad's images reflect the Father's heart of love. Each picture gets inside the very heart of the subject Brad is photographing. The eyes alone reveal an entire world of need, hunger, and gratitude, conveying both the hard reality of deprivation and also great joy and compassion.

Second, each of Brad's photos issues a powerful missionary call. The images you see here pull you in with their subjects—and transport you to areas of desperate need throughout the world. I believe as you peruse these pages, you'll find yourself moved and compelled. And you may ask the Lord, "Jesus, what would you have me to do?" If so, Brad will have fulfilled his calling.

I believe the book you hold in your hands, *The Call to Missions: Living the Book of Acts,* is one of a kind. It is a modern-day look at the Great Commission as told by missionaries themselves. None of the missionaries appears in these pictures, however. Every photograph is of the people who are ministered to, those in need, and those who have come to know Jesus.

The testimonies offered here, in combination with Brad's photographs, are powerful. Together they provide a voice for multitudes who are voiceless.

They also tell a story of God's love for the hurting as few books can.

I thank the Lord for Brad's servant-heart in bringing a hurting world to our doorstep and for taking us to a world God desires to reach. Surely God will use this unique book to stir the heart of many who hope to make a difference in a world crying for help.

I know many times Brad was tempted to give up his mission, and the tears and frustration kept him on his knees. He is well-known in his field, and it would have been convenient for him to give up the call.

From a background of over nineteen years of missions work, and now, after eight years of travail and perseverance, this work is finished. The fruit of his labors may not be fully revealed in a few short years, but in time it will go on impacting lives in college and home libraries, in Bible schools, and in missionary societies around the world.

Thank you, Brad, for this amazing book.

In Christ,
DAVID WILKERSON

In Memory of
DAVID WILKERSON
May 19, 1931 - April 27, 2011
founding pastor: Times Square Church, NYC
founder: World Challenge, Inc.
founder: Please Pass the Bread
founder: Teen Challenge
author: The Cross and the Switchblade
over 50 million copies sold worldwide
loved and missed by millions the world over
www.davidwilkerson.org

overcrowded youth prison
St. Petersburg, Russia

Preface

In 1991 while living in New York City after having had a successful commercial photography career, I was at the lowest point of my life. I had gotten myself deeply involved in the fast-paced nightclub scene of New York City. And I was struggling with an extremely bad drug addiction to crack cocaine. It had ruined my life and career. I had given up all hope of recovery. I was selling and pawning everything I owned to buy more drugs. I was visiting crack houses in dangerous neighborhoods. I had tried everything to quit but could not.

I went to drug rehabs, outpatient programs, cocaine anonymous, and more. I actually thought I would die as a drug addict. One night when I had no hope left, I cried out to God with all my heart. It was truly amazing how God saved me that night—His Holy Spirit came down and touched me in a dramatic way and instantly and permanently delivered me from my major drug addiction. That night I radically discovered Jesus was real! God showed me that through His Son Jesus Christ, He was able to forgive me of my sins and deliver me from my addiction.

While I was not sure what to do next, as I was saved in my loft all alone, a friend led me to Times Square Church under founding pastor David Wilkerson. I knew instantly I had found my home. They were in the beginning stages of starting a missions' program and needed a photographer to document their trips. I reluctantly went on my first trip to Russia where we worked in and visited orphanages and children's camps. God grabbed a hold of my heart on that very first trip. I saw Him in everything that we did, especially helping the orphans, the poor, the lost, the "least" of this world. After that trip, I was hooked on missions' work. I started to volunteer to be part of every trip the church was scheduled to go on.

On a few of the first trips I went on, we worked with orphanages in Romania, war widows in Croatia, refugees in Bosnia and Kosovo, youth prisons and glue addicts in Russia. We did medical outreaches and witnessed demon possession in Guyana, worked with street kids and AIDS orphans in Mozambique, glue addicts in Colombia, saw genocide in Rwanda, and ministered to refugees in Sudan and Uganda. I was witnessing firsthand God's heart and love for every lost and hurting soul in this world. I saw His active involvement, and miracles were happening in front of my eyes. I desired to be as active as possible in missions.

I came back to the States and shared what I witnessed with my friends and employees who were not Christians. I realized that my stories sounded crazy and impossible to them. I had a desire to share these stories with the whole world but did not know how. Christ was larger than life to me, and He was doing a deep work in my own heart.

In 2004, after moving to New Jersey years earlier with my wife to start a family, God gave me a dream that I owed Him my life. I knew that He was claiming my life for His service and fulltime ministry while asking me to lay down my life in His hands! After reading the scripture, "But seek first the kingdom of God and His righteousness, and all these things shall be added to you" (Matthew 6:33 NKJV), I bowed to my knees, laid my life in His hands, and prayed for His total will upon the rest of my life.

To make a long story short, soon after that prayer He birthed this book! I immediately laid down an embarrassing amount of fleeces in which He confirmed all of them—sometimes through dramatic circumstances. I knew He was calling me to write a book on missions! I knew immediately that it should be a testimonial book combined with the photographs God had given me on the mission field.

I did not know that it would take me more than eight years to complete and several more trips around the world, but it is now done. I have been obedient to that call. It is now many years later and He has taken me on some 80 missions trips to approximately 50 different countries. I visited every corner of this troubled and hurting world while capturing environmental portraits and images of the human condition in the most extreme of times. All along while meeting, traveling with, and working alongside some of the most amazing missionaries and humanitarian aid workers, I got to experience firsthand their ministries and the calling God had placed upon their lives. I was also seeing and experiencing God's love for His creation and His desire to reach every lost and hurting soul on earth.

Besides learning that we should all show God's love through our actions and our lives, I know that the most important question that each and every person on this earth needs to answer is, "Who is Jesus Christ?" I am here to spend the rest of my life and with every breath that I take proclaiming that He is the Son of God, the King of Kings, Lord of Lords, Creator and Redeemer, our Lord and our Savior, the Messiah!

May this book take you on a journey where you too will meet Jesus and see God's love for His creation and His deep desire for every soul on this earth to be reconciled back to Himself. May you too be inspired to be part of His Great Commission!

Sincerely,
BRAD GUICE
photographer and author

Acknowledgments

I want to thank *GOD* for birthing this book and giving me the honor of serving Him through the writing and compiling of it. I pray that it pleases Him and He uses it for His glory.

To *LISA* my wife, what can I say to someone I love so much? God birthed this project in front of both of us, and you have been a wonderful helpmate throughout its creation. Many of the ideas for this book you contributed. You gave me so much encouragement at times when I was down and depressed and the end was not in sight. This book could not have been possible without you and your support!

I thank *DAVID WILKERSON,* who before his death believed in this project. His words of confirmation were a huge inspiration for me to complete it. His godly, laid down life was an inspiration for millions of people around the world. Being part of his ministries is a great honor. Thank you, pastor Dave, for all that you did and the incredible legacy you left behind. May this book help to continue that legacy and inspire many for His glory.

CARTER CONLON, God confirmed this book through your sermon "A double portion of the Lord." Thank you for teaching that the heart of God is with the poor, for being a missions minded pastor, and for teaching that the greatest of all is the servant. It has been a pleasure and an honor serving under your ministry. Thank you for all your help and support.

NEIL RHODES, for your encouraging words at the beginning of this project when I first showed you the book proposal. You inspired me not to compromise. I have remembered your words throughout this project. I have made this book a pure offering back to the Lord. Thank you for always being there for me and showing by example your own willingness and heart to go on the mission field.

BETTINA MARAYAG, it has been a long journey from the start of a missions program. Thank you for being such a great friend and for all your help and friendship over such a long period of time, and for believing in this project.

ELISABETH ELLIOT and LARS GREN, thank you for generously contributing one of Elisabeth's writings. Elisabeth, you have been one of the most inspirational people in missions in this last century. Thank you for your ministry, kindness, and giving heart.

DR. PAUL MEIER, thank you so much for everything. It was great meeting you through such a divine appointment. You were an answer to one of many of my prayers during the journey of this book. We were meant to be friends, and you are a blast to hang out with. Thank you for your editing skills, encouragement, mentorship, generosity, and guidance.

RON PEARCE, for opening your arms to me. Traveling with you is so much fun. You have always been someone I looked up to and admired in the world of missions. Your help has been greatly appreciated. I have learned so much from you. Your passion for missions is unmatched. I hope we will team up together many more times in the future.

JOHN WEAVER, what can I say to thank you enough for inviting me to experience your "Extreme Calling." I was able to see and experience things that most people only dream of. You have shown me what it really means to give up everything for a calling and watch God give you back so much more in return. John—you, Jeanne, and the kids are always in my prayers. God's blessings upon you and to quote you…always remember, "The best is yet to come!"

RICK & KIM HAGANS, the two of you and your kids are the greatest! You bring Technicolor to this Christian faith, always giving of yourselves to everyone around you. Rick, you are a living example of 'being all things to all people'. What a wonderful example you are for so many. Thank you for being close friends and for all your help.

IRVIN RUTHERFORD, for taking me under your wing, inviting me to travel around the world with you, teaching me, and letting me experience so much. You are more than a friend; you and your missionaries and missions team are family.

ROGER HAYSLIP, for taking such a special interest in this project. You have no idea how much you helped me with your advice, in seeking publication, and your overall encouragement. Thank you for always being there for me.

TREG MCCOY, you have greatly inspired and encouraged me to finish this book. It has been a lot of fun traveling together, and I thank you for running the TSC Mission's Department so wonderfully and for all the help you have forwarded to me through it.

TAMMY SHANNON, thank you for just giving of your time, efforts, advice, and expertise in publishing when I really needed it.

BOB STEGEMANN, you are one of the special people I met along the way in compiling of this book. I love your heart for God and thank Him for introducing us. Thank you for taking me to Ecuador and into the Amazon rainforest—what an incredible experience! Your ministry of teaching at Bible colleges around the world and ordaining native pastors is a true blessing and a wonderful fulfillment to the Great Commission.

TOM LARKIN, for inviting me to travel along with you for World Aid New York. You hold a special place in my heart. I enjoyed all of our long talks with each other. God has done wonderful things through you. Great things are yet to come.

BRENT HIGGINS and WALKER DEAN MOORE, again I want to thank two very special people I met on the journey of this book project. Thank you for your commitment to missions. Your efforts to inspire young people to get involved in missions is incredible. I pray for God to bless your wonderful ministry.

CHUCK DAVIDSON, special thanks for someone that I consider to be one of the world's best art directors. You have been a creative inspiration for over 20 years of my photography and advertising career. You have always pushed me and inspired me to do great things. Your heart is bigger than the Grand Canyon when it comes to helping people. Thank you for developing my eye for photography, layout,

and design, and my heart to try to make a difference in this world.

JANICE MOSES, my commercial photography agent, for sticking with me through thick and through thin. Especially when I was a drug addict many years ago. You have seen firsthand through me how God can change a life. You have been an important part of my life journey. I thank you for being so supportive of me and this project, and most of all for your loyalty and friendship throughout the years.

KATHI JONES, thank you for your organizing skills and for keeping great records for me throughout this project. A tremendous amount of information was gathered. God certainly brought you in my time of need. Your help has been invaluable.

THOMAS BUSCH, LAURIE SANFILIPPO, and KATHI JONES, thank you for being my "go to" people in editing testimonies all along the way.

FRANKIE GONZALES and NICK SCHMITZ at 3rd Edge Communications for all your initial design ideas, help, and consultations.

LOU MORALES, for all your design talents and having such a wonderful heart for this project. Thank you for coming through for me in a pinch, and all the long hours you put into the initial and final layouts.

Last but not least, I thank EVERYONE who contributed a testimony for trusting me with your stories. This book would not have been possible without you. The response was amazing. Only God could have brought together so many people for a common purpose as this. There were many testimonies that I was unfortunately not able to fit into this book. I am so grateful to all that supported this project. May this book encourage and inspire many through your faithfulness.

A special thank you to all,
BRAD GUICE

13

WELCOME TO THE GREAT COMMISSION

Imagine being on the same mountain with Jesus and His now eleven disciples as Jesus stood in front of them in all of His resurrected glory. What a sight it must have been…

…with the disciples worshiping Him, and Jesus proving to them that He is their risen Savior, putting an end to all of their doubts and fears. Then He speaks with all the importance of someone sharing His very last words, shortly before He ascends to heaven:

"All authority in heaven and on earth has been given to me. Therefore go and make disciples of all nations, baptizing them in the name of the Father and of the Son and of the Holy Spirit, and teaching them to obey everything I have commanded you. And surely I am with you always, to the very end of the age" (Matthew 28:18-20, NIV).

The disciples had witnessed the risen Lord, and they had been taught and trained by Him very well. This was graduation day, and they were no longer disciples—they had become apostles. They were being sent forth to go to "all the nations."

This is the Great Commission! This one command by our Lord has motivated multitudes of people over the centuries to lay down their lives and go to the ends of the earth to answer this Call.

This is still our command today for all who know Jesus; this is for each and every one of us to answer, whether it is sharing about Christ in our own homes, neighborhoods, communities, or going to far away nations. Very few people are great pastors, speakers, or evangelists, but God equips all of us with certain gifts to be used for His glory in answering the Great Commission.

The mission field is where the word of God is tested and a believer's faith gets strengthened. It is a place where God makes miracles happen as the individuals who answer this Call step out in faith, trusting Him to lead them and meet them in their needs and trials. They stand firm in their faith in times of extreme adversities and in the sharing of His gospel. They are truly living the Book of Acts.

I have traveled all over the world spending time with the people that are answering this Call today. They are surprisingly normal people just like you and me, with very little to give of themselves except an overflowing heart filled with a love for Jesus. The difference is that they have taken that step of faith to answer the Call.

They are true servants of God, not caring so much for their own welfare but focusing on sharing God's love with the people they are reaching out to. I have witnessed their humble actions firsthand as they give themselves to the homeless, the poor, the sick, and the dying, while sometimes putting their own lives in danger in the process. I have seen missionaries take off their own shoes and coats on a cold night to put them on a freezing and hungry street child. I have seen them spend their last money on food for the starving. They take no thought for themselves but only show love for the hurting souls they are helping, with full faith that God will take care of their own needs. They are true servants of God, reaching out with His love and sharing the faith that they know will give eternal life and joy to hurting souls this side of heaven.

I have had the wonderful opportunity to work with medical doctors after the devastating earthquake in Haiti, witness missionaries dig out people's homes in New Orleans after Hurricane Katrina, build homes in Indonesia after the tsunami, help dying AIDS victims in Africa, teach forgiveness after the Rwandan holocaust, help the Sudanese refugees reestablish their lives, set up medical outreaches in the most diseased stricken areas of the world, and open orphanages to help with the tragedy of the AIDS epidemic that has been the cause of millions of street children in Africa. I have met believers that have been beaten, persecuted and their families killed for their faith. I also had the honor of meeting and spending time with a missionary that was killed; he had counted the cost of his Calling and paid the ultimate price for living a life of serving God while helping others.

At this time in history with great man-made disasters, natural disasters, economic crisis, famine, disease, war, and human need at a level that cannot be overlooked any more by the compassionate heart of a believer. I believe God is calling all of us to action. I also believe a great Harvest is coming, and we are all being called to be ready and to be involved in it.

It is my prayer that this book strengthens the faith of all you believers who read it—that you see God's love for each and every soul in this world and that God places a call upon many hearts to go into the nations. May it also motivate us all to do whatever we can in answering the Call of the Great Commission, while reaching out to the needs of this hurting world and the communities in which we live. I challenge all of us to put our faith in action. If we cannot go, then give. If we cannot give, then pray. "The Call to Missions" is reaching the world, if need be, one soul at a time.

WELCOME TO THE GREAT COMMISSION!

BRAD GUICE
photographer, editor, and author

The Great Commission

OF CHRIST TO HIS DISCIPLES

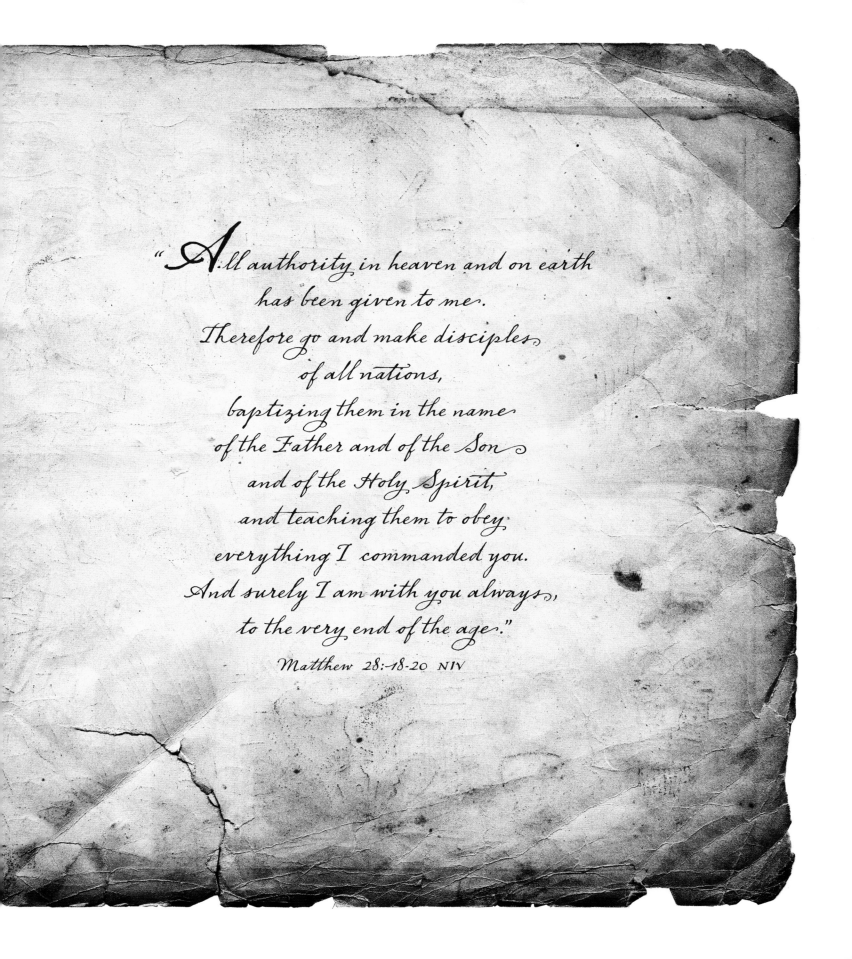

"All authority in heaven and on earth
has been given to me.
Therefore go and make disciples
of all nations,
baptizing them in the name
of the Father and of the Son
and of the Holy Spirit,
and teaching them to obey
everything I commanded you.
And surely I am with you always,
to the very end of the age."

Matthew 28:18-20 NIV

God's Word says, "Greater love has no one than this, that he lay down his life for his friends." *John 15:13 NIV*
God loves us so much that He gave us His very life.

He gave us His Son Jesus,
the greatest gift He could possibly give us.
That's how much He loves you and me.

This is the gospel of Jesus Christ, "the good news":
Jesus died on the cross for the forgiveness
of our sins, and He was buried and rose again
on the third day so that salvation is
available to all people through Him.

He said to them, "Go into all the world
and preach the good news
to all creation." *Mark 16:15 NIV*

"But God demonstrates his own love
for us in this: While we were still sinners,
Christ died for us." *Romans 5:8 NIV*

Jesus said, "So now I am giving you a new commandment: Love each other. Just as I have loved you, you should love each other.
Your love for one another will prove to the world that you are my disciples." John 13:34-35 NLT

"Three things will last forever— faith, hope, and love—and the greatest of these is love." 1 Corinthians 13:13 NLT

"Whoever does not love does not know God, because God is love." 1 John 4:8 NIV

His Heart
FOR MISSIONS WORK

"Lord, when did we see You
hungry and feed You,
or thirsty and give You drink?
When did we see You a stranger
and take You in,
or naked and clothe You?
And the King will answer and say to them,
'Assuredly, I say to you, inasmuch as you
did it to one of the least of these
My brethren, you did it to Me.'"

Matthew 25:37-38, 40 NKJV

✝

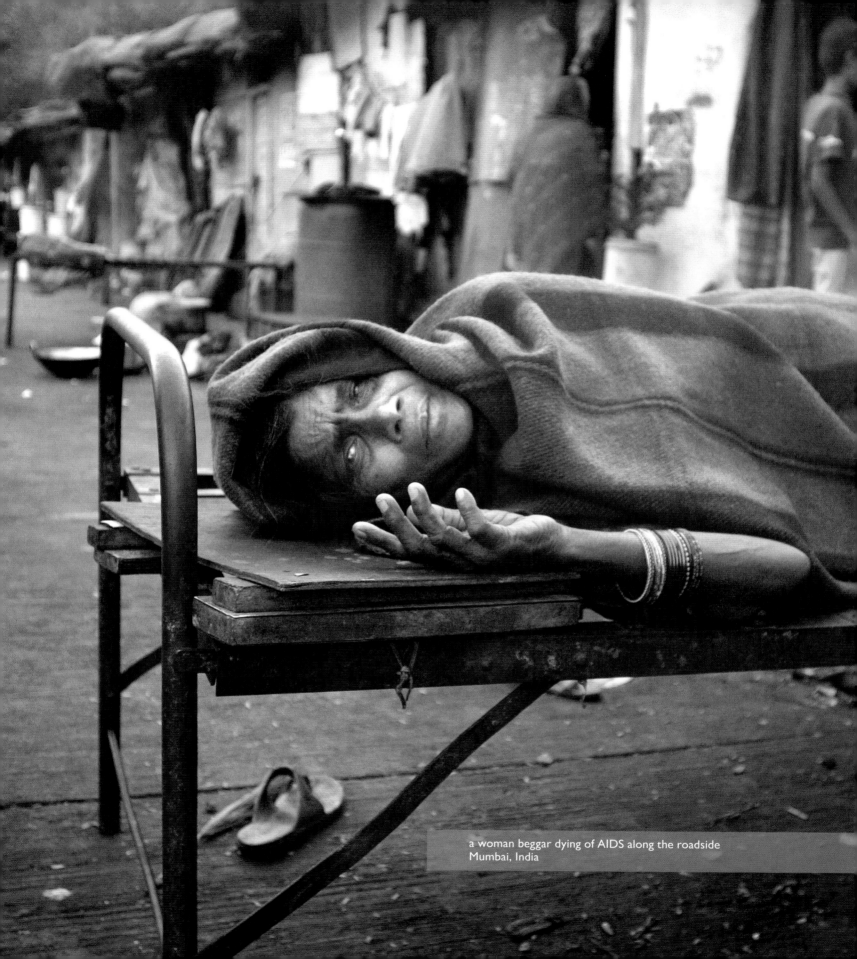

a woman beggar dying of AIDS along the roadside
Mumbai, India

At the Right Hand of the Poor

CARTER CONLON
Senior Pastor
Times Square Church, NYC

So many people today are looking for purpose and fulfillment in their Christian experience. "Where is Jesus?" they ask, in the midst of all that declares itself to be His and of Him.

I must tell you that I have found Christ and His life in a place that He has never left. Psalms 109:31 states: "For he shall stand at the right hand of the poor, to save him from those who condemn him" (NKJV).

Consider for a moment the ministry of Jesus Christ. From the perspective of heaven, sharing life and glory with His Father (John 17:24), from before the foundation of the world, He saw our need. You and I were without resources, without truly victorious lives or lasting hope. He came to us because we had no way to get back to Him. He faced our accuser, and with the sacrifice of His own life gave to us the strength to stand—believing God for another and a better day!

"I have set the Lord always before me: because he is at my right hand, I shall not be moved. Therefore my heart is glad, and my glory rejoiceth: my flesh also shall rest in hope" (Psalms 16:8-9).

With His own blood, Jesus purchased for Himself a peculiar people (Titus 2:14). In an "every man for himself" society, those who belong to Christ are not marching away from, but rather toward the mountains of human need in our world. They possess inward resources that do not cower before the magnitude of the task. Jesus calls these people His Church.

"Then said Jesus to them again, Peace be unto you: as my Father hath sent me, even so send I you" (John 20:21).

The heart of God beats within this earthly Body of Christ. An enabling love, which caused God to give His only begotten Son, moves in them and through them.

My story began with just a little seed of caring springing to life in my heart. Years of self-focus had made me dull to most needs other than my own. Jesus promises new life—His life—which leads those who are His into that which concerns Him. How fulfilling it is to know Christ with the intimacy that allows us to look away from ourselves and walk with Him where He truly is!

"If any man serve me, let him follow me; and where I am, there shall also my servant be" (John 12:26).

In Luke 4:18-19, Jesus stood and defined the reason why God had become a man on the earth. "The Spirit of the Lord is upon me, because he hath anointed me to preach the gospel to the poor; he hath sent me to heal the brokenhearted, to preach deliverance to the captives, and recovering of sight to the blind, to set at liberty them that are bruised, to preach the acceptable year of the Lord."

He came to neither analyze nor inspect but rather to move into the center of human capacity and become a door of redemption. He gave His life for this cause.

I have walked with Jesus and found the purpose of His life being interwoven with mine. Sharing His love with prisoners on two continents, walking through war-torn diseased, and unspeakably poor masses of humanity, I have learned more about His life than in any amount of study. There are sorrows and yet there is unspeakable joy every time someone reaches out to take the hand of God's forgiveness, promise, and strength!

The Call today remains the same as then. Jesus calls for every person who is weary and heavy laden to find his rest in Him. It is a passionate call from the heart of God who loves those whom He has created. He also calls those who know Him as Lord, Savior, and Friend to walk with Him until the day His work here is complete.

"Come, my beloved, let us go forth into the field; let us lodge in the villages; let us get up early to the vineyards; let us see if the vine flourish, whether the tender grape appear, and the pomegranates bud forth: there will I give thee my love" (Song of Solomon 7:11-12).

The once extremely dangerous Auca Indians of the Amazon rainforest / Ecuador
Waodani indigenous tribe in which 5 missionaries were killed in 1956, now a Christian community

But I don't feel Called

ELISABETH ELLIOT
Famous Missionary and Author
www.elisabethelliot.org

A seminary student once stopped me to ask the question that troubles many young people today. It is not new... I struggled with it when I was a student, as I suppose people have for many centuries. "How can I tell if God is calling me? I don't really feel called."

Usually the question refers to a life's work. Nobody seems to stew very much about whether God is calling them to run down to the grocery store or take in a movie. We need groceries. We like movies. If the refrigerator is empty or there's a good movie in town, we jump into the car and go. Even Christians do this. Spiritual "giants" do it, I guess. They don't even pray about it. But this matter of the mission field. Oh, God, do you want me there? Shall I risk everything and launch out to some Third World backwater, some waterless desert, some dreadful place where there are starving children, refugees, Marxists, and/or dictators? Are you asking me to drag my wife and my children to a place like that?

The call of God to Saul of Tarsus was dramatic—he was blinded, knocked flat, and clearly spoken to. God got his attention. But later in Antioch, the Holy Spirit spoke to certain prophets and teachers. "Set apart Barnabas and Saul for me, to do the work to which I have called them." That was good enough. Barnabas and Saul obeyed the divine call, even though it came through other men.

It was during the mass of the Feast of St. Matthias, in a chapel in the midst of a great, silent forest, that Francis of Assisi heard the call of God. It was not through an angel or a disembodied voice from beyond, but through the reading of the Gospel for that day: "Go preach the message, 'The kingdom of heaven is at hand!'...Freely you have received, freely give" (Matthew 10:7-8). When the young man heard the words read by the priest, he felt that God had finally illuminated his path. He did not, however, trust his feelings. He asked the priest to explain the passage. The priest said that Christ's disciples were to preach repentance everywhere, to take nothing with them, and to trust God alone to supply their needs.

"Francis thrilled with happiness at this revelation and exclaimed enthusiastically: 'That is what I want! That is what I seek! That is what I long to do with all my heart!' On the instant, he threw away his staff, took off his shoes, and laid aside his cloak, keeping only a tunic; replaced his leather belt with a cord, and made himself a rough garment so poor and so badly cut that it could inspire envy in no man."

St. Francis of Assisi
Omer Engelbert

There are at least six lessons in this short story:
1. The man wanted God's direction.
2. He went to church, where he could hear godly preaching.
3. He listened to the Word of God.
4. He asked for help from one who was his spiritual superior.
5. He accepted the help.
6. He acted at once.

It is significant that he found in the words of the Lord the answer to a deep longing in his heart.

In C.S. Lewis's Preface to *Paradise Lost*, he describes Aeneas' unfaltering search for the "abiding city," his willingness to pay the terrible price to reach it at last, even though he casts a wistful side-glance at those not called as he is. *"This is the very portrait of a vocation: a thing that calls or beckons, that calls inexorably, yet you must strain your ears to catch the voice, that insists on*

>

being sought, yet refuses to be found." Then there were the Trojan women who heard the call, yet refused to follow all the way and wept on the Sicilian shore. "To follow the vocation does not mean happiness," Lewis writes, "but once it has been heard, there is no happiness for those who do not follow."

Yes. My heart says yes to that. What agonies I suffered as a young woman, straining my ears to catch the voice, full of fear that I would miss it, yet longing to hear it, longing to be told what to do, in order that I might do it. That desire is a pure one. Most of our desires are tainted at least a little, but the desire to do the will of God surely is our highest. Is it reasonable to think that God would not finally reveal his will to us? Is it (we must also ask) reasonable not to use our powers of reason, given to us by him? Does it make sense to go to the grocery store because groceries are needed than to go to foreign lands because workers are needed? If we deny the simple logic of going where the need is most desperate, we may, like the Trojan women, spend the rest of our lives suspended. 'Twixt miserable longing for the present land and the far realms that call them by the fates' command.

Aeneids, V, 656

While Virgil wrote of mythical heroes, his lines echo the more ancient lines of the Psalms, which are rich with assurances of God's faithful guidance of those who honestly desire it, and of the lasting rewards of obedience.

"Blessed are those whose strength is in you, who have set their hearts on pilgrimage. The Lord bestows favor and honor; no good thing does he withhold from those whose walk is blameless" (Psalms 84:5,11 NIV).

"The Lord is near to all who call on him, to all who call on him in truth. He fulfills the desires of those who fear him" (Psalms 145:18-19 NIV).

It is the sixth lesson from the St. Francis story that is most often overlooked. Obedience is action. Often we do not have any instant light on the particular question we've been asking God, but he has shown us something we ought to do. Whatever it is, however unrelated it may seem to the "big" decision, do it. Do it at once. We thus put ourselves in the path of God's will. A single step taken, if we have his Word as a lamp for our feet, throws sufficient light for the next step. Following the Shepherd we learn, like sheep, to know his voice. We will become acquainted with his call and will not follow a stranger's.

ELISABETH ELLIOT
famous missionary who spent two years ministering to the Auca tribe members who killed her husband and four other missionaries in the Amazon rainforest
www.elisabethelliot.org

"He is no fool who gives up what he cannot keep to gain that which he cannot lose" — *Jim Elliot*

"People who do not know the Lord ask why in the world we waste our lives as missionaries. They forget that they too are expending their lives... and when the bubble has burst, they will have nothing of eternal significance to show for the years they have wasted." — *Nate Saint*

missionary martyrs who lost their lives trying to reach the Auca Indians of Ecuador

Auca Indian with his spear
Amazon rainforest / Ecuador

Garbage City, where families live and survive by sorting trash
Cairo, Egypt

Moving from Sympathy to Love

GARY WILKERSON
President: World Challenge Inc.
Founding Pastor: The Springs Church
Colorado Springs, CO

Most of us are touched by pictures of the poor and needy; they tug at our heartstrings. Seeing children suffer is disturbing, anger evoking, and can easily draw tears from even the most stoic among us.

In the past few years, I traveled to many of the sites you see on these inspired pages. As amazing as these images are, they can never really show the horrors of extreme poverty, of civil wars that enlist child soldiers to shoot other twelve-year-olds, and epidemics that devastate whole populations, leaving them without farmers or teachers, not to mention mothers or fathers. Or of entire populations without the Word of God revealing faith, hope, and the greatest—love.

It has been said that a picture paints a thousand words, but neither a thousand pictures nor tens of thousands of words can truly tell the story of the real sorrows of human suffering in an accurate and full way. We, in the affluent West, cannot truly know the ravages of extreme poverty, and what's worse is that we far too often close our eyes to the poor.

Today, there are over six and a half billion people on earth, and well over a billion live on less than 23 cents a day. That's three times below the level called extreme poverty. While over one billion poor have no safe drinking water, we, in America, consume 26 billion liters of bottled water yearly. Every sixteen seconds someone in the world dies of hunger, while two out of every three Americans are overweight or obese, partly due to the eleven billion dollars we spend on ice cream each year. Eighty percent of the world lives in substandard housing; fifty percent in slums, while the average home in the U.S. is now 2,349 square feet. Fourteen million children are orphans because of HIV/AIDS, while American parents shop an average of six hours a week and spend only forty minutes playing with their kids.

The world cannot afford for us to be unaware, unconcerned, and unmoved. We must go beyond our emotions, beyond sympathy. As we become more aware, that awareness can lead to more prayer; and more prayer always leads to God demanding, orchestrating, instigating, and ensuring actions that make a real difference. God uses truth to set freedom in motion. God is on the move on behalf of the poor.

It is one thing to feel sadness when viewing images of the suffering, but God requires those of us who have been given much to also give much. Our sorrow and sad emotions don't suffice. Sympathy is natural and given to us by God, but God wants more than our sympathy. Sympathy thinks about the poor. Love compels our actions, especially those of us with the outlandish blessings so common in the West.

Traveling as an evangelist and relief and development worker with World Challenge has taught me this one prevailing and vital truth: sympathy helps the poor, but love overcomes poverty. Love works.

Our inspired acts of mercy and charity are a perfect starting point. What comes next, however, requires a huge, forceful, and relentless engagement in changing the conditions that keep people bound in the evil of deadly, senseless poverty. When we are doing the works of Jesus, conditions change. We start by meeting the immediate needs, and we continue until there is lasting transformation, all the while giving what we can with love in the name of Jesus.

If I lived in extreme poverty I could say:

"When I am in need, without food or shelter, when my children lie sick with no hope for medicines, and you knock on my door, I will gladly accept your charity. Give me food and medicine. I will not tell you your money is going to waste; you are not throwing it down the drain. You are not creating a dependency; you are not perpetuating my poverty. I will be grateful for the gift. It will save my family."

>

"But if you have to knock on my door every month for years on end and hand me a basket with food and clothes for my children, I will begin to wonder if there is not a better way. I will begin to wonder if there isn't a way out of this vicious and demeaning cycle of poverty. Isn't there a way for me to live without crying myself to sleep after putting hungry children to bed? Isn't there a way for me to break the shackles of this endless, senseless and brutal poverty?

"I see a day coming when you will come to my door with your basket, your food, and your money, and I will tell you, thank you, my friend, but I no longer need it. Your charity helped me in my crisis, but I have now overcome this plague of poverty. I have work and food, and I can take my children to the doctor when they are sick."

There is a time for charity when a boy is lying on a worn blanket in the dirt, and he has not eaten in days. He fled hundreds of miles on foot because of the men who drove into his village with machine guns, burning houses and raping women. At this time he needs the help of one who cares. He needs charity; he doesn't need to learn to fish. That can come later. In times of crisis, charity is our first response. But as the crisis subsides and the help has been freely given, then comes the time to help that boy become hopeful and believe he has a future. He needs assistance to create opportunities.

The poor will be with us, but they don't have to die of poverty. The poor will be with us, but we don't have to turn our backs on them. The poor will be with us, but it is not the way things should be. Jesus says the poor will be with us, quoting Deuteronomy 15. It is a passage most of us have heard, but few realize that the same chapter tells us clearly, "There should be no poor among you." There will always be the sad reality of extreme poverty, but there will also be the reality that it is not what God intended; it is not what He wants us to resign ourselves to. It is not the preferred status of heaven.

As a matter of fact, God suggests an all-out campaign to be certain we are doing all we can. The reason the extreme poor are with us is that we are not doing all we can. We allow injustice, tolerate unnecessary suffering, and are far too often unaware of the vast needs around the world and of the many opportunities we have to make a real difference in the world.

Don't just read this book. Don't just look at these pictures. Don't just let a few tears run down your cheeks. Get up and do something. God will lead you if you ask Him. He will not only show you the need, but He will lead you into being a part of the solution.

GARY WILKERSON
President: World Challenge Inc.
Founding Pastor: The Springs Church
Colorado Springs, CO

There will always be poor people in the land.

Therefore I command you to be openhanded toward your brothers,

and toward the poor and needy in your land.

Deuteronomy 15:11 NIV

Children of the Twa Tribe, once an endangered people group
Burundi

All Things to All People

How can we reach people more effectively around us? How can we show the world God's love and the full magnitude of what Christ did for us on the cross?

The body of Christ, like the world itself, is fascinating and diverse. Having had the privilege of seeing many believers at work around the world, most serving in small congregations and ministries, I've seen how despite the different personalities and cultural backgrounds, the Spirit of God takes people and forms in them a common characteristic—living for others instead of living for themselves, being a servant to all. They become whatever is needed to reach those that the Lord has placed around them.

The apostle Paul the greatest missionary of all time wrote, *"To the weak I became weak, to win the weak. I have become all things to all men so that by all possible means I might save some"* (1 Cor. 9:22 NIV). In this scripture Paul was sharing the tactics behind his missionary heart. He not only shared the way he would go about ministering the gospel to a broad diversity of people, but he also gave us guidelines on how we should mirror ourselves after him. The goal is not only that we will become more effective in our ministering and reach as many people as possible but that we will also show the love of Christ in and through our actions.

How can we expect people from all different cultures and backgrounds to listen to the gospel message if we are not willing to live among them and learn their culture to understand them more fully? We need to feel for their circumstances and to share in the things that oppress them. Paul never compromised the gospel in his efforts to become all things to all men or disobey any biblical principles in his striving to reach his audience. But Paul was prepared to go to incredible lengths to minister to people in their circumstances and even become like his audience to better win them for Christ.

There is no better way to reach a hurting person than to comfort their pain, and to be willing to hurt with them.

There is no better way to reach a person than to speak to them on their level while fully understanding their lives and sympathizing with the circumstances they are in because we ourselves are at least willing to be alongside them in their circumstances comforting them. There is no better way of mirroring the love of our Savior who died for us while taking upon our sins so that we could be reconciled to Him.

Through the years, many people have blessed and challenged me with their willingness to surrender to this calling. Only heaven will reveal the ones that have delighted the heart of God the most, but as I look back through my life at these people that have touched me with their personal journey, one Iranian woman who suffers from chronic fatigue syndrome combined with fibromyalgia stands out. Having withstood the rejection of family after giving her life to the Lord and then battling an illness that left her in constant pain, she embraced God's call on her life for the deaf community. Through my time in ministry, I have watched this woman embrace the burden for the deaf and live it out. She started by learning sign language and then taught others to sign. A ministry developed to reach the deaf in the church and then to the deaf community in New York City. Today they offer simultaneous translation during services and travel to other countries to minister to the deaf around the world. She has given her life to reach the deaf and has not stopped allowing the Lord to push her to be more than she can physically be in order to win some. Not all, but some.

"When I am with those who are weak, I share their weakness for I want to bring the weak to Christ" (1 Cor. 9:22 NLT).

TREG MCCOY
Director of Missions
Times Square Church, NYC

husband and wife goat herders
northern India

Testimonies
FROM AROUND THE WORLD

The man who saw it
has given testimony,
and his testimony is true.
He knows that he tells the truth,
and he testifies so that you
also may believe.

John 19:35 NIV

†

Western Wall / Jerusalem

EUROPE + MIDDLE EAST

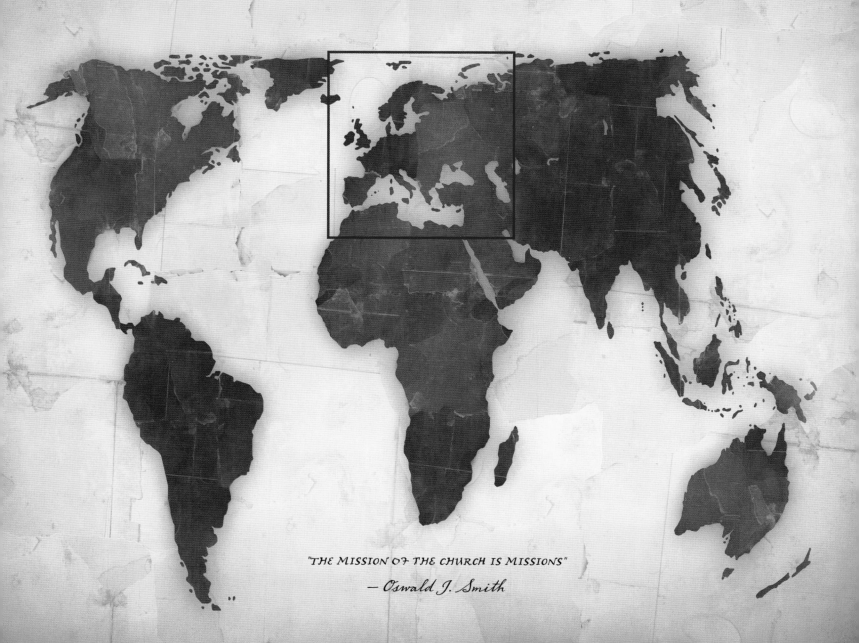

"THE MISSION OF THE CHURCH IS MISSIONS"
— Oswald J. Smith

glue addicts on the streets of St. Petersburg

Sergé

In the summer of 1996 Sergé was fourteen years old. Early that summer he made a decision to go to St. Petersburg where he would live on the streets. His mission in going to St. Petersburg was both very simple and essential to his family.

He would go there to try to earn money to buy winter shoes, coats, and school supplies. These would be needed if he and his younger brother and sister were to go to school next fall. Because Sergé comes from one of the poorest villages around St. Petersburg, Russia, neither his mother or father can find work. The odd jobs they do find barely supply food each day. Some days they do not eat. Obviously there was no hope of extra money for shoes or school supplies, so Sergé was allowed to go to St. Petersburg.

Unlike many of the street kids who beg or steal, Sergé was too proud to do either. Instead, he looked for work. Because he is such a hard worker, he soon earned a reputation among street merchants that allowed him to find work easily. If everything worked out OK, these odd jobs during the course of the summer would provide the funds Sergé wanted for shoes, coats, and school supplies. However, everything did not work out as he had planned.

When he went to live on the streets, Sergé had become a street kid, and the streets are not a safe place for any child much less a very small boy like Sergé. Periodically older street children would rob him of all the money he worked so hard to earn. The police provided no help. Instead, periodically they too would raid the shack he and some other boys lived in. During the course of those raids, they would take everything the kids had, including the money Sergé had saved to buy shoes, school supplies, and coats.

By midsummer Sergé started to realize that he would not be able to amass the money that he and his younger brother and sister needed. Discouraged, Sergé started to join the other street kids in sniffing glue. He knew it would kill him, but somehow that no longer mattered. Instead, the glue seemed his only hope. It covered the pain of his hunger, loneliness, and discouragement.

In early August, Sergé met two missionaries who were visiting Russia for the summer. They had come to preach in a nearby youth prison. Each day they would meet with Sergé and about five or six other boys and bring them food. Eventually Sergé turned to Jesus. In mid August, Sergé learned some-thing that he felt provided needed encouragement. He learned that if he would seek first the kingdom of God, that God would provide the things he needed. That day Sergé invited Jesus into his life. The next day with a Bible in hand and promise from God in his heart, he returned home.

Shortly after this happened, the missionary team left Russia as scheduled. About six months later, an interpreter who had worked with the team e-mailed one of the team members. She told them that she had heard from Sergé and that he was doing fine. God had provided all the needed resources, but she and others from the local church hoped that the missionary team would return. It seems that the local church was so encouraged by what had happened to Sergé that they wanted to see if a permanent ministry could be started. At first, Russian officials resisted the idea of a Christian ministry to street kids. Then one of the officials met Sergé again herself. She was so shocked by how he had changed that she not only opened the door for the start of a permanent ministry, but she actually encouraged it.

In October of 1997, Sergé died in an accidental fall. The missionary who had led him to Christ was asked to do the funeral. At the grave, Serge's father, who was not yet a Christian, asked the missionary to stand with him at the head of the casket. This is a spot reserved in Russia only for the parents of a child who has died. The father explained to the community that he wanted the missionary to stand in this spot because when Sergé came back from St. Petersburg, it was like he had been born again. Other non-Christians agreed. The missionary explained that he had been born again but not because of meeting any human. He had been born again because he had met Jesus. By the time he died, Sergé had led almost one hundred other children to Christ. He did this through his testimony about how Jesus had faithfully provided for all his needs.

Today the ministry that was inspired by Sergé's life still functions. Weekly it serves several hundred children. It includes a school, shelter, outreaches, and a day center.

I know this story to be true because I was that missionary.

runaways, orphans and glue addicts / St. Petersburg, Russia

Still other seeds fell on fertile soil, and they produced a crop that was thirty, sixty, and even a hundred times as much as had been planted. Matthew 13:8 NLT

vision impaired orphanage / Zelenogorsk, Russia

Religion that God our Father accepts as pure and faultless is this: to look after orphans and widows in their distress, and to keep oneself from being polluted by the world. James 1:27 NIV

a lesson learned about the heart of God

Pure Religion

It was a hot August day and we were driving several vans through the woods of Zelenogorsk, Russia, a rural city an hour and a half outside St. Petersburg. The road was lined with tall pine trees on either side.

Dappled sunlight lit the dust being kicked up from behind our vans as we made our way down a bumpy dirt road. We were headed for an orphanage, one of many orphanages that were tucked in and hidden away in the back woods of Zelenogorsk.

This was our church's second mission trip after starting a missions program. In the beginning days of our missions program, we were inexperienced and sought after God's help. It was all very foreign to us; we had very few guidelines of any kind on how to do missions. We were a group of young, zealous individuals excited and eager to serve the Lord any way we could.

The one thing I remember most about those first days was praying. We prayed! We started everything in prayer. We ended everything in prayer. We prayed for hours and hours. We had all-night prayer, once a week. We could not pray enough. We sought God's will and His guidance. And most of all we prayed for His heart! We really wanted and desired His heart for the nations and His heart for the lost.

One of the first projects we did as a young missions program was a clothing drive. We constructed large cardboard boxes that we painted and decorated, then placed them in the lobbies of corporate buildings all over New York City. We asked people to donate all their unwanted shoes and clothes.

The response was incredible—something that none of us could have ever expected. God opened up the floodgates. We collected so many clothes that, no kidding, we had to rent a warehouse in which to store them. We had Missions Night sorting parties, where we folded, sorted, and stacked everything. The warehouse was filled to the brim with hundreds of stacks of clothing and piles of shoes. Many stacks reached as high as eight feet tall. We did not know where God intended all these clothes to end up, but one thing was for sure—He certainly filled

our storehouses to overflowing! Needless to say, we started shipping large containers of clothing on every missions trip that the Lord led us on.

So here we were in Russia, we came to minister to the dozens of children's youth camps throughout Zelenogorsk. These camps were originally used to indoctrinate people into communism; now they were youth summer camps and orphanages. There were 150 of us from our church scattered throughout these camps. We taught English, gave Bible studies, ran vacation Bible school, and performed dramas, puppet shows, and music. In the process we fell in love with the Russian people.

On one particular day, our vans were filled with these collected clothes and shoes as we headed through the back woods of Zelenogorsk toward an orphanage. Our Russian interpreter was guiding us down the long, dusty, bumpy dirt roads that he said would lead us to an orphanage. We finally saw buildings appear through the tall pine trees. As we approached, you could see that the grounds had not been taken care of in years. The grass was very overgrown; paint was chipping off fences and walls. The orphanage appeared as if it had been long forgotten about by the world.

Then we saw the children; they were so adorable. They ran up to us as if they had never had visitors before in their lives. They greeted us with so much excitement, smiles, and laughter, while tugging at our clothes begging us to play with them. They were dressed in old, dirty, tattered clothes that looked at best like they were from an old 50's vintage store. It was as if we stepped back in time.

Their shoes were in awful shape. Most of them were missing laces with holes in the front and their toes hanging out. Many of their shoes barely had any soles left; I even noticed several of them detached and flapping open as they walked.

>

41

The children followed us as we made our way to the main office to meet the headmaster of the orphanage. The orphanage was an old pre-war brick building that had been terribly neglected due to obvious lack of money. As we entered the building, we saw just how bad the building really was. Electric wires were hanging out of the sockets, and the walls and ceilings were covered in watermarks and mold. In the reception area was an old desk, a couch with the stuffing and springs sticking out, and a classic old tube TV sat in the corner of the room with an unrecognizable static picture on it.

Just then the headmaster walked in. She was an old stern-faced Russian woman with deep wrinkles and tough skin. It was obvious that she had lived an extremely hard life, lacking any pleasures or normal conveniences we were used to. You could tell by the look on her face that she questioned our motives for being there, at the same time surprised that anyone would visit.

We greeted her with the few Russian words we knew and spoke to her through our interpreter.

Her countenance changed abruptly when she heard we were there to bless the children with clothes and to minister to them.

The next couple hours were some of the most special hours of my young missionary life. While some of us played games, sang songs, and taught them about God, others took the old shoes off these precious orphans' feet and fit them with the shoes and clothes we had brought. Seeing the pure joy upon the children's faces, we realized that we had been part of something so special that had gone full circle. From our initial prayers, the collecting of clothes, and now being on the other side of the earth handing them out to these deserving orphans, we realized that this only could have been part of God's plan and that He had led us there.

Our time was sadly up as we got back in our vans to drive back to our camp. The children did not want to see us go. They grabbed for us through the van windows; some of them had tears in their eyes.

It was then that I saw the headmaster standing on the steps of the orphanage. She was crying uncontrollably, tears rolling down her face. What used to be a stern, hard face on this Russian woman was now transformed into a soft face amid a puddle of grateful tears. I could only imagine what her thoughts were as we had given all the glory to God and told her over

and over that He had led us to her orphanage. She was deeply moved that anyone, including God, had come to bless her kids in this far removed, forgotten place.

That moment will forever be etched in my memory. Seeing the tears on her face while pulling away in our van with the kids running after us yelling; "Spasiba, spasiba," meaning "Thank you, thank you," I had to fight away the tears in my own eyes.

Our van ride back to our camp was incredibly quiet as no one spoke a word for the entire 30-minute drive. You could tell everyone was in deep thought and incredibly moved by the day's events. With the only sound coming from the hum of the engine, it was an extremely contemplative moment.

You see, we had prayed for God to lead us and to show us His heart, and He had done just that! James 1:27 says, "Pure and undefiled religion before God and the Father is this: to visit orphans and widows in their trouble, and to keep oneself unspotted from the world" (NKJV).

God does not want us to limit our faith to the inside of a church building. Pure religion in God's eyes is not a strict adherence to religious rules and practices. Instead it is for us to have a heart of love and compassion that stirs us into action through our faith. This is completely opposite of the world's view of religion. The more humble our actions are to the hurting, needy, and forgotten people around us, the more pleasing it is to God. Orphans and widows are normally considered the poorest of the poor because they have no one to take care of them. They are the least of these of this world and often need the help of others just to survive.

True servanthood to others is the giving of ourselves without expectation or hope of gaining anything in return for our efforts. When we love and go out of our way to help those that are helpless we truly show God's love to those around us. This is putting the Word of God and our faith into action. Helping orphans, widows, the poor, the sick, and the homeless is difficult work because of the complexity of their lives and their extreme needs are burdensome to meet.

God calls us to keep ourselves unpolluted by the world and to help those who are helpless; and when we do, we truly see our heavenly Father in action and experience His heart and love for every soul in this world. This is religion that is acceptable to God.

orphanage / Zelenegorsk, Russia

elderly women / St. Petersburg, Russia

The Lord does not look at the things man looks at.
Man looks at the outward appearance,
but the Lord looks at the heart.
1 Samuel 16:7 NIV

TERESA CONLON
President: Summit International School of Ministry
Pastor: Times Square Church, NYC

a Russian grandmother meets God

The Woman who cleaned the Toilets

The missionary's words rang prophetically in my ears, "When you get to Russia look low, then look lower; that's who you will preach to." *How strange,* I thought, *because we are going to Russia to minister to children in summer camps.*

When we arrived at the camp, we eagerly began our ministry to children: teaching Bible stories, gospel songs in Russian, and where permitted, English classes.

Then I noticed the grandmothers in the camp who cleaned the toilets. Little esteemed and largely exploited, these older women worked twelve-hour days, dragging buckets and mops around from one foul smelling toilet area to another in order that their grandchildren (mostly oblivious to their sacrifice) could have the opportunity of attending a summer camp.

Every day I looked for them and noticed their swollen legs, their exhaustion, and the humorless, hopeless expression on their faces. And strange to say, I began to yearn for them. I became consumed with the desire to reach out to them and love them and tell them about Jesus, who was putting these yearnings in my heart for them.

We started having teas for them and serving them nuts and cookies from the goodies we had brought from home. No such luxuries were found in our wilderness camp-grounds. They were amazed and at first, skeptical. "Why are you doing this for us?" they asked through interpreters, alternating between skepticism and astonishment.

We sang for them, shared the gospel, and served them with joy. One older grandmother, Babushka (Grand-mother) Vera, especially caught my attention. She was as wide as she was tall and came only to my shoulders. I was gripped by a supernatural love for her. There is no describing this except for the first time in my life I experienced firsthand the all-consuming love and yearning Christ has for a soul. I devoted all my energies to see her know the love of Christ. One day while walking with her with my arm around her shoulders (and she beaming in the attention of it all), I told her how extraordinarily loved she was by God. She stopped, spat on the ground, and said, "I'm fat and I'm ugly." Her actions were saying how could she—a fat and ugly woman—be loved.

At another Bible study we passed around nuts. Babushka Vera, conditioned by a lifetime of famine and hardship, counted the number of people in the room, the number of nuts in the bowl, and reached in and took one. Smiling at her, I invited her to take more. When she realized she was allowed to have more, she reached in and took a handful but put the contents in her pocket, patted it shut, and said, "For Genia." That was her grandson. She would only take one for herself, but she could reach out for a handful for a grandson.

Oh how I understood the beauty in this soul that Christ so loved! She was unselfish. She knew the misery of hunger, and she would deny herself so that a grandson would not suffer as she had.

At another night of Bible study, my determination grew that this woman would know the love of Christ. We ministered all day to the children, but these women worked till nine o'clock at night, so we would start after that. One night into our grandmother's Bible study came some young, big, tall guys. *Oh,* I thought, *if these guys get saved they would have quite an impact around this camp. I should tailor my Bible study to them.* Suddenly my heart was gripped the voice of the Lord, "I have sent you here for them—the toilet cleaners. That's who you are to minister to." So being reproved, I conducted the Bible study to minister to the grandmothers, irrespective of who was listening.

>

The next Bible study time arrived. Right in the middle of the study, Babushka Vera sprung to her feet and danced as a young girl, laughing and crying and saying "Slava Boghu; slava Boghu" (Praise the Lord, Praise the Lord). We witnessed a miracle. Grandmother was saved, and the light and the glory of being chosen, loved, and forgiven flooded her being. Her whole countenance shone with an unearthly light; everyone noticed.

Shortly after this, a camp decree reached us. No more Bible studies. I was shocked. We were ministering to the women they literally didn't care if they lived or died. They barely noticed them and then only with contempt. We had Bible studies with the children and that was permitted. Why did they want to shut down our loving and caring and ministering to this bunch of "worthless" (in their eyes) people? Then the Lord whispered to my heart, "Teresa, when you teach the children, they can teach children; when you sing with children they can sing with children; but when you love these women, they can't love them—they are threatened. This is power they know nothing about."

With such a heavy heart I watched the hour approach for our usual evening Bible study time.

Shortly after 9 p.m., I watched Babushka Vera make her way to our usual spot with her dirty bucket and tired legs. She sat there defiant. She seemed to be wordlessly proclaiming to everyone in this camp, "I have found a Jesus who will never leave me or forsake me. I come to the place where I first found Him. You will never take Him from me." I cried as I watched her sit there and testify of Him the only way she knew how. After much prayer, mysteriously the Bible study ban was lifted. And several days before our leaving the camp, we resumed our studies with our Russian grandmothers.

Our parting time was searing. My heart was bound to this small woman; Christ and His triumphant and tender love had knit us together inseparably. I heard later that summer that this toilet cleaning grandmother was responsible for many conversions in this camp. She did not have much formal Bible knowledge, but she had something better. She had a glory in her face that radiated a love and joy that touched many hardened and dreary lives as our poor words could not. I thought I went to Russia to teach the children. I was sent for one woman who scrubbed toilets and who King Jesus was determined to have as His bride.

Blessed are the poor in spirit,
for theirs is the kingdom of heaven.
Blessed are those who mourn, for they will be comforted.
Blessed are the meek, for they will inherit the earth.
Blessed are those who hunger and thirst for righteousness,
for they will be filled.
Blessed are the merciful, for they will be shown mercy.
Blessed are the pure in heart, for they will see God.
Matthew 5:3-8 NIV

old peasant woman / Lenin Square, Moscow

STEVE PARSONS
Music Ministries
Cardiff, Wales

sex offenders in prison

Grace in unexpected Places

It started out as a missions date booked in my diary, an outreach concert to be held in Cardiff, Wales. Little did I know how much the next couple of days would radically affect my life and ministry.

The concert was held in a sports hall, and 400 teenagers and adults gathered on a warm summer's evening to listen as I sang my songs and shared the message of God's love. However, as I sang my songs that night I felt disturbed. All around the hall were posters with the photograph of a pretty sixteen-year-old girl who had been brutally raped and murdered just the week before. Police were offering a reward for information. I'd seen the poster just before walking on stage, and it sickened me. *How could anyone do something like this?* I asked myself.

At the end of the event, I gave an invitation for people to accept Christ as their Savior, and many from the crowd made their way to the front of the hall to pray and talk to one of our team. It was during this time that we encountered a thirteen-year-old girl. It was evident that she was frightened; and as her story emerged, it became clear why. Her father routinely sold her to his friends for sex.

That night as I lay in bed, I was angry and frustrated. Many people had accepted Christ that evening, but all I could think about were the encounters I'd had with two horribly abused young girls.

The next morning the Chaplain at Cardiff Prison called. His name was Martin, and he wanted to know if I would come in later that day and minister to some of the men. I was not ready for what he said next. "Steve, I want you to come in and speak to the sex offenders."

I met Martin at the prison gate, and we made our way inside. I'd visited prisons before, but this time I was on edge. I'd never spoken to these men, and neither did I want to. I felt like Jonah must have when God asked him to speak to the unbelievably cruel city of Ninevah, where human bodies lined the main highway hung on wooden poles stuck through their bodies. But rather than get swallowed by a whale, I accepted Martin's invitation, mostly because he's a nice guy. But secretly I wanted nothing to do with these men. Martin took me to the prison chapel and left me on my own for a while so he could go and get the men. As I sat there in that little chapel, I felt

sick. All I could think about was that frightened thirteen-year-old girl we'd met the night before. The photo of the other young victim flashed through my mind repeatedly. "God, I don't want to do this," I prayed quietly. "What am I going to say?"

And then in they came.

I'm not sure what I was expecting—probably evil looking monsters with glaring eyes! But as the dozen or so men sat down on their chairs, I was stunned. They just looked so normal. We started the service, and Martin suggested we read some scripture. One of the men read aloud from Romans 8, "Nothing shall separate us from the love of God." Another read John 3:16, " that whosoever believes in Him…" Those amazing words started to soften my hard, judgmental heart. Finally, before I spoke we sang the hymn "Amazing Grace." God's presence filled that little chapel with a wonderful atmosphere.

By now tears were rolling down the cheeks of some of those men, and I could hardly sing as tears rolled down mine. These men who had done wicked things were in desperate need of grace. So was I.

It didn't take me long to realize that I was not in that prison to just speak—I was there to learn.

That day I realized that I was no different from those men. Sure, my sins were different, and the consequences were different. But I needed forgiving and cleansing just as much as they did. We are all in need of God's amazing grace.

We live in a difficult world. The hideous things that humans are capable of doing and the pain inflicted upon others are indicative of just how fallen we are. Acts of violence and abuse against the innocent often leave us full of outrage towards the perpetrators. Yet when those same people turn to Jesus, He meets them with His amazing offer of grace. Friends, the price has been paid. God hates sin, but He loves sinners—sinners like those men, and sinners like me.

For it is by grace you have been saved, through faith—
and this is not from yourselves; it is the gift of God.
Ephesians 2:8 NIV

men's prison

Shepherd / Ocna Mureș, Romania

Preach the Word; be prepared in season and out of season;
correct, rebuke and encourage—with great patience and careful instruction.

2 Timothy 4:2 NIV

RAY WRIGHT
Romania

testimony of what God can do through what little we have to offer

Fishes and Loaves – the importance of short-term missions

I became a Christian at the impressionable age of seventeen, just one year before leaving for college, where I became actively involved in a student-led campus ministry. As part of the leadership team, I met regularly with staff members to pray and plan campus ministry activities.

During my junior year, the primary staff worker took a sabbatical and was replaced by a man who led the organization's yearly mission trip to Eastern Europe, where, at that time, evangelism was illegal and believers suffered under Communist persecution. He shared amazing personal testimonies, such as meeting secretly in corn fields to train pastors in personal Bible study, and traveling to underground churches to teach and encourage the flock. He told me of a world and a life I was not aware of and challenged me to participate in one such trip. I sensed the Lord leading me to go.

The following summer, I was behind the Iron Curtain, camping at a refugee camp in Yugoslavia. I remember the gravity of the situation and having to lean on the Lord for protection and guidance. We had to memorize complex driving directions and train schedules to avoid a paper trail of our itinerary. I saw a physical iron curtain of barbed wire separating Western and Eastern Europe. At the border crossing, I watched car doors and seats being dismantled and searched, as our van of smuggled Bibles was waved through. Our small team visited underground churches and evangelized persecuted refugees.

I remember the first time we brought Bibles to an underground Romanian church, awestruck by the intensity of the prayer and worship. I recall the pastor turning to our small team and saying, "You will sing for us, then you will preach to us." It was common for them to call upon anyone, including visiting teams, to preach to them. They were far too accustomed to the government coming and grabbing their pastors out of the pulpit and throwing them into jail. There was no time to prepare anything. Whatever the Holy Spirit had deposited earlier that morning was my sermon. I felt inadequate, realizing that the lives of these giants of faith were teaching me far more than what I was able to offer them.

At our campsite, the Lord stretched me in every way. For example, I had to use a learned second language like German to share the gospel with an Iranian couple and some Albanians. Every day He unfolded more and more the meaning of a Spirit-led life, and worked in me an ever-increasing yearning to walk in His strength. Most of the refugees I befriended came from Romania, and their stories of escape and torture broke my heart. Some had their teeth kicked in by the secret police, others had their homes and churches razed by bulldozers, while others lost their jobs or families because they professed Christ. I developed a special burden in my heart for the Romanian people, spending nights around a campfire, lining up verses from the book of John in the Romanian and English Bibles. I journaled, "Lord, give me this language!" I came away from that experience forever changed, compelled to live a poured-out life, and wanting to become a full-time missionary. It was difficult to return home; I entered the workforce, but I felt out of place. I sensed the Lord calling me to Romania, but I was confused because Romania was a closed country. I began to consider serving in other Eastern bloc countries, thinking perhaps I heard wrong. As time passed, I could not shake off this burden.

Shortly thereafter, God started to sovereignly shake up the nations. Glasnost provided a new openness in the Soviet Union and surrounding republics. Poland, Czechoslovakia, Hungary, and Germany each experienced significant movements towards freedom. I remained convinced that there could be no change for Romania due to the fierce, iron grip of its dictator. But on a cold winter day, people took to the streets crying, "God exists! God exists!" In a week, the tyranny ended with the dictator's execution. God heard the cries of the oppressed, and the country was now miraculously open to the gospel!

Two months later, I entered Romania for the first time. Not knowing where to go, I set out for the home town of

>

a Romanian immigrant I had met just before leaving America. Arriving late at night and without the benefit of lights or street names, I asked a bicyclist in a newly-memorized phrase, "Where is Lake Street?" "This is it," he replied. The Lord had faithfully directed me to my host family! They graciously offered me a room, and unknown to me, slept on the kitchen floor so I could have a bed—another humble reminder that I still had a lot to learn about serving.

I was given a tour of the town's hospital, which had a ward for abandoned children. I was horrified to meet a six-year-old girl who could not walk or talk, not because of a handicap or birth defect, but because no one had ever talked to her or took her out of her crib while she was growing up! The children just sat in wet cribs, malnourished, and swatted flies from their head, with no one to care for them.

The abject poverty was overwhelming. There were long queues for basic necessities like milk, bread, and fuel. Children wept whenever I gave them a banana or an orange. Someone said to me, "It is a miracle you are here—it is in the soul of every Romanian to leave." A newspaper headline read, "The last one to leave, turn out the light." I knew I was where I was supposed to be but not what I was supposed to do, nor the scope of all that God wanted to do in that country.

From that initial exploratory short-term mission's trip, the Lord raised up an anointed team of both resident and visiting missionaries who bore much fruit with a simple vision to "plant Christ." An orphanage now rescues abandoned children; some have been adopted into families. Churches have been planted in poor areas and among the neglected Gypsies. A feeding program provides hundreds of children their only warm meal each day. Personally, God blessed my language studies far beyond my meager efforts around that campfire years before. I enrolled in the local university's language program, attending each winter day in a classroom without heat, arriving each day by literally hanging outside an overcrowded tram. But the Lord reaped far more than I sowed. I was able to help with the translation, printing, and distribution of the book, *The Cross and the Switchblade*. Later I had the privilege of translating a pulpit series

for publication and the initial manuscripts of the Teen Challenge curriculum for people addicted to drugs.

I think we tend to underestimate the impact that short-term mission trips can have. When my college mentor encouraged me to spend a summer abroad, I had no idea that it would ultimately result in real, tangible lives being rescued, people getting saved, being fed, clothed, and children adopted into families. I also could not fathom that God was about to overthrow an entire nation's evil regime to make a way to reach the suffering and the oppressed.

When I look back on my life and think about God's Call, I notice that there is an intertwined relationship between the many decisions we make in response to Him and the events that ensue. It's a process that involves putting ourselves in a position where we are able to hear Him. In my particular situation, I was just an ordinary teenager, wanting to be used by Him, and willing to go on a mission's trip. To this day I stand in awe of all that He has done. I share these thoughts in hopes of encouraging ordinary young people like me that every decision we make is important to the kingdom of God.

Short-term missions is not only a vital part of the process of reaching the nations, but of birthing young missionaries with a burden for God's work and Call upon their lives, and His desire to reach multitudes of people who are in desperate need. Like the little boy who brought Jesus five loaves and two fish, He can take our few loaves and fish that we bring to Him and multiply them beyond what we ask or think possible.

"Here is a boy with five small barley loaves and two small fish, but how far will they go among so many?" Jesus said, "Have the people sit down." …and the men sat down, about five thousand of them. Jesus then took the loaves, gave thanks, and distributed to those who were seated as much as they wanted. He did the same with the fish. When they had all had enough to eat, he said to his disciples, 'Gather the pieces that are left over. Let nothing be wasted.' So they gathered them and filled twelve baskets with the pieces of the five barley loaves left over by those who had eaten" (John 6:9-13 NIV).

Bring to God what little you have to offer, and watch Him multiply it, for His glory!

Gypsies / Romania

a daughter's legacy

Selflessness

"Dad, I want to go on a mission's trip!" What beautiful words for a father to hear from his ten-year-old daughter! Tiffany was expressing her interest on going on her first mission's trip.

A call was made to the Mission's director of our church inquiring about any opportunities that would be beneficial for a ten-year-old girl. After prayerfully considering the various opportunities presented, an orphanage in Romania seemed to be a good fit. Summertime when school is out in Romania as well in the USA was decided as the best time. We also asked a friend of Tiffany's if she would be willing to accompany her.

Shortly after expressing her desire to go on a mission's trip Tiffany was diagnosed with a type of brain tumor known as Anaplastic Oligodendroglioma. The only hope the surgeon offered Tiffany was that maybe if she survived the next five years, a medical cure would be found. Tiffany underwent surgery, and in the following months she also had treatments for chemotherapy and radiation. Unfortunately the final recommended chemotherapy treatment took place at the same time as our planned departure for Romania. The treatment drastically lowered her immune system, and Tiffany's doctors advised us to postpone this long anticipated mission's trip. Disappointed? Yes, me even more so than Tiffany. I knew how excited she was to make this trip and what she had just experienced medically the previous seven months. Tiffany took the news about having to postpone the trip for another year in stride and amazingly her enthusiasm actually increased with anticipation during the entire next year.

The next summer and the mission's trip finally came and what a joy it was to watch Tiffany interact with the children at the orphanage. She had a realization even at her young age that she was on a mission. Her actions were out of pure love for the children, never any concerns for herself. She was in Romania for a purpose. She understood the orphans' plight and wanted to show them as much love as possible. Tiffany's friend who accompanied her wanted her to take personal time off during the day. This was frustrating to Tiffany because it interfered with the reason she was in Romania.

While at the orphanage, Tiffany talked via phone with her mother back in the USA, "Mommy, Mommy we have to adopt this beautiful little girl named Eva right away!" These were the first words out of her mouth. "We can bring Eva back home with us, and I'll take care of her. She always wants me to pick her up, and she won't let me put her down. I really love her as a sister already." Mom tried to explain to her that this should not be a quick decision and that we would have to pray about it.

Seven months from the time Tiffany came home from Romania, she departed to her heavenly home. Up until Tiffany went home to be with Jesus, her special dream was to adopt little Eva.

At a time in her little life when most others would have been understandably concerned about themselves, Tiffany's only desire was to pour love out to others. There was no wallowing in self-pity or focusing on the question "Why me?" She instead had an unmistakable confidence that she knew where she was going. She had incredible peace that came from that all-knowingness that could only come from her own strong relationship with God.

Tiffany's short life and actions spoke volumes to all who knew her. My wife and I look back at her life and have learned a valuable lesson, one that we should all learn early in life—complete selflessness. Life is so short, and we need to make the most of the time we have here. We need to focus on the moment and the people we have around us. We need to love them and show them Christ in us and in all of our actions.

"Do nothing out of selfish ambition or vain conceit, but in humility consider others better than yourselves. Each of you should look not only to your own interests, but also to the interests of others" (Philippians 2:3-4 NIV).

One Calling, one mission's trip, and one incredible legacy that she left for her parents to cherish.

"*I tell you the truth, unless you change* gate to orphanage / Ocna Mureș, Romania
and become like little children, you will never enter the kingdom of heaven.
Therefore, whoever humbles himself like this child
is the greatest in the kingdom of heaven." *Matthew 18:3-4 NIV*

a farmer holding an unexploded bomb that struck his home / Kosovo

"Even though I walk through the valley of the shadow of death,
I will fear no evil, for you are with me;
your rod and your staff, they comfort me." Psalm 23:4 NIV

LUIS MORALES
Kosovo

The Spirit of Fear

In 1996, I came to know the Lord Jesus Christ after having spent the eight previous years in a skinhead gang. I committed my life to Christ in a studio apartment I lived in, all by myself, with the guide of a prayer in the back of a Chick cartoon tract.

I never attended church before, but I knew that God had heard my prayer that night, while I was seemingly all alone in that dark place.

Almost immediately after, I was in church, and God was beginning to burden my heart for overseas missions. After watching videos at the Thursday night missions prayer meetings, I felt so challenged in my heart for this type of work. All I wanted was to give something back to God for all of those years I had spent on the streets working against Him. I wanted my life to have an impact on this generation.

My first short-term trip was in 1997 to Colombia, and from then on I was hooked. This was the capacity that I wanted to serve God in. It wasn't until spring of 1999 that I finally had the desire to step out for a long-term commitment. In March of that year I spent a month in Romania, working in an orphanage. The work challenged me, and I felt that working with orphans was a work that was very close to the heart of God. During my stay in Romania, the war in Kosovo broke out, and I felt curious over what was happening in a country that I had never heard of before. My plan was to go to Macedonia to work with the refugees for a few weeks and then move back to Romania for a one-year commitment. God has a way of changing our itineraries in the strangest of ways.

Kosovo would never have been a place that I would have chosen, partly because of the risks involved, partly because I never saw myself ministering in a Muslim country. When I arrived there in August of 1999, it was a mess. The country had been in total anarchy. Ethnic cleansing was the horrible objective of the war, and mass graves were being found throughout Kosovo.

I later arrived in the city of Pristina with its bombed-out buildings and bullet holes in every wall. Fires were still burning, and smoke was rising up out of the city. The Serbians had come through the city, marking the Albanian's homes with spray paint. Then they went through the city looting their homes while raping and killing people. Those that they did not kill, they rounded up and put them on freight trains to expel them out of the country. Now that the war had ended, there were reports of Albanians taking revenge on the Serbians. So here I was in a very lawless society. The harshness of the culture was enough to repel any prospective missionary. But within two weeks of being there, God began to do a work in my heart. I grew to love the people there, people who had suffered through extremely difficult circumstances and lost family and friends in the process. My short-term commitment in Kosovo turned into long-term.

I saw God do some wonderful things in Kosovo. You see for me, Muslims coming to Christ is a bigger miracle than limbs growing back or sight being restored to the blind. God also did some wonderful things for me personally. I became engaged while there to my wife, Myranda, a woman whom God brought into my life, someone who had the same passion for missions as I did.

The first place I lived in Pristina gave me the creeps! It appeared to have been used as a Serbian hideout; I even found a Serbian officer's uniform underneath my bed. So I temporarily moved into the local church building. We were working side by side with their people.

One night at about three in the morning, I heard the doorbell ringing. The two pastors of the church, Arthur and Driton, and a sixteen year old were also staying there that night. Being a light sleeper, I woke up and opened the door, thinking it was some of the young kids from church out late. Five gunmen entered with handguns and masks over their faces. They immediately put me on the floor and taped my hands tightly behind my back, along with my

>

feet, mouth and eyes, in gangland style. A couple of the gunmen had silencers.

I panicked, and fear came over me. It was 3:00 in the morning and I found myself with a gun to the back of my head. I could feel the hard, cold steel being pushed firmly into the back of my skull. My attackers cursed at me and kicked me, and then went on to the other captives and did the same. I honestly wasn't feeling like the angel of the Lord was encamping around us at that moment. I started praying…My body tensed to brace myself for the impact of a bullet going through my skull! *This is it! Would I feel anything?* I thought to myself. I knew that missionaries died in situations like this, especially in Muslim countries where Christians are targets of violence.

I had a million thoughts rushing through my mind. For the first twenty or so minutes, moments of real fear came upon me as I thought of the reality that this could be the end of my life. So I found myself with my face being pressed against the hard floor, praying against the spirit of fear. This was the reality for me. I started to pray and said, "Lord protect us; help us to be calm; take away this spirit of fear!" And He did calm me. The breakthrough was subtle but real. My faith at that moment gave me that eternal peace when we know that our final resting place is in Him. I felt His peace and that He was with us whatever the outcome. The situation lasted for almost two hours.

The breaking point came when the main attacker reached into the aquarium we had and killed the fish. It was as if he had to kill something so as not to kill us. They stole all the money they could. Praise the Lord they decided to let us go. Only afterwards did I realize just how really close we were to death. I found out later, that at the same time this was happening, the Lord had laid an urgent need for prayer for my safety on the heart of my fiance's father back in the states.

Why do I share all of this? Because even after that experience, my heart for missions still burns bright. Many years later as I write this, I have left my job, and we have sold our house. My wife, Myranda, and I have three children. We are now preparing to go to Zambia to work with street kids. It has been several years since the incident that night in the church in Kosovo, and I feel that the call to overseas missions is clearer today than on that night. There have been fears for our children (we have three girls) and for our own lives. There is also the understanding that the world we live in today is more hostile as a result of 9/11. But the Bible has made it very clear to us, "For God has not given us a spirit of fear, but of power and of love and of a sound mind" (2 Timothy 1:7 NKJV).

What are my options at this point? Should I remain in the rat race and continue to build my own empire? The borders of my kingdom being a driveway and a self-contained safe community, or should I cast my cares on He who loves me and respond to the voice that asks, "Whom shall I send, and who will go for me?"

I have counted the cost and still continue to do so, especially as I look down at my peaceful sleeping girls who are safely tucked under the warm covers of their own secure beds. I can worry to the point of not being a part, however insignificant, of the Great Commission, living my life in the shoulda-coulda-woulda realm (and in debt), or I can respond to the Call, despite all the risks involved. And the risks are real! But so is our God, and He promises that no one who has left houses or lands or families or dead-end (but well-paying) jobs for the sake of the kingdom would not fail to receive more in this lifetime and the life to come.

"Be strong and of good courage; do not be afraid, nor be dismayed, for the Lord your God is with you wherever you go" (Joshua 1:9 NKJV).

"The Lord is my light and my salvation; whom shall I fear? The Lord is the strength of my life; of whom shall I be afraid? Though an army may encamp against me, my heart shall not fear; though war may rise against me, In this I will be confident" (Psalm 27:1,3 NKJV).

We have been rescued from our enemies, so we can serve God without fear.
Luke 1:74 NLT

war widows dressed in black as a sign of mourning / Bosnia

survivor of the Vukovar Massacre

"*All this is from God, who reconciled us to himself through Christ and gave us the ministry of reconciliation.*"

2 Corinthians 5:18 NIV

JACQUELINE MEIHSNER
missionary to Kosova

a challenging testimony of forgiveness and reconciliation

Reconciliation

JOURNAL ENTRY—FEBRUARY 18, 2000, KOSOVO (8 MONTHS POST-WAR)
I stepped outside the church to get some fresh air. Our weekly prayer meeting had not yet finished but I needed some moments alone simply to regain my composure.

My heart was so grieved, and I knew the Lord's was too. The girl that sat next to me in prayer still did not know the whereabouts of her brother. He was taken by masked men at nightfall in front of her house. She was not the only one missing a loved one—3,600 other boys and young men were captured and remain missing today. Mass graves were still being uncovered. Every week bodies were being returned by the Red Cross to families for a proper burial. Not including those who were taken as prisoners, more than 12,000 Albanians were killed in the ethnic cleansing that took place under the Serbian regime led by Slobodan Milosevic. Women now widowed with children told us how they could hear their husbands scream as they were burned alive in a nearby house. As I stood next to the water spout just outside of the church, my mind seemed to be flooded with these and other horrors of war I had listened to during my first six months on the field. My heart was broken with those who were truly broken-hearted. Just as real as the snow that had fallen the night before was now melting from the warmth of the sun, the Lord began speaking words of comfort and words of truth to me outside of that church. He assured me that He is greater than the wickedness of men's hearts…that He has the power to purify even the vilest of men…that He is the living fountain that never dies…the spring that never runs dry.

Miraculously, seven years after the Lord spoke those words to me, I am seeing their fulfillment.

What follows is a testimony of a fifteen-year-old boy's experience during the war, which I believe clearly paints the picture that Jesus intends us all to paint—the one of the beauty of the cross. Suffering and death are indeed part of it, but victory over sin and death are too. And in the end, there is forgiveness and newness of life!

"It was just past six in the morning when I received firm instructions from my father to go and release all of the animals we had and tell the rest of the family to leave the house because the Serbian forces had entered our village. But it was too late. The gates of our house were crushed beneath the big blue tanks that came rumbling into my town that spring day. I was grabbed by a masked solider who asked me where my father was but I did not answer him so he put the barrel of the gun into my ear. Then he asked my mother for money. My mother gave him all the money we had, which was 80 Deutschmarks (about $100 US at that time). The soldier got so angry that I thought he would kill me, but I was not afraid. I became without feelings. My father taught me never to surrender even if it hurts.

"They captured my father that day. We heard the shots that killed him.

"My father was part of the Kosovo Liberation Army. He was a patriotic man who struggled and fought to free his countrymen from an oppressive regime that ruled harshly for almost ten years. Many months before the invasion of Serbian troops, I used to keep guard for my father as he slept. When he was awake, I slept. At the time of these 'watches,' thousands and thousands of houses had already been burned, men were taken prisoner, and many more ethnic Albanians systematically murdered.

"The same day they killed my father, we walked all day and into the night in order to cross the border into Albania and find refuge for our family. My youngest brother was only two months old at the time, my sisters then nine and seventeen. We stayed in Albania nearly three months until the NATO forces and Kosovo Liberation Army succeeded in driving out the Serbian regime from Kosovo."

>

61

"I had harbored such hate, and the echo of the sounds of those shots, which killed my father, that I heard the morning of April 27th planted a vengeance in my heart..."

"When we returned, nothing looked the same. It was as if hell had broken through the earth. So much pain filled my heart. I cried that day as I approached the broken gates and stood in front of my burned house and in front of the bodies that were slaughtered. My father, three uncles, and many cousins were killed that morning plus nearly 500 other men from my village.

"I had harbored such hate and the echo of the sounds of those shots, which killed my father, that I heard the morning of April 27th planted a vengeance in my heart that followed me for many years. I actually prepared myself to take revenge on his killers as is customary in our culture (the Balkans). That was until one young man who was helping to build us a new house gave me a Bible. Little by little I began to experience peace and love, something I had not known for a very long time. But a deep loneliness still remained in me

"Then one day I was asked a question, 'What would you do if you came face to face with a Serbian?' Anger arose in me and I told this person never to ask me these kinds of questions again. But he went on to say that I needed to ask God to deliver me and give me strength to forgive those who killed my father.

"That night God challenged my heart; He asked me if I loved Him more than the anger that was inside of my heart toward the Serbian people. I went on my knees near our old house, and I cried before my God, telling Him that I forgave the men who killed my father, my uncles, and my cousins. That night I forgave

the Serbian nation. That night for the first time in a very, very long time I didn't feel alone."

JOURNAL ENTRY: December 23, 2007:

"Sunday service. Pastor Jeton (pronounced Ye-ton) asked the church to share the specific visions the Lord had given them. Then he said that the Lord had given him a vision to minister to people of other countries. I immediately thought he was going to join a couple of other local pastors here who already ministered in Albania and Macedonia. However, these were not the places the Lord had spoken to him about. Tears filled my eyes and the presence of the Holy Spirit could be felt so strongly in that room that day when he said the Lord was calling him to share the gospel with the people of Serbia—a people who had ravished his land and his people, destroyed his home, and brutally killed those he loved and held most dear."

"All this is from God, who reconciled us to himself through Jesus Christ and gave us the ministry of reconciliation" (2 Cor. 5:18).

The fifteen-year-old boy in the testimony above is now a young man. He is Pastor Jeton. As the Lord has given to him this ministry of reconciliation, he has given it to us all who call ourselves followers of Jesus.

Please take a moment and allow the Holy Spirit to search your heart. What have you done with the ministry of reconciliation the Lord has given you?

refugee camp / Bosnia

*Yet in all these things we are more
than conquerors through Him who loved us.*

Romans 8:37 NKJV

KIM O'CONNOR

Kosovo

a praise testimony of God's love and protection

On Fire for the Lord

I feel full of God's peace and assurance as I write this to you—pecking at the computer keyboard, looking through one eye but bursting with eagerness to share with you the goodness of our Lord and Savior Jesus Christ.

Last night, I was in Pristina, Kosovo, where I now serve by teaching English to many Muslim children with the Bible and songs. I entered a room of the compound, happy that I had managed to prepare the name lists for semester two, when the lights went out. I went to light a candle, and suddenly the room was on fire. Gas was leaking in the room from a butane lamp canister, and it exploded, burning one side of my face, my stockings, and my right hand. I beat at myself to put out the fire and screamed for help to put out the fire in the room.

Some brothers from the church here were fortunately still in a nearby building, and they quickly put out the fire and took me to the hospital. They also took me to a British K-FOR army medic, who after examining my treated face, hand, and legs gave a similar analysis—first degree burns. I was quite shaken, but quietly a song kept going over and over in the back of my mind. It went like this: "Victory is mine. Victory is mine. Victory today is mine! I told Satan, get thee behind. Victory is mine!"

I thank God that these words are true! Brothers and sisters, I thank you so much for your faithful prayers. Those prayers have carried me through completing the first term, which was quite a battle! It has been difficult to teach with chaos on all sides, from the many organizations coming through the building where I teach, to the power shortages, the Muslim chants and their call to prayer, water shortages, and miscommunications.

You see, Satan saw that he could not bring disunity on the teams that came. He saw how God used a small Gideon army: a little Puerto Rican woman, Maria, with a sweet spirit who had experienced much in her life but whom God used to encourage us; Wilma from New Jersey with a humble and patient spirit, who sings in the choir and who completed hundreds of registration cards and attendance details; Carlos, with a diligent and authorita-

tive spirit, who is in his first year as a believer but is filled with the wisdom and grace of a believer of ten years; and then me, a little Jamaican girl still uncertain and adjusting to the cultural changes from Russia to Kosovo. And God chose this little Gideon army to take hundreds of screaming, pushing kids and establish a regular class system with small groups of twenty to twenty-five so that kids could hear the gospel of Christ and be taught about it.

And Satan saw. He saw that water shortages and no baths for days didn't take away from the joy of the good news or a cheerful countenance. Instead we were encouraged to share the Lord, knowing that these little ones, who were experiencing the same conditions, still came and without the comfort of the Holy Spirit that lives within us. So it moved us to meet them with a smile that they would know His comfort and experience His love. Satan also saw that power shortages didn't deter us from candlelight lessons, that hour by hour children were being fed with the stories of the goodness and faithfulness of God in the fire with the three Hebrew boys or with Jonah in the darkness of a fish's belly. I'm sure it infuriated him to hear little lips singing: "Whose side are you leaning on? Leaning on the Lord's side!" And it probably increased his rage when he saw that children, weak from observing the fast for their Muslim Ramadan, still came to class, and that Jesus looking into those tired and hungry faces, provided the bread of life, honoring their faithfulness to come with His words of comfort and His strength.

Here's one praise report: Last week, a little twelve year old pointed to the Bible and asked, "Teacher, can I look at that?" Then he stood quietly throughout the following lesson reading it. Another praise report: One adult woman singing, "Cast your burden on Jesus" said, "I know what is cast and what is burden, but what is Jesus?" and the Muslim woman beside her immediately responded, "Jesus is Zoti. Jesus is God." Can you imagine? It's no

>

"Nothing, neither challenging conditions nor shortages, spiritually dark chants or burns can separate me from the love of God. And so even now, I praise and sing: 'Where then, O death, is your sting?' I know that Jesus has the victory, Hallelujah!"

---

wonder that Satan is so angry. Brothers and sisters, I am convinced that Satan hates me, and that he hates all believers sharing the good news of Jesus Christ. He saw that God's will was being done despite his devices, so he attacked my physical person. But I am also equally and fully convinced that Jesus Christ, the Son of the living God, the Alpha and the Omega, the Lord of heaven and earth, loves me. And I am convinced that the Father has said to my Lord Jesus, "Sit at my right hand until I make your enemies a footstool for your feet," and He is doing just that!

Brothers and sisters, nothing, neither challenging conditions nor shortages, spiritually dark chants or burns can separate me from the love of God. And so even now, I praise and sing: "Where then, O death is your sting?" I know that Jesus has the victory, Hallelujah! I can rejoice in these momentary afflictions, waiting even more eagerly to return to Kosovo to begin the new term in January following my Lord! And let me tell you, it is a delight to follow Him. Do you know that verse, "I will never leave you nor forsake you"? It's true! He is here. He was here with the concerned help of my Kosovon brothers and with the speedy response and love of my church brothers and sisters.

I was taken to Macedonia last night. A doctor who was recommended to me arrived this morning to look at my stumpy missing eyelashes and swollen face. She marveled at how God had protected my eyes. One is swollen shut with fluid and I have quite a few blisters, but I can see! And the story does not end there. This doctor sent me to her colleague, who is a Serbian burn specialist and a Christian! She gave me a tetanus shot, antibiotics, and then made a number of small incisions to drain my face, reassuring me that there shouldn't be scarring. But what most encouraged me was that after the medical procedures, she

put her hands on me and prayed for my healing in Jesus' name! Can you imagine the incredible peace I feel knowing the loving care of the Lord and feeling His gentleness? He truly lays a table before me in the presence of my enemies! It fills me with joy overflowing to know that I can trust Him. For with the prayers and His peace around me, I know that I can just take this time to rest and enjoy Him!

Be blessed and strengthened in Him, brothers and sisters! Our God is an awesome God, and He is eternally faithful! I implore you to continue praying because I know that the battle isn't over yet, but press on in faith! He cares about all that concerns us. He is coming soon so that we can be where He is.

I want to encourage those who may be burdened with feeling the weight of sin all around us: the poverty, disease, death, violence, and war, or to see the hard faces of those rebelling against God as if all of creation is truly groaning in expectation of His coming. But I encourage you to look up. He sees. Our God sees! And we can lift our faces toward heaven and thank Him for another chance to celebrate that Almighty God fulfilled His promise and came to us. I encourage you to whisper His name "Immanuel—God with us" and smile!

On another note, dear brothers and sisters, I'm still a woman, so I ask you to pray that my hair and eyelashes grow back! It's a silly request, but His eyes are on the sparrow and I know He watches me.

Editor's note: This was taken directly from an e-mail that Kim sent out after the accident. Kim has since been completely healed from this incident and is beautiful inside and out!

And we know that in all things
God works for the good of those who love him,
who have been called according to his purpose...
What, then, shall we say in response to this?
If God is for us, who can be against us?...
Who shall separate us from the love of Christ?
Shall trouble or hardship or persecution
or famine or nakedness or danger or sword?...
No, in all these things we are more than conquerors
through him who loved us.
For I am convinced that neither death nor life,
neither angels nor demons,
neither the present nor the future,
nor any powers, neither height nor depth,
nor anything else in all creation,
will be able to separate us from the love of God
that is in Christ Jesus our Lord.

Romans 8:28-39 NIV

God's reconciling power to mend a century's old family feud

One New Man

Arabs and Jews are brothers; they are descendants from Abraham. It is the longest standing family feud in the history of man.

When I was in college I was at a point in my life where I was seeking God as a Jew. I was seeking truth! I came across different books that pointed to the Bible and the New Testament. I began reading the Bible, and it became increasingly more Jewish to me and much more real. I started questioning who Jesus is.

I wanted to know if He is the Messiah. I spent days in my dorm room praying and asking God to reveal who Jesus is. The revelation finally came that He is my Messiah! I can say this because it came to me when I was alone. No one was there witnessing to me, and no one took me to a church. As a Jew I could say it was not because somebody prosely-tized me. I was just a Jew pursuing the truth.

I had a true encounter with God. I prayed the sinner's prayer alone in my room. I felt brand new, born again. Up to that point I had been partying, going out to nightclubs, and doing drugs. I threw away my drugs and broke up with my girlfriend. I started to run around, telling everyone I knew that Jesus is the Messiah! That went on for months, but I started to get confused again as many Jewish people told me He is not my Messiah and that He is only for the Gentiles. I went on a spiritual journey for several years even though I knew it was real. It had been an extreme struggle giving myself fully over to Christ as a Jew.

It was years later when I finally surrendered my life to the Lord and had a desire to go to Israel. I made my plans to go on vacation. I was still a young believer of two years. I had a vision that the store in which I was working would be closing down. I shared this with a friend. I believed I had gotten a word from God that I was going to Israel for a longer period of time. Two days before leaving to return from vacation, I was told my store was closing and my job would end. I knew God had spoken to me, and He was calling me to stay in Israel.

I felt it was my home and ended up fully moving there and becoming an Israeli citizen as a Jew. I had no desire to go back to America.

It was September 2000 and the second intifada started in Jerusalem. Riots began after Ariel Sharon visited the Temple Mount. Fear and hatred took over the country. There were uprisings all over with protests, burning tires, and mobs in different Arabic neighborhoods. Violence escalated quickly from rock throwing to machine gun fire, mortar fire, car bombs, and suicide bombings. Tanks made their way out onto the streets. Thousands lost their lives. It was a difficult time in the body of Christ and high tensions developed between Jewish and Arab believers.

I remember I was driving home away from Jerusalem when I made a wrong turn and drove into an Arab village. A fear came upon me like it never had before—a fear for my life—but nothing happened. The next morning after return-ing home I was filled with fear, hatred, and a mistrust of people I did not know. Even though I felt that Arabs and Jews could be brothers through Christ, I was not living it. I felt God speaking to me and drawing me to go into my office to pray. I knew it wasn't going to be a good thing. God immediately started to confront me by asking, "What are you first—a Jew, an American, a Christian, or an Israeli?" He wanted to know where I put my identity! He pointed out to me that first I am a child of God, a believer and follower of Jesus Christ. He showed me that my love for my brother or my sister, whoever they may be—whether Jew or Arab—is primary. He showed me that I was not to have fear based upon someone's nationality and that my security is in Him.

Following this I did some conferences where I tried to reach out to Arab believers. At one congregation I visited, there was a young man in his twenties who came up to me and started pouring his heart out. He told me that he felt God had a plan for his life, yet everything was going wrong: he had lost his job and his car, and felt like Job. I really did not know what to do with this young man. When I left, he was deeply on my heart. Later I came back a second time, and he shared again the same thing. He was an incredible musician and worshiper. After this second visit he ended up calling me, asking for my help and advice. I told him that he needed to come see me. I felt that he needed to take a step toward me, but he was reluctant. I prayed for him, and no more than a half hour later he called me and said he was on a bus on his way to see me. I picked him up, and it was very strange that I really did not know him at all. We did not even talk much.

I took him to my house where we talked for a few minutes and then we started praying. As I started to pray for him, the Spirit of God just fell in our living room. He started weeping and asking God back into his life, repenting from different things. God incredibly knitted our hearts together at that moment. God spoke to me that I needed to mentor this young man. The circumstances felt very odd, as he was an Arab from a different congregation and an Arab village. I asked if he would be all right with me being his mentor. I asked, "Is this something you want?" He said he wanted me to meet his pastor. I called his pastor since I was concerned that he would think I was stepping into his sphere of authority. But instead, he was excited as they had been praying for people to come to help.

I went to his village two days later and met with the pastor, his wife, and this young man. I will never forget our time together. We were sitting in front of the church, looking at this young man when his pastor asked him, "Is this something you want to do? I think this is from God." The young man was torn as if he were a disciple making the decision to follow Jesus. He knew it was a big decision, as I would be pouring into his life. The moment he agreed, the peace of God fell on him, on me, and onto the pastor and his wife. This unity was built between an Arab pastor and myself, and we instantly became like brothers! In Hebrew they call it a *Kesher*, which means when you meet someone for the first time and there is a soul connection that is bound in your spirit. We all became like family. The young man became like my younger brother, and his mother became like my mother. She treated me like her son.

For about two years I visited him and his family weekly, pouring into his life. He lived in an Arab village, and I would go in each week to meet him. One time he told me to park in front of some stores. All these people were there staring at me. They knew I was Jewish and was not from that village. A fear came over me again. I felt God say to me that He had given me authority in this village, and nothing would happen to me unless He allowed it. From that moment on, I felt His complete favor wherever I went in the village. It was amazing. God said to walk in His love, *"There is no fear in love; but perfect love casts out fear"* (1 John 4:18 NKJV). And that is exactly what happened.

I continued to pour into this young man's life. We became the best of friends, and I helped his family get their house together. I saw him grow in responsibility as a Christian leader and a worship leader. God broke that fear powerfully as He can only do and created the "one new man in Christ Jesus" where there are no Jews, or Gentiles, or Arabs.

The hope for Israel is Yeshua the Messiah and the unity that comes through Him. There can be mutual respect, but true love for the Jew and the Arab can only come through the Messiah. And yes, Arabs and Jews are brothers; they are both descendants of Abraham—one through Isaac and the other through Ishmael. It is the longest standing family feud in the history of man. Because of Christ, not only believing Jews, Gentiles, and Arabs are reconciled to God, but they are also reconciled to each other. Jesus' death on the cross put to death any remaining hostility among them. To this day this young man and I are still close, and his family is still like family to me. God can, does, and is creating the "one new man!"

For he himself is our peace, who has made the two one and has destroyed the barrier, the dividing wall of hostility, by abolishing in his flesh the law with its commandments and regulations.
His purpose was to create in himself one new man out of the two, thus making peace, and in this one body to reconcile both of them to God through the cross, by which he put to death their hostility.
Ephesians 2:14–16 NIV

children walking along a dangerous road lined with land mines / Sudan

AFRICA

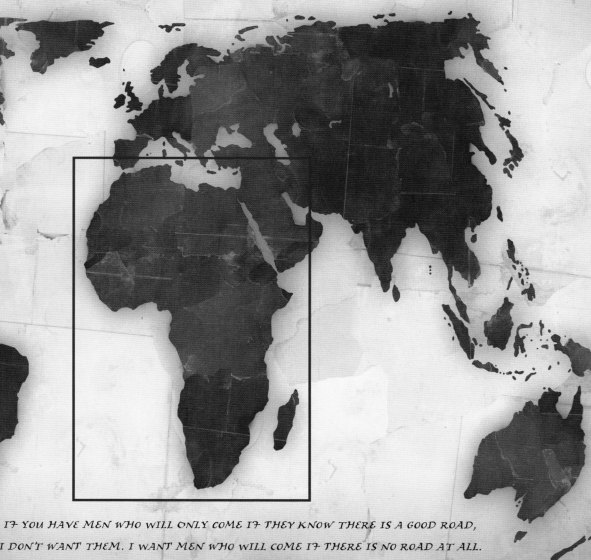

IF YOU HAVE MEN WHO WILL ONLY COME IF THEY KNOW THERE IS A GOOD ROAD,
I DON'T WANT THEM. I WANT MEN WHO WILL COME IF THERE IS NO ROAD AT ALL.

— *David Livingstone,*

FAMOUS MISSIONARY TO AFRICA

Genocide Site in Rwanda

1.3 million dead in Rwanda, 300,000 dead in Burundi, 3 million dead in Congo

Love your enemies, do good to those who hate you, bless those who curse you, pray for those who mistreat you. Luke 6:27-28 NIV

LEOPOLD BANZUBAZE
National President: Foursquare Church of Africa
Chairman of Disarmament, Burundi

ethnic genocide in Burundi and Rwanda

Loving your Enemies

What is genocide? It is one of the most evil of heart issues involving pure hatred and anger for another ethnic group so strong as to go all the way to seek them out and eradicate them, erasing any memory of their existence.

Burundi, Rwanda, and the Congo have had a long history of civil and ethnic unrest as a result of decades of unresolved conflict, hatred, anger, and fear between the Hutu and the Tutsi tribes. The situation came to a boiling point on October 21, 1993 when the first democratically elected Hutu president of Burundi, Melchior Ndadaye, was assassinated by a group of Tutsi officers. Extremist Hutus killed thousands of Tutsis in revenge, and the Tutsi army then swept through the countryside. There were reports that the witchdoctors in the rural villages helped to provoke the hostility. The conflict resulted in the death of an estimated 300,000 people, the flight of 500,000 refugees, and the internal displacement of 1,000,000 persons. These figures are for Burundi alone, but what happened there was soon overshadowed by the events in Rwanda.

The increased hostility in Burundi helped spark cross-border violence into Rwanda, which resulted in more large-scale killings on both sides. On the evening of April 6, 1994, Rwandan President Juvénal Habyarimana and Burundian President Cyprien Ntaryamira's plane was shot down as it was landing in Kigali International Airport, Rwanda. This set in motion in Rwanda some of the most gruesome and bloodiest atrocities of the late 20th century, resulting in Hutu militias launching their plans to destroy the entire Tutsi civilian population.

Death squads conducted mass killings of Tutsis and pro-peace Hutus who were called traitors. They went through the streets killing people with grenades and guns, while setting up roadblocks. But the genocide was carried out by hand on a large scale as people were brutally and individually killed with machetes and clubs. Politicians, officials, and soldiers deliberately incited the killers. Officials even assisted in the rounding up of victims to be slaughtered and provided suitable places for the murders to take place.

Thousands of Tutsi women, children, and babies were targeted in schools. When the residents of a farming village Rukara heard of the rampage coming their way and the massacring of entire villages, up to 1500 people sought refuge in the sanctuary of a Roman Catholic church where they were all brutally slaughtered mostly by machetes.

It was well documented that the government-controlled radio station broadcast hate messages, which incited more murders, such as, "The enemy is still there. Find them! Kill the cockroaches!" They also were conscious of the risks of international scrutiny as they also broadcast, "No more corpses on the roads, please!" Mass gravesites were disguised by covering them with banana leaves to hide them from cameras and aerial photography. But the real terror was that many times the victims' cold-blooded killers were friends, neighbors, and co-workers.

The international community was shamefully and embarrassingly slow in responding to the crisis and struggled to even use the word "genocide," so they did not intervene until it was much too late. In the first 100 days of genocide, about 1 million people were killed, perhaps as many as three quarters of the Tutsi population. An estimated 250,000 to 500,000 women and girls were raped. Two million Hutus fled to the Democratic Republic of Congo. Although the killing in Rwanda was over, the presence of Hutu militias in the Congo has since led to violence and years of massacre there, causing millions of deaths.

What can any of us say to such horrible atrocities? To any common man this seems so far from reality, an almost impossibility of extreme evil and hatred. How can such madness take place? How can such insanity exist in this world? But more importantly, how do we react? What would God want us to do to curb the violence and to start the healing process?

>

I was a pastor at the time of the genocide in Burundi. I had just started the Foursquare Gospel Church of Burundi when the massacres began. I heard God's voice tell me to preach the gospel of reconciliation. He gave me a mission to reach out to Burundians who are from a different ethnic background than myself, which was a dangerous calling, needless to say. I was very persecuted during this time, but God protected me. I went from village to village during the uprisings and murders, sharing about Jesus. I was obedient to God, and I was glad I was because many people were saved. I was preaching to people who wanted to kill me. I told them how Jesus paid the ultimate price by dying for our sins, but that through Him, we can be forgiven of the awful things we have done and be reconciled back to Him. By accepting Christ into our hearts, He could take away our anger and hatred for one another, and give us a new heart filled with love, compassion, and forgiveness. Through the process of preaching to my enemies, I experienced God's love and mercy firsthand. I preached and people listened. It was amazing to see people's hearts truly changed in front of my eyes.

I could have been killed many times preaching in camps up country and in the villages I entered, but God kept me safe! He proved Himself faithful to me. I eventually was arrested and thrown into prison. I saw God's hand in that also. Prison life was difficult, but I soon discovered that many politicians were also thrown into prison at that time. I started being bold and began preaching in the jail, and many of the politicians ended up getting saved. Now years later, our current president of Burundi is a Christian who is not ashamed to preach the Gospel. I believe that God is going to change the situation of our past in our country. I believe He can change people's angry hearts into hearts filled with love.

But it is not easy; the deep-rooted pain and anger that exist because of the massacres is almost an impossible topic to even talk about let alone minister to people in the aftermath of the genocide. Lost family members and loved ones, the memory of vicious crimes committed against them, and the anger over their losses cause the hatred on both sides to continue to grow and keeps building from generation to generation. It is very insidious with seemingly no end or way out.

Jesus teaches us to love, pray for, and forgive our enemies. Jesus said, *"If you love those who love you, what credit is that to you? Even 'sinners' love those who love them"* (Luke 6:32). It is hard to love those who have hurt us the most. But God calls us to rise above the evil that was acted out against us and love our enemies!

Forgiving and loving someone does not justify the wrong that was perpetrated against you. You can forgive someone without pardoning the act. Forgiveness immediately starts a healing process that goes all the way down to the root of the anger, bitterness, and pain. It releases the hold that this pain has upon both sides of the circumstance. Forgiveness leads the way to compassion, understanding, deep healing, and restoration. By forgiving, you bring peace, hope, gratitude, joy, and love back into an otherwise impossible situation.

Since the genocide, I have been given the job of Chairman of Disarmament for the Government of Burundi. It is my job to help disarm the people of Burundi, to help eliminate the over abundance of guns, machetes, and weapons. However, I also know that you can take away the weapons, but the hate can remain.

The real solution and hope for Burundi is to disarm the heart to stop the decades of hate and anger that exist deep in the hearts of the people and instead fill their hearts with love, joy, peace, patience, goodness, faithfulness, gentleness, and self-control—the gifts of the Holy Spirit. The hope is there for Burundi because through Christ, all things are possible!

"If your enemy is hungry, feed him;
if he is thirsty, give him something to drink.
In doing this, you will heap burning coals on his head."
Do not be overcome by evil, but overcome evil with good.
Romans 12:20-21 NIV

Love your enemies and pray for those who persecute you.
Matthew 5:44 NIV

genocide site outside of a church where thousands were killed seeking refuge / Rukara, Rwanda

TALLAT MOHAMED
Regions Beyond Evangelism
Mali, Africa

lessons learned on obedience

All the way to Timbuktu

I grew up in British Guyana. All my relatives were Muslims. My mother died a couple weeks after my birth, and my father decided to get rid of me. My aunt found me in the garbage dump. She raised me. She sent me to Islamic schools and raised me in the ways of the Koran.

I remember there was this lady that lived in my neighborhood who would tell me that Jesus loved me. I told my aunt, and she warned me to stay away from her. I was so curious to find out more about Jesus, so I would sneak out to talk to this woman.

Who was this Jesus? I had never heard of him before. She said Jesus loved me. I did not know love; our family had no love and did not show it to each other. I did not even know what it was like to receive a hug. That woman was the first to tell me the story of Jesus.

As I grew up, I got into drugs and joined a gang. One night we went into a Christian Church and broke up the chairs, the windows, and a guitar, tore up Bibles, broke up the pulpit, and just made a mess of the place. The next day I heard a voice tell me to go back to that church. I did not want to go; I was afraid that they may want to get back at me for breaking up their church. I decided to first fill my pockets with rocks and to bring in a two-by-four that I placed by the door to protect myself. I expected them to try to beat me up. I sat in the back while a man preached. When it was all over, people came up to hug me and they told me they loved me. I told them to stay away. They reached out their hands to shake mine and invited me to come back. It was so strange—I had broken up their church and they loved me back! I went home that night and thought that these people had something that I needed. They had a peace in them that I had never before seen or experienced.

The next Wednesday night I came back and brought all my gang members with me. We all sat in the very back. When they gave the altar call, all fifteen members of the gang stood up and accepted Jesus. Today fourteen of those members are in ministry.

I went off to Bible College. Since then God has made me an evangelist. I work with churches in different countries. With my name being Mohamed, I am easily able to go to places and countries other people have extreme difficulty going to.

I have been to more than 100 countries through the years. I take a few weeks off in November usually to pray and ask God where He would like me to go next. The Holy Spirit always leads me. I write down the countries and start planning in advance.

One time I was praying and the Holy Spirit said to me, "I want you to go to Timbuktu." I stopped and thought; *Where is Timbuktu? This must not be the Lord!* Then I heard it again: "Timbuktu." So I looked at a map and there it was in the country of Mali in Africa right next to the Sahara desert. But as I investigated it online, I found information that I did not like. Many of the early Christian efforts in Timbuktu ended in death for the individuals. My wife and I had a one-year-old baby girl, and I did not want to run off to a dangerous place. I instead replaced Timbuktu with a couple countries I felt were safer.

In other words, I was in complete disobedience! Things started to go bad for us. People were not sending money for our ministry. There was no money for anything. Everything kept going down, down, down… It was like Jonah's story. Nothing was happening, and I could not make anything happen! The Lord taught me my first lesson on obedience. You never advance past your last act of disobedience. The Lord told Jonah to "Arise and go to Nineveh." When he did not go, the Lord did not change his words the second time around. It was still, "Arise and go to Nineveh."

The second lesson I learned is that when you are in disobedience, it affects everyone around you—your ministry, your wife, and your children. Even the dog and the cat are affected. But I thank God for His mercy and His grace. Deep down inside I knew I was disobedient, but I still didn't want to go to Timbuktu!

A whole year went by, while my ministry was doing very poorly. We had barely enough money to buy food. One day I was unshaven, wearing jeans and a t-shirt, walking in a Wal-Mart. This little man came up to me and asked, "Sir, are you a Christian minister?" I did not know what to think of him or his question. In fact I looked nothing like a Christian minister. I look Muslim if anything. I answered him, "As a matter of fact, yes I am! Why?" He stared at me, told me his name, and said, "I am a pastor from a local Baptist church. Can I pray for you?"

I took a second, thought about it, and since we were in the back of Wal-Mart, I said yes, all along thinking no harm could come from it. This little man put his hands on my shoulders and started to yell loudly, "God make this man obedient!" He continued to pray very loudly. With my head down, I heard people walking around us. I heard one man say, "Wow, that guy must really be disobedient!" After what seemed like a long time, he finally finished his prayer and I excused myself while saying, "Thank you, thank you." I quickly made my way to the opposite end of Wal-Mart, as if I was hiding from him. I was a little embarrassed and kept thinking about what he had said and prayed. I turned around, and there he was again. I was in a corner and could not escape. He came walking up to me. I said, "Do you want to pray for me again?" He said, "No, I want to give you something." He reached into his pocket and pulled out a ten dollar bill and said, "Here, put this toward your trip to Timbuktu!" I stared at him in disbelief. He said, "Do you think God can't talk to a Baptist?"

So I was soon off to Timbuktu. I made my plans, God provided just enough money, and within a month I was on a plane to Bamako, Mali. I got a four-wheel drive Land Cruiser, a guide, and an interpreter. We drove for such a long time—fifteen to twenty hours. We drove through the Sahara Desert with nothing in sight for as far as you could see, over areas that had no roads, just sand. We got to the Niger River where we took a pontoon boat across to the other side. We finally arrived in the afternoon on a Saturday. As we pulled up to a gate there was a big sign saying, "Welcome to Timbuktu." I had finally arrived!

Timbuktu is a city of approximately 30,000 people in the middle of the Sahara Desert. It is a major desert trading post that is getting smaller and smaller as the sands of the Sahara Desert keep creeping in on it. So there I was in Timbuktu in the middle of nowhere. I did not know the men I was with, and I felt helpless not knowing why I was there or where I was supposed to go. I had no plan. I

owed the driver two hundred dollars, and I was out of money! I did not know how I was going to pay him. I had obeyed God and there I was! *Why am I here, God?* I wondered. *Now what?* We asked a fourteen-year-old boy for directions. The boy said that he was told if people came, that he was supposed to take them to Mr. Nock. *Who is this Mr. Nock,* I thought to myself. I said, "Yes, yes take us to this Mr. Nock!" We got back into our Land Cruiser and drove into the city. As we pulled up to a house, a dark, handsome looking man in a long flowing robe came out. He said, "Mohamed, Mohamed, welcome! What took you so long—you are a year late? What happened?" I said, "Do you know me?" He said, "We have prayed, and God showed us you were coming. Anyway, follow me; we have rooms and food for you to eat." He led us to a large compound, where he had everything prepared for us—very nice rooms and a large, wonderful meal of lamb. We were so hungry.

Afterward we sat in a big room and he said, "Tomorrow we have the big meeting. The mayor is coming; his name is Mohamed! The congressman is coming; his name is Mohamed. Several other important people are coming; all their names are Mohamed." I joked, "Are you having a Mohamed convention?" He said, "No, no, just a lot of people have that name."

The next day a bunch of Islamic people showed up, and it was amazing. We preached the Gospel. I don't know if my Islamic background and my name being Mohamed helped, but God was so good that day. The Holy Spirit was there, and many people ended up getting saved. Some German people came to the meeting also. One came up to me and said, "The Lord told me to give you some money; here is four hundred dollars." That was the third lesson I learned on obedience: the place of your obedience is also the place of your provision. It was enough to pay the driver and get back to Bamako. News of that meeting even made it in their local newspaper.

On our way back to Bamako, the Lord spoke to my heart and said, "Someone's destiny always depends on your obedience." This was the last lesson I learned on obedience. I think about this all the time. How many of us have a Call upon our hearts to which we need to be obedient? There are many people's destiny and salvation attached to those Calls. I encourage you to be obedient. God will provide for you. Answer the Call!

ROBERT STEGEMANN
Missionary Ventures International
Zambia

a student witch doctor who finds God

Housewarming for the Witch Doctor

As a missionary, one of my main jobs is to teach at many of the thirty Bible colleges that our ministry runs throughout the world. These Bible colleges are rising up wonderful men and women to become native pastors and missionaries.

Teaching throughout Africa in countries like Zambia, Nigeria, Malawi, and South Africa, I have met many people who were connected to witchcraft, spiritualism, and other occultic practices. Witchcraft has an extreme stronghold on many of the villages we visit. Witch doctors are looked up to and admired.

Celine was one such woman who was serious about her witchcraft and was studying under the head witch doctor in her village. She had plans to make her living from this practice.

Over a period of time she had became extremely sick and was sent to a clinic to see the local medical doctor. The doctor told her she had a disease that would soon take her life and like so many Africans seeking medical attention, she was sent home to die. But God had another plan for her.

The witch doctor that she was studying under gave her roots, cast spells, and did other things to try to cure her, but she only grew worse. A missionary couple who were students from the Bible college where I taught, had made friends with Celine over a period of three years. They lived in a nearby village and had been sharing the love of Jesus with Celine. As her sickness progressed, she became desperate and called them to come to her. They quickly responded and were soon sitting by her bedside. In love that day they were able to lead Celine to Christ.

The very next day, a missionary friend and I received a message to quickly go to the village to minister to this dear sister. We all arrived at the village to see Celine. She had waited patiently all day for us to come. We gathered around her and prayed for her that the Lord would deliver her from all demonic presence, and she deeply repented of her sins of witchcraft. That day we saw the powers of darkness broken in this dear lady, and evidence of God's love took over her broken life and began to heal her. To see the Holy Spirit minister to her was a wonderful thing, She became a new creation in Christ. God not only set her free from Satan's grip, but we witnessed her physically get healed.

Following our prayers, Celine was so excited that she wanted to get rid of everything that related to magic or the occult that the witch doctor had given her. She began by going into her small two-room hut made out of sticks, twine, and other gathered brush. She collected every item she had used for casting spells and performing witchcraft. She even dug a root from under her front door. What she did next surprised all of us, as she carried everything that she had gathered to the witch doctor's hut in the middle of her village. Celine then asked permission from the head elder, who was the only other Christian in the village, to burn down the witch doctor's hut. He gladly gave her permission. She started a fire and set the hut ablaze. She was very determined and made sure she burned the witch doctor's entire house down.

People from all over the entire village came to see what was happening as big billows of dark smoke rose up into the clear blue sky. What a great sight it was! Celine proudly stood there as great testimony to everyone of God's delivering and healing powers. It reminded me of the book of Acts when the people gathered together and burned their magic books.

Celine is now out sharing Christ with others in her village. I happened to be back in this part of Zambia on my last visit. My wife and I saw this wonderful lady standing by the roadside, still serving the Lord and sharing the love of Jesus with all who would listen. God is so good!

As for my wife and me, God has opened an unusual door for us. We are now pioneering a two-year Bible college on the Galapagos Islands. The school will be at Charles Darwin's front door. What makes this exciting to me is that I was an avid Darwinist before my own salvation. I am excited to see what wonderful plans God has in store for this new region!

family involved in witchcraft / Maputo, Mozambique

A number who had practiced sorcery brought their scrolls together and burned them publicly... In this way the word of the Lord spread widely and grew in power. Acts 19:19-20 NIV

BRAD GUICE
Photographer
Nigeria

a miracle testimony of God stopping a storm

The God of Heaven is Stronger!

It was a warm, sultry evening as the large crowd of 500,000 people started to gather in the polo field for the first night of our International Outreach. A Muslim mosque towered ominously behind the stadium as the main silhouette in the skyline.

I remember looking up at the ever darkening sky and seeing the black storm clouds rolling in above our heads. There were loud crackle sounds in the distance as lightning bolts were starting to give us a dramatic light show on the horizon. I remember thinking to myself that the outreach was definitely going to be rained out…

It was October 2002, and we were in the province of Jos, Nigeria, for our churches second ever International Outreach. The first outreach was to the Philippine Islands, which was marked with wonderful success. After the Philippines the Lord had laid a burden for Africa on our pastor's heart, so when the door to Nigeria opened, we immediately took it.

The outreach to Nigeria had been about a year in the planning stages, and we had spent months praying and fasting for the event. A little over two hundred of us had come for the outreach. One hundred choir members, along with musicians and sound technicians, were there to conduct worship. The majority of the remaining group of people were from our missions department. They were there to conduct medical and dental clinics, along with outreaches to orphanages, hospitals, people in the streets, as well as helping set up and run the outreach.

The hour for which we had all been preparing for so long was quickly coming upon us. The choir started to file in and line up in performing order on the stage. The band was in position and was tuning their instruments. Our pastor, elders, and missionaries came in and took their seats.

Unbeknownst to us, in the back of the polo field over 200 witch doctors joined together dancing, chanting, and casting spells upon us. We did not know that six months earlier when we had placed billboards all around the province advertising the upcoming outreach for Christ, the witch doctors had publicly announced they would stop our outreach! They boldly stated, "Just wait and see! We will show you the witch doctor's power is stronger." They were so bold in their statement of their plan to stop the outreach that the news of it had spread over the whole province and the crowd that night was waiting to see what would happen. What we did not know was that first night was going to be the big showdown.

The seven o'clock hour arrived, and the worship music began. Immediately the first raindrops fell, light at first. Our pastor stood up and started to pray boldly for the start of the crusade. Just then a downpour started as the rain came down on us from two different directions. The wind whipped up and blew so hard that a twelve foot wall next to the choir blew over, sending the choir running for their lives and crushing the pulpit. There was a moment of chaos as we removed the wood wall and cleared the stage, making sure that no one had been hurt. All the time the rain continued to pour and the wind blew so hard you had to brace yourself against it.

In the midst of the chaos, a missionary stood up and took the microphone. He boldly raised his hand and said to the audience, "How many of you believe that the God of heaven can stop this rain? Raise up your hands to the clouds and join me in prayer: In the name of Jesus we command the rain to stop!"

Thousands of hands were raised up to the clouds, as the crowd joined in interceding to stop the storm.

I remember thinking to myself, *I can't believe the boldness of his prayer. If God does not answer this, what will happen to everyone's faith?* Then I realized that I needed to take control over my own thoughts of unbelief and join in. I lifted my hands in prayer.

We were entering into a prayer of the magnitude of asking God to part the Red Sea! It was amazing hearing the crowd cry out to God. A couple minutes later, the rain and the wind stopped!

Our pastor took the microphone as he now had the whole crowd's undivided attention. He rebuked a few witch doctors who were trying to cause a distraction in the crowd, and God caused them to lie down prostrate on the ground unable to move. For the next two hours, we could see and hear the loud crackling of lightning all around the polo field, as it was obvious that it was pouring rain all around us. It was as if we were standing in the middle of the parted Red Sea. God appeared to be using it as a reminder of the miracle He was doing.

The sermon that night was anointed by the Holy Spirit as our pastor spoke on God's power, His grace, His love, and receiving salvation through His Son Jesus Christ. It was a sea of palms that night as people raised their hands to accept the Lord into their hearts. God held off the rain until the last note of the last worship song was played. Then the rain started to come down. No sooner than everyone had boarded the buses to leave, rain came pouring down in buckets.

I witnessed this miracle firsthand as I photographed and videotaped the entire event. There were also, of course, more than 500,000 witnesses!

The next day our pastor was visiting businesses in the city. When people recognized him they said, "There is the man of God from the outreach!" One business invited him in to pray with all of them—a group of ten Muslim women. The whole city was buzzing with the news as everyone proclaimed, "The God of heaven is stronger! Stronger than the witch doctors!"

We had two more nights of our International Outreach after that. God made sure that nothing stopped His gospel from being spoken. The province of Jos had been a region plagued by years of major religious and civil unrest. For a good period of time after we left, there was a peace that settled over the region; now, unfortunately, the conflict is back more serious than ever.

I know the impact of that night had a major influence over the entire region, and to this day you can still hear people proclaiming, "The God of heaven is stronger!"

*The disciples went and woke him, saying,
"Master, Master, we're going to drown!"
He got up and rebuked the wind and the raging waters;
the storm subsided, and all was calm.
"Where is your faith?" he asked his disciples.
In fear and amazement they asked one another,
"Who is this? He commands even the winds and the water,
and they obey him."*
Luke 8:24-25 NIV

DR. IKO IBANGA
Executive Director: Pro-Health International
Nigeria

a miracle testimony of the Holy Spirit's healing power

The Great Physician

We go on roughly thirty to thirty-three medical outreaches per year where we bring health care aid to the poor, tribal villages of Nigeria and other African nations. We often travel into the bush areas, reaching out to native people that have never seen a doctor.

For many of them, seeing us will be their only opportunity to get health care in their entire lifetime. We have a data base of 3000-4000 health care workers (physicians, surgeons, dentists, opticians, nurses, and pharmacists that generously donate their time to Pro-Health International). Our doctors come from all over Africa, Europe, and the United States. Each year we have more than 500 doctors that go into the field with us.

On one such occasion we were on a one-week medical outreach to Agpor, Nigeria. Many of the tribal people traveled for days to get to us, some carrying their sick over long distances and rough terrain. Thousands and thousands of people began camping outside our facilities waiting to receive medical attention. Our staff carefully screened people by their illness and importance of medical attention. Over the next few days, we gave out general medical care, preformed surgeries, dressed wounds, pulled teeth, dispensed medicines, performed eye surgeries, gave out eyeglasses, and more importantly, shared the Gospel and prayed with these hurting people.

The week went by as our doctors worked compassionately and selflessly through long hours to try to meet all of their needs. At the end of the week, we had taken care of several thousand patients. We were all very tired, and our time had once again come to an end. But as usual on these medical outreaches, our available time was not enough to reach all the people's needs. We once again found ourselves facing thousands of people who were still waiting for and needing medical attention.

Our tired medical staff gathered together in front of the large crowd to address them to let them know our time had come to a close. We told the crowd we were sorry, but we could not stay any longer and that we would like to pray for them. Our medical team started off by worshiping the Lord. The crowd soon joined in as

everyone sang songs of praise to our Savior.

We were all fully immersed in worshiping when a large commotion came from the back of the crowd. There was an excitement with whooping and hollering coming from the people as every head turned to see what was happening. It started from the very back of the crowd and moved steadily forward as if a slow, large, powerful wave was flowing over the people. It was the Holy Spirit! There was an overall sense of surprise, amazement, and joy as the Holy Spirit swept over the crowd and healed people!

Many of the sick were healed as the wave progressed toward the front of the crowd. There was an overall sense of surprise, amazement, and joy as the Holy Spirit swept over the crowd, healing supernaturally many of those that our tired medical crew had not been able to help.

Just then, a crippled woman in her 30s, whom all the people seemed to recognize and know very well, came walking forward from the back of the crowd rejoicing. The crowd went wild with excitement. Amazingly she was healed!

None of us will soon forget that moment as we witnessed the wonderful grace and healing power of the Holy Spirit poured out on these very needy and deserving people. The Lord, in all of His grace, stepped in and wonderfully accomplished what we could not.

As physicians, every day we are made aware of our medical limitations in the care of our patients. It is wonderful when God reminds us that He is the Great Physician, and He is not limited, and nothing is impossible to Him!

blind boy with mother at medical outreach / Nigeria

Crowds came from the villages around Jerusalem,
bringing their sick and those possessed by evil spirits,
and they were all healed. Acts 5:16 NLT

crowds waiting for medical outreach / Nigeria

"Be quiet!" said Jesus sternly. "Come out of him!"
The evil spirit shook the man violently and came out of him with a shriek.

Mark 1:25-26   NIV

DOLORES ROBLEDO-SMITH
Nigeria

demon possessed woman at a medical outreach

Still setting the Captives free

Every night on this missions trip, before going to sleep, I would read my Bible and pray. This night was different. The eerie chanting that pierced through the night skies was echoing from east to west. When one voice ended, another would take over.

The Holy Spirit simultaneously prompted me from casual prayer to intense intercession until I fell asleep from sheer exhaustion.

Upon awakening early the following morning, the Lord gave me a vision. I saw myself standing before a great sea of precious Nigerian people as far as the eye could see. With a microphone in hand, I was being filled with the Holy Spirit's Gospel message tailor made for them. My response was, "Have your way, Lord; not my will but your will be done."

After meeting with our team leader for morning devotions, worship, and prayer, we boarded our vans once again to assist Dr. Iko Ibanga and the medical mission team. We had helped out the entire day before and what an experience that was, unlike anything I had ever known. It was a scene straight from the book of Acts. Droves of needy people walked for miles and miles with all kind of injuries and diseases. Some carried their sick loved ones on homemade carts. Women carried their little ones on their backs. They balanced jars or baskets on their heads that held rations of food and drink for a day spent desperately waiting to be seen by a doctor.

My heart broke as I was totally overwhelmed with emotion. I understood how Jesus was moved with compassion for the lost and needy. I knew that if God didn't show up, our being there would be in vain. I realized my faith was being challenged in ways I had not known before. Hot tears uncontrollably streamed down my face as I petitioned God for His divine wisdom, strength, and intervention.

My other team members Max and Carl and I were again assigned to join the Nigerian pastors who had a small tent set up across the field, opposite the building where the medical team was set up. We were to minister to those who desired prayer, so they announced to the people to form lines like we had them do the day before. We each had prayed for hundreds upon hundreds of people and knew we needed more help. Other team members had joined us to help out as well. I shared with the guys what I believed the Lord had placed on my heart. Although the medical needs of these people were great, their spiritual needs were greater still. Every two hours, one of us would share our testimony and give an invitation to receive Jesus as their personal Lord and Savior. We knew that if they would receive Jesus into their hearts and lives, they would have all they needed.

When the guys shared their testimonies, hungry hearts gave their lives to Christ as far as the eye could see. We would continue to pray for the sick until noon when we took a much needed break. While resting under the tent, one of the Nigerian pastors rushed over to me and bid me come pray for a woman who he thought was experiencing an epileptic attack. As we followed him through the crowds that had formed around her, I immediately knew that this was demons not epilepsy. (Biblical accounts and personal experiences revealed that demons seem to manifest when they sense the Master is present to deliver.)

We witnessed these demons violently throwing her down on the rocky soil, tormenting and tossing her around like a rag doll. I turned to the team and asked them to pray in the Spirit. As we stood there watching and praying, the woman looked at us and began telling the crowd in a mocking voice, "Oh yes, I've been delivered in the name of Jesus." I then heard the Holy Spirit telling me she had been involved in voodoo, and that if she would give her heart to Jesus and renounce these works of darkness, He would deliver her this day.

I stepped out into the clearing toward the woman, and when she saw me approaching, the demons violently threw her down to the ground again. This time, I got on my knees

>

next to her. After silencing the demons who were hurling insults and curses at me, I asked the woman her name. Struggling to get the words out of her mouth, she finally said her name was Sarah. I proceeded to tell her that God Almighty had revealed to me that she had been serving Satan through voodoo, and that if she turned away from these acts and give her life to Jesus Christ, the Son of the Living God, He would deliver her this very hour.

Struggling to respond because the demons were trying their best to interrupt, distract, and torment her, she finally answered yes, she wanted Jesus as her personal Lord and Savior. As I began leading her in a sinner's prayer, the demons would interrupt with profanity, and I would have to silence them over and over until I could get Sarah back on track again. After we prayed, there was a stillness. Finally, Sarah spoke and stated she felt a little sick. I knew she had yet to come to a full deliverance. The guys helped Sarah up and I led them to the tent. After a while, she began to vomit chunks of meat as we continued in prayer. When she was through, she dropped to her knees, lifted her hands to heaven, and declared in a clear voice, "It's over, Jesus Christ has set me free. I've truly been delivered!"

Tears of joy overwhelmed all of us as we gave thanks and worshiped the Lord. I told her she needed to tell the people what God did for her. She stood up to adjust her clothes and her turban. We went out of the tent to the crowd of witnesses that were looking on the entire time in wonder and amazement.

The Nigerian pastors interpreted in two dialects so there would be no misunderstanding what God had done. When she finished, I took the microphone from her and preached the Gospel in the exact way that God had shown me in a vision early that morning. Needless to say, hundreds turned to God in true repentance, receiving Jesus as their personal Lord and Savior. The Holy Spirit truly had His way. Just as in the book of Acts, God made an open display of the enemy and triumphed victoriously. Jesus is the same yesterday, today and forever. May He forever be praised!

"Jesus rebuked the demon, and it came out of him;
and the child was cured from that very hour.
Then the disciples came to Jesus privately and said,
"Why could we not cast it out?"
So Jesus said to them, "Because of your unbelief;
for assuredly, I say to you,
if you have faith as a mustard seed,
you will say to this mountain,
'Move from here to there,' and it will move;
and nothing will be impossible for you.
However, this kind does not go out
except by prayer and fasting."
Matthew 17: 18-21 NKJV

bush girls / Abuja Territory, Nigeria

CONNIE DEBARTOLO
Zambia

God awakening a woman on her death bed

Raised!

I was called to go on an International Outreach to Zambia, Africa in October of 2004. It was a multi-task call. I worked on the press conference, I had the opportunity to preach, and I was part of an AIDS outreach team.

It was the latter of the three that I would like to share…

My team was scheduled to visit a location where there would be people who have the AIDS virus gathering to meet us. Unfortunately confusion with transportation and scheduling caused us to be very late, and when we finally arrived at that location, no one was there. We were told that many that were stricken with the virus had to travel a long way and had to make the long return back home to their villages to rest.

But that didn't stop three of us from our team!

Over the years, I had heard many stories of miracles from the mission field and my prayer for this trip was "to see in the supernatural" as I had read in the Bible.

The mission: Two of us would venture out with a small group of local women while the other teammate went with one other local to visit and pray for a dying man. So my friend and I ventured out on our own as we were determined to spend some time spreading the gospel of love and hope!

We walked through areas that were heavily oppressed and received dark stares from the locals. We walked deeper and deeper into the village until we reached this one particular house with a man sitting on the porch. We stopped and asked him if we could talk to him. "Yes," he answered but then looked away. He had nodded to us and then nodded to the house as if giving us permission to enter. I sensed that there was someone in the house. So we slowly and reluctantly entered and walked through one room until we got to the back of the house. We were shocked at what we witnessed!

There was a women lying on a cot with tons of flies landing on her as well as circling around the room. The humming of the flies and the odor in that room was overbearing. The room was dark and dirty, with no light at all. She was lying on a very dirty sheet, dying, weak, extremely skinny, with puss coming out of her ears, and bedsores all over her. She had AIDS! We were in the presence of a woman in the extreme last stages of the disease.

I remember bending on my knees and whispering in her ear to see if we could get a response from her, and if we could pray for her. There was no response. I turned and saw children running to see what was happening and peaking through the open doorway. We lifted her up and started to pray for her. Moments later the power of the Holy Spirit came upon us. I laid my hand on her back.

Suddenly, light entered the room! The room was much brighter. The flies left; Jesus was there!

The women opened her crusty eyes, and they were bright and glowed as if something was happening inside her. She was meeting her Savior Jesus. "You were dead but now you are alive." Those were the words that kept going through my head. Strength came upon her, and she was able to talk. We shared the Gospel and spoke about Jesus and heaven and how beautiful she will be when she gets there. She acknowledged our words and had hope.

As we were leaving we asked the locals to bring her to our medical outreach clinic so she could see a doctor and get medicine for her infections. I am not sure if she ever made it to the clinic, but I do know that she did make it to heaven! And that she is with Jesus…

Jesus pulled her out of a pit of death that day and raised her to be with Him. I do not know that she lived much longer after that, but she did come alive long enough for her to hear about and except Jesus into her life. More importantly, she definitely set her path for her eternal destination. My prayer was answered. I witnessed the miracle of Jesus waking up and raising the dead and giving her the gift of eternal life.

PETER & VICKI SORENSEN
Executive Director: African Prison Ministries
South Africa

how God stretches us

Way out of the Comfort Zone

The bang of the steel door closing behind me seemed to shudder through my soul. My flesh wanted to be anywhere other than where I was—a prison in West Africa. Having just stepped through the main door of this decrepit colonial-era facility…

…I glanced around the courtyard looking for the precious sons God had called us to claim back from this terrible place of darkness.

I had never before visited any prison anywhere. I was totally out of my comfort zone, standing in a place that was as foreign as another planet. In anticipation of our arrival, the administrators had assembled the entire prison population in the courtyard. As my eyes first fell upon our captive audience, my immediate thought was that the gathered prisoners more resembled impoverished, sickly refugees than wards of this small West African government. These men were more bones than flesh, dressed in rags that wouldn't qualify to check the oil in a car. Coupled with the most terrible smells I had ever encountered, the sights and sounds of that very first prison visit will be forever etched in my mind.

Just two months earlier I was minding my own business, working on Wall Street in downtown New York City. I had the corner office as the chief executive of a small financial services company servicing large corporations and their billion dollar transactions. As a committed Christian in that role, I was doing my best to fulfill the Great Commission by proclaiming the Lord's truth whenever and wherever I could. I was always focused on reaching out to the lost, even praying with clients over business lunches as they personally faced the challenges of life. On several occasions I had the privilege of nervously sharing my faith before groups of clients during business meetings. As satisfying as it was to take a stand for Christ in the business realm, I always had a deep desire to do more.

At this same time, my mother was working as a missionary in West Africa. A general fear of sickness and disease kept me from visiting her on the mission field, but I would often phone to hear of her adventures and share my encouragement. On one such call she mentioned, "I will be visiting a prison here tomorrow." Deeply intrigued, I phoned her back the next day to hear of her experience and the very difficult conditions in the prison she visited. As we said our good byes and I replaced the receiver of the phone, an image passed through my mind. It was the picture of the Prodigal Son in rags at the end of his

reckless adventure. With this image still fresh, I phoned my mother back with an idea I felt could be God-inspired.

"Mother," I said, "could you go back to the prison and ask the warden if he would allow us to host an outreach there, a Prodigal Son banquet?" She agreed and when I called her back the next day, she shared the warden's enthusiastic response of "Yes, come do whatever you like." Thus began the biggest adventure of our lives. It was this passing idea, which I believe came from God, that began my transition from Wall Street to full-time prison work in Africa. You see, on Wall Street, people are trained to seek out opportunities. As a Christian, I had never seen a more incredible opportunity on the mission field than in the prisons of Africa.

So there I was, with the blessing of my wife and family, standing in front a crowd of the most miserable and unfortunate men I had ever seen. Following the example in Scripture of the father's homecoming banquet for his lost son, we purchased a cow in the marketplace in this African village and had a wonderful group of church volunteers prepare a feast for these sickly and starving men. I explained to these men that they had a Father in heaven wanting to spend eternity with them, and who was prepared to claim each of them as a son. Given the opportunity, the response to this gospel message was overwhelming. Nearly every inmate in that prison indicated a desire to follow Jesus that day and I walked out of that prison in tears.

It was that day that I knew He had a calling on our lives. I have since left Wall Street, and my family and I have moved to Africa. My precious wife has also embraced the opportunities in the prisons here as she ministers so effectively. From that first outreach, we have hosted Prodigal Son banquets in many countries throughout Africa and have seen thousands respond to the gospel message. Since taking that step, we have experienced the most fulfilling and exciting adventure of our lives. For us, even as committed Christians, answering God's call to the prisons of Africa was the most life-changing and rich experience of our lives.

ELIZABETH CANTU
first time missionary
Zambia

sharing a personal testimony to prostitutes

Six Prostitutes on their way to Heaven

"Maybe because you came all the way from New York City, they will listen to you," the pastor told me, then added, "I've tried and tried to bring these six prostitutes to the Lord, but they just won't listen to me."

I stared at the pastor and felt myself begin to shake from head to toe. This was my first mission trip. The group I was in had gone house to house witnessing with two local pastors. This was a new and exciting experience for me. Most of the people we talked to were willing to listen, and many came to the Lord.

But now one of the pastors was asking me to go with him to talk to the six women without the rest of the group. I didn't know if I could do this by myself. Several excuses for not going with him came to my mind: *I can't separate from my group, we have to go back to the hotel, it's late, the bus is waiting…*

Instead, I heard myself say, "Yes, I'll go with you." Why had I said this? What could I possibly say to these women? If the pastor hadn't had any success, what made me think I would? We were in one of the poorest compounds in Lusaka with dirt streets and humble, one- or two-room houses. He led me to one of them at the end of a narrow, dirt road. We walked into a dark room that was bare except for a bed that stood in the center. Still nervous, I sat at the foot of the bed while he went to find the women.

The room was almost pitch dark, and it was hot and oppressive. I could feel the atmosphere of voodoo and black magic around me. I began to pray and to plead the blood of Jesus. I was still shaking when the pastor walked in, followed by six young women. They were scantily dressed. They kept their eyes intently on me. They sat on the floor in front of me, and their eyes never left my face. All six faces held the same expressions—boredom, with just a tiny bit of curiosity at what a woman from America could possibly say that would be of any interest to them.

The pastor sat next to me as I began to speak. I talked about the sacrifice that Jesus made to save us, about His love for us, about His saving grace. I talked and talked, but their expressions never changed, their eyes remained empty. I continued to talk and they continued to stare. "Lord," I prayed in my spirit, "how can I reach these women? How can I tell them of Your love in a way that can touch their hard hearts? How can I explain that in You they have everything?" "Tell them your testimony," the Holy Spirit told me. So I began…

I was happily married for twenty-eight years. I had four children and a successful business. It was a beautiful life. I had everything. And then, it all ended suddenly because of adultery. Without warning, I found myself alone with a daughter who was twelve (my other children were already married).

My perfect life had been shattered, and all the pieces lay at my feet. Night after night, through tears, I would stare at all the pieces, not knowing how to begin to put the pieces together again. Then our business was gone, and I lost all financial help. I had nothing left. Twenty-eight years of marriage and hard work gone, destroyed because of sin.

All I had left were memories and pain, and a young daughter who needed me. And then I turned to God, and He began to put the pieces of my life together again. He guided me and comforted me, and I held on to His loving hand as He pulled me up to my feet again. Slowly I began to live again. I read Psalm 91 over and over again, and I knew that the Lord would be my strength and my refuge forever. And now, He is my Husband, my Friend, my Provider, my Comforter, my Healer, and my loving Father. He will never abandon me or betray me.

I swallowed hard, realizing I had been crying. I couldn't see the faces of the women, and I closed my eyes tightly to clear my vision. When I opened them again, I looked at them and saw their tears. They had been crying too. The Lord knew my testimony would soften their hearts so that the seed of His love could be planted.

"Do you want this Jesus I am talking about to come into your hearts too?" I asked. They nodded. I turned to the pastor. " Would you please lead them in the sinner's prayer?"

women gathered in flea market / Lusaka, Zambia

God demonstrates his own love for us in this:
While we were still sinners, Christ died for us.
Romans 5:8 NIV

DANNY & SUE JAYNES
Directors: GlobeLink Foundation
Ghana, West Africa

teaching the ways of God on the mission field

Hugging God

Before becoming a full-time missionary, I was in the insurance business and was an Associate Pastor of a church in Texas. Now we serve as missionaries in the upper regions of Ghana, West Africa.

We do a lot of traveling into various remote villages. Our primary focus is to plant national missionaries (native missionaries from Ghana) in these villages and to disciple people in the ways of Christ. To accomplish this task, we employ several methods to reach the people. Sue, my wife, is a licensed nurse, so medical outreaches are routine. Sue's medical training is the primary door we use for entrance into these villages in which she can see on the upwards of 150 people per day.

I myself have developed an effective, quick, and unique method of building huts for the national missionary to live in within the village they are to be missionaries. I do this by simply using plastic bags filled with dirt and then covered with chicken wire and cement. I also discovered a method of putting Christian movies into local languages so those hearing them in their mother tongue receive the complete message of the videos. In our time in the villages, we encounter numerous opportunities to share the Gospel one-on-one with people. Each time is a unique experience and most times very rewarding.

While recently on an outreach into a remote village in the north, I was asked to pray for an elderly man who had several sacrifice stones in front of his hut. It was routine for him to make sacrifices to his ancestors on the stones. I got permission not only to pray for him but to also converse with him through an interpreter.

I started the conversation by asking the man how many gods he thought there were. He quickly replied, "Three." Then he proceeded to name them. It was then that the interpreter explained to me that the three gods were his father, grandfather, and great grandfather. I asked him if any of them made the sun, moon, trees and clouds. He replied with a definite no. I explained to him that the God that did make all those things gave us a book, and that in the book God explained that He would send His Son into the world to die for the sins of the world, and that if we will place our trust in the Son and follow Him faithfully the rest of our lives, that there was no need to make any more sacrifices. In fact, I explained to him that every time he made a sacrifice, he was telling God that His Son's death was not enough. The elderly man looked into my eyes with an excited and sincere look and said, "If someone would tell me of this book, I would obey it!" I had the honor of taking a stick and drawing two roads in the dirt and explaining the broad way and the narrow way to him. I told him that he must be very special in God's eyes for

God to send a missionary from the other side of the world to talk to him about Jesus. I prayed with him and encouraged him to find someone to continue teaching him the Bible and also warned him that he will no longer be able to stand before God on judgment day and use the excuse, "No one told me the truth."

Another day we did an outreach to a people group that had migrated from the north of Ghana into the central region of the country. Sue provided medical services for many in the village while our son Micah and I were busy building one of our plastic bag huts. In the evening, we set up and showed a Christian movie to those in the village and had an altar call afterwards. I noticed that one young Muslim man seemed very irritated by the movie. The following day when the team went back to the village to do one-on-one evangelism, I deliberately looked for and conversed with this young Muslim through an interpreter. I asked what he received from the movie the evening before and the man replied, "You Christians do not know how to pray!" I asked him to explain this statement, so he said, "Well, sometimes you stand up to pray, sometimes you bow, sometimes you look up, and sometimes you close your eyes. We Muslims we know how to pray correctly!" I then asked if he had children. He answered yes. I asked if his children ever hugged him, and if so, how did that make him feel? He answered that his children do come to hug him and when they do, it makes him feel very good to receive their hugs.

I told him that praying is man hugging God, and that it makes God feel good for us to hug Him. I asked if his children ever hugged him on his legs, one on one side and one on the other? To which he answered, "Well, yes." I then asked him if he ever stopped his children and told them to stop hugging him this way and that they should stop at the doorway and bow to him ten times before he would receive their love. The man laughed and said, "No, of course not!" I then explained to him that God is the same way. He does not care if you hug Him in the front, on the side, or the back; He just wants His children to hug on Him. The man was very satisfied with this illustration that was provided about the posture we take while hugging, loving on, and praying to God.

This is much of our ministry, one-on-one evangelism while serving God and others. Just a reminder—have you hugged God today?

old Muslim couple / Nigeria

"*As the heavens are higher than the earth,*
so are my ways higher than your ways
and my thoughts than your thoughts." *Isaiah 55:9 NIV*

street musician in central market place / Maputo, Mozambique

Muslim children / Nigeria

JERRY HAMPTON
Elder and Director: Prison Ministries TSC
Zambia

two men given a choice

Two Men sitting in a pile of Trash

This is a simple testimony, or is it? It is one that is at the basis of everything we believe in and know as reality as Christians. I saw it illustrated in real black and white terms this day.

It was October 2004. I was part of our churches international outreach to the country of Zambia in Africa. Zambia is a country that has been devastated by poverty and AIDS. Everywhere you look, there is tremendous need. It's as though many of the populace, in general, has given up the fight for daily living.

In addition to the planned ministry in the prisons of the capital city of Lusaka, we were also part of street ministry. Street ministry on this particular day was basically going door to door, witnessing and praying for the local citizens. We had finished our work and were making our way out of the neighborhood. I was with a young local man named Thomas who had been wonderfully saved and was escorting me through the community. He was a delightful young man with a great smile, clear eyes, and the love of God in his heart. As we were heading back to the rendezvous point for the rest of the team, we came upon the local trash dump. Even before I actually saw it, I could smell it—rotted garbage, discarded clothes, broken furniture, and everything else you can imagine were everywhere. As we rounded the corner and saw the crater of filth, we could see the small fires in and around the dump where there was a meager attempt to burn some of the garbage. The smoldering garbage caused for an overall smoky environment.

On the edge of the dump was a small makeshift shelter of cardboard, sticks, and plastic, where two young men were tending the dump. I think they had nothing else to do but scavenge whatever they could. We sat down with them and began discussing who they were, what they do, how they got there, and where their families were. They were both from families who had died from "the sickness" as they call AIDS. They had no future, no hope, no energy, and no life in their eyes. You've heard the expression, "I'm in the dumps"—these young men were literally there. We began to share that there was a way out, a hope, a future, and it comes from having a life with Christ!

As we continued our discussion, one of the young men began to respond and asked questions about the reality of God: can there be hope, can there be a life? As we answered his questions, he began to cry—not out of pain or sorrow but out of a hope that what we said was true. His tears were also pleading with us to end his pain of depression and loneliness. We offered to lead them both in a prayer of salvation, but only the young man who was crying accepted our offer. We began to lead this one to the Lord and his tears turned into rivers of joy as he accepted the love of our Savior! The other young man refused to accept our prayer.

As we were leaving, my young associate Thomas offered to take the new believer with him. The young man accepted! We left the dump with one in tow and the other left behind. It was a combination of joy for the one and sorrow for the other. Both were in the same circumstances at the same place and heard the same story of salvation. It reminded me of the story of the two thieves on either side of Jesus while on the cross. After the one thief showed repentance and reverence Jesus replied to that thief, *"I assure you, today you will be with me in paradise"* (Luke 23:43 NLT).

When we were walking away, I turned to look back over my shoulder. The other man that we had left behind was sitting there playing with his shoelaces. He was comfortable in his makeshift cardboard shelter looking down at his dirty, worn out shoes. He still had the look of hopelessness upon his face. He had no real idea what was offered to him that day. Even though we had explained it to him, he still did not understand the eternal consequences of his choices. He was content with his life of sitting in trash and salvaging through it as a method to sustain his life. He knew nothing else. I could not help but wonder if he would come to the saving knowledge of who Jesus Christ is before his own life is done on this earth.

Two days later at the stadium where we were holding our evening meetings, Thomas came up with the young man from the dump. As he parted his way through the large crowd of people, I saw a changed man. He was bathed, with new clothes and a brand new smile from a new heart. Thomas had taken him home and began to clean him up in more ways than one. The young man had hope and a future! I could not help but look at him with love and excitement, that excitement that causes all the angels in heaven to rejoice when just one soul is saved. I was so happy for him and his newfound life in Christ. I also thought about the glorious moment when we all reach heaven. It will be much more of an exciting moment when we all see what God has prepared for us in our eternal home.

This memory keeps it fresh for me. We are offering a simple message of love and salvation to everyone we witness to. It is a message that is easy for someone with blinded eyes to turn down and even scoff at, but one of great joy and eternal consequences for all that accept Jesus as their Lord and Savior. We live for that moment when someone looks up and comes to the reality that Jesus Christ is Lord. What an exciting eternal moment!

MYRANDA MORALES
missionary to orphans
Zambia

a man led by the Holy Spirit

A big pot of Beans & an Answer to Prayer

A few weeks ago in my personal time with the Lord, I was deep in prayer, asking the Lord to give me the sensitivity to feed anyone who comes to my gate hungry. You see, we have been struggling with all the needs here in Zambia. It is hard to see the grinding poverty and children begging for food on the streets daily.

My husband and I have been on the mission field for less than two years, and we have already noticed that it is so easy to grow cold, get hardened, and turn away from what you see. Our day-to-day ministry can sometimes get mundane. So on one particular day, I was going about my day as usual. I homeschool our three daughters, and my husband was out working hard at the orphanage, going about his daily chores and routines.

I was about to cook lunch. For some crazy reason I wanted to cook a big pot of beans. I noticed how I had too many vegetables in my fridge, and I was worried about them going bad. I soon found myself putting a large amount of beans and cut up vegetables into an oversized pot, wondering who was going to eat all of this food.

A few minutes later our gardener comes to our door to tell me someone was at the gate who wanted to talk to me. I proceeded to the gate to find the tiniest old man I had ever seen standing there! This is what he told me:

"Madam, I have not been able to feed my children in more than two days. I prayed last night, and God gave me a vision of your gate. God told me, 'Go to this gate and my servants there will help feed you and your children.' "

Now understand something—this man had no idea what he was going to find upon arriving at our gate. He had no idea who we were or what kind of greeting he was going to encounter. All he knew was that God gave him a word, and he had the faith to believe that God wasn't going to let him down. So with the utmost faith and courage, this man being led by the Holy Spirit walked a total of fourteen miles on an empty stomach to come and find our house with the gate the Lord had given him a vision of.

That day I was just going about my day as usual. I wasn't looking for any great ministry to fall in my lap. I had even forgotten about my prayer that morning. But God doesn't forget our prayers! Because of God's faithfulness, we got to be a part of that man's miracle, not because we are so special. Even in his own words, this man said God told him that His servants there would feed him and his family. That is all we are—His servants. We only are servants willing on a daily basis to do His will, willing to be led by Him even in the mundane things such as making a big pot of beans.

This little man didn't have to put his children to bed hungry, and his faith in God was bolstered beyond any words possible. And God used that moment to remind us of why we are here and the importance of living our lives daily to the glory of God. It was probably the most humbling awesome moment I have had in my Christian walk so far. As simple of a moment that this was, the precious man left my house with big bags of food and tears of gratitude flowing from his eyes.

Do you think that God sent him to test the sincerity of our hearts? Does it matter? Isn't that the heart of God, "When I was hungry you gave me bread." Don't we all need to learn that lesson and live out our lives this way?

The moral of this story is that nothing is mundane in the kingdom of God! Cook those beans to the glory of God and watch what Jesus will do with your life! Be willing to serve Him in the simple things, humble yourself in the day-to-day simple tasks of everyday life in which we serve Him. Don't always think that your ministry has to move mountains every day. God knows you are there and will use you through your humble servant actions for His glory. Oh how God encourages us!

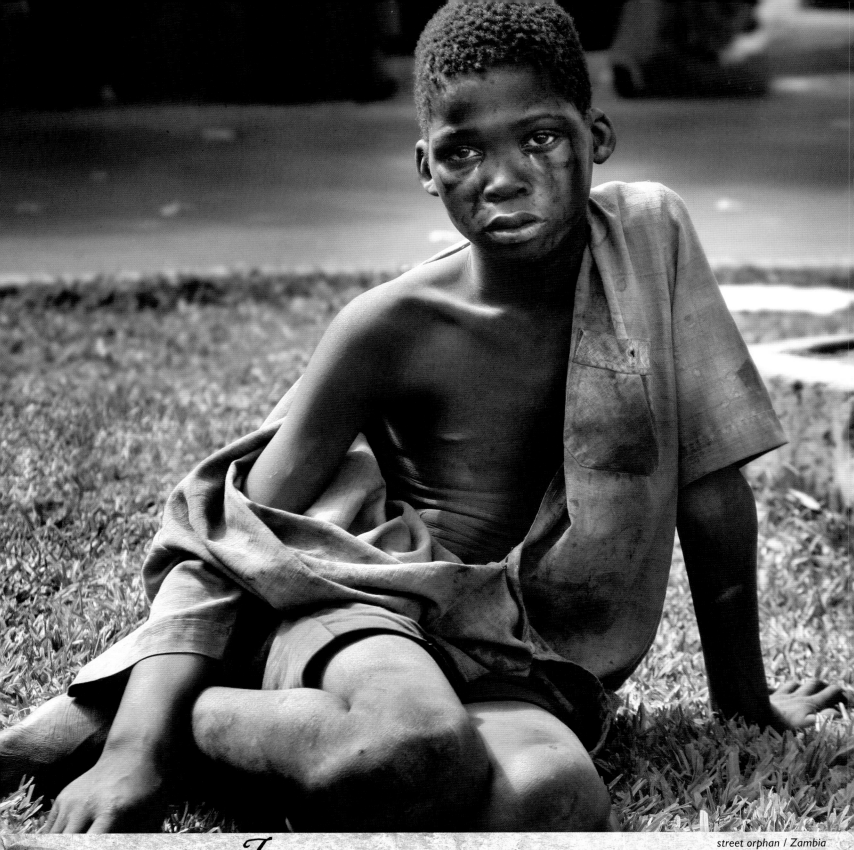

street orphan / Zambia

"I am the vine; you are the branches.
If a man remains in me and I in him, he will bear much fruit;
apart from me you can do nothing." John 15:5 NIV

SAUNDRA WIKELUND
Founder: Emma's Kids orphanage
Zambia

The Fruit of Our Labor

I grew up in West Virginia, one of a large family of twelve. As a little girl I was raised in the Nazarene church. I remember the day I walked up the aisle, with my knees all wobbly, to respond to God's salvation plan. I was twenty years old, but I still get the chills thinking about it.

When I got saved, I just wanted to tell somebody, anybody, and everybody about the Lord! Something was exploding inside me. I just could not shut my mouth. I would give tracts out at the local filling station and leave them on restaurant tables. I had a lot of zeal. The chaplain at my work said, "Saundra, not even I can tell everyone about Jesus!" But I just wanted to be able to stand in front of Jesus someday and make Him proud.

But I never thought I would end up in Africa. I did not know anything at all about Africa. I just was not interested in it. I thought I was called to Central America. I had determined that that was where I was going, and I was full steam ahead.

Then one day, Rolland, our mission's director, sat my husband and me down and told us there was an open door for us to go to Africa. He said to my husband, "Rodger, we need you to build a Bible dormitory there. You may be there six months or maybe a year. Who knows, you may just like it there." I thought that was the funniest thing I had ever heard! I did not think that was possible. I felt like Sarah laughing; there was no concept in my mind at all that I would go to Africa, let alone like it there!

Just about that time my mother got sick with cancer. She was the most important person to me. So I put everything on hold. My mother's last verbal request just before she died in 1997 was, "I want to go to the mission field, I want to go now!" Sadly she never got the chance. Later I would name the ministry, "Emma's Kids," in her honor.

We have been in Zambia since June 1997. We went there with one thing in mind, and the Lord birthed something totally different. When my husband, Rodger, and I first came to Zambia, our primary objective was to build the dormitory to help with finishing a project that was started

years earlier. Rodger is a builder and a teacher, while I am a registered nurse. While Rodger knew what he would be doing, I did not have any idea what God would do with me.

When we first arrived, we moved up to the copper belt to a little town called Mufulira to start our work. We did not have a stove or a refrigerator. I did not want to be there, and I was still grieving my mother's death. I had a deep hurting feeling inside. I would privately cry and grieve and say to the Lord, "I don't want to be here, Lord. How can you get me out of here? I am not really happy here, but I love You!" I never planned on being there long so I did not even seek out a refrigerator or a stove.

Every day I would go around town buying food, and I would cook it outside on a little grill. This put me in contact with the street kids. I would just turn my head on them because I knew I could not help all of them—not because I did not have the compassion but because the sheer vastness of the problem was just too overwhelming.

One day, a little boy named Patrick was begging. I gave him about 25 cents, which he took into the store to buy bread. I watched him devour the bread that day, and I felt sorry for him. I saw him often. Then within a short period of two or three days he found out where I lived in the apartments. He came knocking at my door. I thought to myself, *What have I done now?* I was scared that all the street kids would start coming to my apartment. I was concerned for my safety and fearful of being robbed. But this little boy, Patrick, was so sad looking and hopeless. So I asked him, "Please come with me to church tomorrow." He came and when the altar call was given, this filthy little boy stood up in his old, ripped clothes and bare feet. He walked down the aisle with his arms raised high up in the air to accept the Lord into his life. When this happened, something in my heart changed.

>

That was the first street kid I had contact with. But little did I know that God had much more in store. The next day I ran out and bought him new clothes and shoes. He was so excited. He had two friends that saw his new clothes, and they all wanted to go to school so badly they asked me to help them. I put Patrick in school for twenty-five dollars. I then prayed to God, "God if you supply me the fifty dollars, I will put the two other boys through school also." I shared it with our mission's department back in the United States. Soon after, I got an e-mail back saying that everyone was giving money to help put the kids through school. Our director, Rolland, said, "I am going to make this a project and call it, "Saundra's Kids" because it needs a name." That is when I felt the Holy Spirit warn me about pride! I did not want my name on anything. Pride is the reason for many ministries failings. When you take any glory away from the Lord, you are a thief because it all belongs to Him! That is when I thought of "Emma's Kids," naming it after my mother.

I have not been able to keep up with God ever since! All I ever wanted to do was feed a couple kids and send them to school, but God had bigger plans. People think I know what I am doing but I don't. God is truly leading this ministry. It belongs to Him! Emma's Kids has literally exploded. I say that respectfully, as it has been a daily surprise seeing what God is up to.

We now have over 300 orphans. Many of them call me Mom. For most of them I am the only mom they will have. God has also increased our ministry beyond children. We now also take in widows. We have over 2000 acres of land, an agricultural and missionary training school, and a medical center. We have a school—Emma's Kids Christian Academy—with ten classrooms. Our farm is ten kilometers in the bush of the most un-evangelized area of Zambia. Where our kids come off the street is considered the witchcraft capital of Zambia. Let me share a few stories of our kids with you.

I went to the police station one day; they had a little boy six or seven years old. His stepmother had brought him in trying to help him. His grandmother had raised the boy in witchcraft. She would take him into the graveyard to do rituals and actually raid the gravesites, taking dead body flesh to cook and eat. They also cut him in three places on his hand; it looked like a tattoo, but it was where they put their blood into his to mix it. They dedicated him to the devil and cursed him. The little boy shared with us all of these horrible things. The people in a local village had even discussed burning the boy to death because he was a witch, and they were scared of him. The stepmother said the boy

was out of control and very hard to handle. The police and stepmother gave him over to us at Emma's Kids, so we took him to our compound. The grandmother would come to our gate and try to lure him back to her. We took him to our chapel where many of us prayed for him. Now that little boy is serving the Lord; he accepted the Lord into his heart, he was delivered, and is now as happy as any child could be. We have now legally adopted him and he is ours or better said, he belongs to Jesus now.

One of our kids was #1 in Zambia for three years with Bible memorization through the ACE program. We sent him to South Africa, and he placed #2 on the continent of Africa. Another one of our kids is in the best academic and most expensive school in Zambia because his scores were so high. When we found him on the street, he had been stoned. His bones on his feet and legs were sticking out of his skin with bad infections. He is now in the top five in that school. Tell me that God does not love everybody and chooses the most unlikely to show His love through.

Another boy, Isaac, was fifteen years old and living on the street. We found him in front of the food market stealing food and hanging out; that's where we find most of our kids. He went unnoticed for a long time; he was one that just did not stand out very much. I saw him begging and fighting with the other kids. I went into the village and saw that he slept in the dirt, on top of an old feed sack. When he came to Emma's Kids and walked into the chapel, he gave his heart to Jesus. He is an incredible child, and he is being mentored at our property. He is sold out for Jesus; his dedication to the Lord is beautiful. You just know God is going to use him. He wants to be a pastor.

One evening someone was walking home to the village about eight o'clock at night. They heard a cry and thought it was a puppy. They did not have a flashlight. There were dogs all around the object making the sound. They went from hut to hut until they found someone with a flashlight. They went out and found this little newborn baby about one day old with the umbilical cord still attached. They took him to the hospital, but nobody claimed him. Everyone called him the Dump Baby. It made national news. We saw him for the first time at three months old with just a rag wrapped around him. The hospital barely had enough money to take care of him. We took him home to Emma's Kids and named him Moses. He is now our child as we were able to personally adopt him. He is the smartest little boy. He accepted the Lord when he was three years old, then again when he was four, then at five years old, and again at seven. He just says to me, "Momma, I just want to make sure I am saved and I go to heaven".

But he knows that he has had an intimate experience with the Lord, and he loves Him so much! He is a straight A student and an incredible athlete. Now when I bring him back with me to the States, he has the track coaches turning their heads as he is faster barefoot at nine years old than all the runners on the high school track team.

There was another little boy named Efrim who was struck by lightening. We found him out on the farm. He could not close his eye, it was fixed open with liquid running out of it. We brought him in to the capital city of Lusaka for surgery then to the United States where they were eventually able to save his eye. He now is doing wonderful and is one of our highly anointed young men.

Then there was Mpuntu. As he tried to walk the streets begging, he was mocked by the other street kids because of his extremely bad clubbed feet. He dreamed that one day he could be like the other kids and wear shoes. When he came to Emma's Kids we took him to a shoemaker. At the end of the day, he came running as happy and ecstatic as he could be, holding up his shoes for everyone to see, even though they were just strips of leather sewed together to fit his feet. His feet were so severely twisted that even doctors back in the United States said he was beyond help. But I have never seen a kid with such pure faith who trusted God as much as Mpuntu. He trusted God even though his condition seemed permanent. He loved the Lord so much that he began preaching God's Word, and he would dance around praising God in front of the other kids with his clubbed feet. His faith made me not lose hope as I continued to try and find a doctor who was willing to help him. God opened the door for him to have surgery. He now walks around as a healthy young man wearing real shoes! God has done exceedingly abundantly above all that Mpuntu could have asked for or imagined. He truly is a testimony of God's love!

On another day I went to the town's social services. They had a young boy seven or eight years old. His mother had gotten mad at him and put his hands in boiling hot water as punishment. His hands were so badly burned and scabbed we thought he was never going to be able to use his fingers again. We took him to the hospital, and they worked on his hands for weeks. They put his mother in prison. We brought him to our premises and put him in one of the dorms. He had so much hurt, bitterness, and anger locked up inside him. He became so rebellious, cussing and causing problems, that we had to expel him for the protection of the other children. He went to the village to live on the street. Soon he came back to us; he saw the goodness of God. He accepted the Lord and now dances in praise and sings worship for the Lord. He has an incredible voice. At the last school break he came to me and said, "Mom, I want to go visit my mother. I know what she did to me, but I love her and want to go visit her." I sent him to her. He was so proud to show her how wonderfully he had grown up. He told her to her face that he loved her and forgave her. It was so beautiful—only God can do those things!

The first thing we do when a child is rescued off the street is sit them down and tell them the Gospel. We tell them the love story and connect them with Jesus. We have rescued so many orphaned children; we have directed our efforts at helping the real street children who are truly helpless. We have witnessed God doing miracles in these children's lives. There are also many runaways on the street that we help with food, invite them to church, and try hard to reconcile them with their families and give them the Gospel. The needs are just so great, but we worship a great God!

But what keeps us going is the fruit of our labor. The testimonies are endless, and the lives that God has changed are precious. Kids are being saved and given the chance to succeed in life. They can go on to achieve and accomplish much more than what I can. My prayers for them are filled with so much hope. God can and is lifting them up to be used for His glory! They can go on to impact their own villages, communities, country, continent, and the world. All things are possible through Christ!

"If you remain in me and my words remain in you, ask whatever you wish, and it will be given you. This is to my Father's glory, that you bear much fruit, showing yourselves to be my disciples."
John 15:7-8 NIV

One million AIDS orphans in Zambia; 700,000 homeless children on the street

Sell your possessions and give to the poor. Provide purses for yourselves that will not wear out, a treasure in heaven that will not be exhausted, where no thief comes near and no moth destroys. — Luke 12:33 NIV

TOM LARKIN
World Aid New York
Zambia

the street children of Lusaka, Zambia

Now I know God is Real!

It was late, about 10:30 p.m. We made our way into the center of Lusaka into the bowels of the marketplace. The streets were eerie and dark. There were burning fires and piles of garbage everywhere. Eyes were peering out of the darkness at us.

We kept walking and walking for some time till we came to the area our guide was leading us to.

The children were asleep inside sewage pipes and ditches. They were packed on top of each other like sardines, trying to gain some warmth from the cold of the night. We woke them up. There must have been some 150-200 kids as they came out of the darkness. They were filthy with tattered clothes and most in just their bare feet. There was a stench of drugs about them. Many of them clung to their plastic bottles with a drug called *sticker* in them. It is a mixture of benzene and glue that they inhale. Many of them say it relieves the pain of being on the streets and helps them to keep warm at night.

The kids were so happy to see us. We gathered them up and sat them down under a dingy street lamp. We had come out there that night to see the street kids. We had visited several orphanages, but we did not understand what a street kid was till that moment. They are mostly AIDS orphans, victims of an epidemic who were plunged out onto the streets to live like animals. They have no mother or father, all of them living in the gutter with no safety net. Nothing about their existence resembled a life that a normal child should have. They had been forced into a life of begging, stealing, and wandering the streets looking for a way to survive. They had joined together in large groups to find some form of comfort.

They were gathered in front of us with all their little faces looking up at us, wondering who we were. Among them were children as young as five years old with runny, snotty noses, filthy head to toe. Our group was made up of mostly pastors and preachers, but they were stunned speechless in front of these children. We had the opportunity to preach the Gospel to them. We told them about the love of God and shared the thought that the King of the universe came down from heaven just for them. We spoke of all of His glory. We wondered if they understood what we were talking about.

We brought food and milk to hand out for them to eat. We asked the children if they would pray for the food. There was this little boy maybe nine years old that raised his hand. He said this prayer, "Oh God, now I know you are real because tonight, before I went to sleep, I asked you to bring me bread, and you brought these people here to feed me." Our whole group started crying as people recognized what this child had said. We had come across continents, walked down back alleys, and we didn't know where we were going. We did not hear a voice say, "Go to this street, go to that street," and yet we were sent to the exact place at the exact time where God had heard the cry of one of His little children. He was just crying out to see if God was real, and if anyone cared. God had sent us there for that moment.

I left that night with a breaking in my heart that would not go away. A burden started to develop in me to return to those kids. From that experience we went back to Zambia in May 2005 with a local pastor named Rueben guiding us. He had come out with us that first night and had developed the same burden.

This time we had returned to Zambia just to minister to street children. We would go out to the streets at night to find them, and during the day we would bring about 300 kids to a transient center for a Bible study and to a medical clinic, and just talked to them about their lives. It was amazing to watch these kids go from being a piece of garbage to being a child of the King. They came to recognize that God really loved them.

Kids were praying for things. When they asked us for clothes and a place to stay, we would tell them not to ask us but to ask God! One time the kids prayed, "God can we have a place to stay tonight with a roof over our heads, blankets, and something soft to lay on?" The director of the transient center said it was impossible. Then to our amazement and theirs, a van from a UN agency drove up and dropped off new mattresses. Then another van drove in and dropped off blankets. The director walked back over to us and said,

>

"We are not supposed to do this, but tonight all the children can spend the night on these new mattresses and use these blankets." The children were seeing the Lord move on their behalf. Their prayers were being answered right in front of their eyes!

One night in the streets with rats all around, with filthiness and garbage everywhere, I was looking at my wife sitting on the ground comforting the children, rubbing their backs, and loving them. I was wondering when was the last time these kids were comforted and loved. Life on the streets is so vile; there is never any rest, and there are fights, violence, sexual abuse, and even murder. It is like the devil is driving them. It is a horrible life on the street.

I was feeling such peace, and I was overwhelmed with love for them. I realize that it was the Lord starting to love the kids through me. It was not an emotional thing anymore or that I felt pity anymore for them. It was a supernatural love for them. I was just looking at the kids and the Lord said to me, "Many people are calling for a revival. It is a carnal thing; it is about themselves! It is about "Touch me, God! Bless me, God! Give me finances and prosperity!" And He said, "If you want to find Me, you will find Me here! I am with the poor and the brokenhearted." At the time I don't think I really grasped what that meant. Later on I thought of Matthew 25:37-40 where the people asked, "Lord, when did we…feed you?" The Lord answered, "Whatever you did for the least of these, you did it for me."

One day we had this idea to take the street children to Pastor Reuben's church on a Sunday morning. So we rented buses, loaded them up with about two hundred street children, and drove them to church. Pastor Reuben's church had a congregation of about two hundred and fifty people. As the kids came swarming in, most of his congregation got up and moved to the back. They were afraid. It was as if the seas had parted in the front. They had left all the front rows open, and all the kids jumped into the seats. Pastor Reuben was horrified to see the reaction of his congregation and how they were not receiving of these children. He went to apologize to the children, and they said, "It is OK, Pastor, most people don't like us and are scared of us." The image in my mind was here were these vagabonds to the natural man but treasures to Christ. It reminded me of the scripture:

"For if there should come into your assembly a man with gold rings, in fine apparel, and there should also come in a poor man in filthy clothes, and you pay attention to the one wearing the fine clothes and say to him, 'You sit here

in a good place,' and say to the poor man, 'You stand there,' or, 'Sit here at my footstool,' have you not … become judges with evil thoughts?" (James 2:2-4 NIV)

Over the next year and a half, Pastor Reuben's church dwindled from two hundred and fifty people down to eight! People left the church—they didn't want to be around the street kids. He paid a price but gained so much in return. Pastor Reuben's testimony was that he realized he had been a religious man and targeted people that would look good in his church, people who would tithe and bring in money. He said, "Now I recognize that everything I thought I knew about religion and God has been turned upside down." Pastor Reuben lost everything in a sense but gained a church of street children, and he is now running the ministry.

We continued feeding the kids in the streets. We knew that there was more work to do than just this. For a six month period I felt like the Lord was saying to my heart, "Would you go all the way for these children?" "Yes, Lord," I would say, not counting the cost or thinking of the implications. For six months that was all I heard from the Lord. Then one day He answered His own question. "Would you go all the way for these children because I went all the way to the cross for you!" My mind raced with the thought that the Lord didn't just come and say, "Love your neighbor, do good to others, and love your enemies!" He did all that, then He went all the way to the cross for us; He brought us in, and it cost Him everything!

The idea of feeding children, getting them a house, and beginning an orphanage sounds so nice, but it is costly to love. To have the love of God for people is costly. It has been filled with heartaches, headaches and losses for us. Yet God has opened up an orphan's home, which is filled with so much joy and love. We have thirty-two boys currently. They are going to school while growing in Christ and testifying of the greatness of God. We are now opening our second orphan's home. We still go to the streets and feed the children. God has done miracles, and we have recognized that He is the Father to the fatherless. He loved them before we knew them. He sent us over continents and overseas to share His love for them.

It has been a privilege to be involved and watch God show His love for these children. But the question still lingers for all of us to answer: Are we willing to go all the way for the Lord? He went all the way for us!

street kids hanging out inhaling "sticker," a mixture of benzine and glue

large crowds gathered and waiting for medical outreach / Ngozi, Burundi

I tell you the truth, anyone who gives you a cup of water in my name because you belong to Christ will certainly not lose his reward. Mark 9:41 NIV

ROGER HAYSLIP
Director: World Challenge Inc.
Orphanage Care / Support & Frontier Missions
Burundi

the simplicity in the word of God

A Cup of Cold Water

We Christians love to hyper-spiritualize. It makes us feel so—well, spiritual. Sometimes God's idea of spirituality is not what we imagine, and the Gospel is far more simple and down to earth than we think.

In the summer of 2007 my wife and I participated in a nationwide medical outreach and evangelistic campaign in the tiny African country of Burundi, fresh in the aftermath of civil war/genocide. God taught me a lesson there I will never forget.

Our particular team was responsible for running a medical clinic in the town of Ngozi, far upcountry from the fairly secured capital of Bujumbura. Tensions still ran high, people were in desperate need of every kind, and we had government-issued soldiers with weapons manning the parameters of the complex for security reasons.

Word of free medical care, something these impoverished rural people could never hope to afford on their own, traveled quickly. People came by foot and bicycle from miles around, and they waited in long lines under a scorching equator sun (some of them for days on end). Onlooking bands of roving orphaned children were kept at bay outside the rope boundaries by the soldiers. The desperate and crowded scene instantly brought to my mind the story of when Jesus fed the five thousand.

My wife helped greet people, register and escort them to and from the doctors or pharmacy in an orderly fashion. As a minister, it was my responsibility to oversee a prayer station in between the clinic, where patients were first assessed by a doctor, and the pharmacy, where they went afterward to get their meds and/or exit. Our prayer team's specifically assigned mission (with interpreters) was to individually encourage, share the love of Christ, and pray with every single person as they passed by.

The first day or two, many of the people were aloof to our gentle spiritual wooing, indicating by facial expression, body-language, or spoken word that they either already knew God, were not interested, or were very uncomfortable. A few even exhibited thinly veiled agitation.

We "spiritually-minded" Christians can be such slow, dull learners. In this case God used the only unsaved interpreter in our midst to get our attention. Danny, who was deeply moved by all we were doing for his people, nevertheless pointed out that men, women, and children were wilting under the sun's intense heat, and that most of them had not had anything to eat or drink for hours (even days) on end. "We have to do something. We must at least get them some water," he said.

After somewhat dejectedly having observed people's overall reaction for several days to all things spiritual, I was ready to listen to God's voice from wherever it came. I recognized it coming out of the mouth of this very pleasant and still unconverted young interpreter. We immediately made arrangements through the soldiers and government officials to secure truck-loads of water and bread to be delivered daily from that point on. We began administering it one-by-one at the prayer station so that all of these precious people in such dire need would at least have something basic to eat and drink.

It was one of those you-had-to-be-there moments to fully understand or believe the level of transformation that then took place. It was as if a huge celestial key had turned closed hearts wide open. The entire atmosphere and attitude was completely changed. Whereas previously people overall had been long-faced, standoffish, and could barely conceal their hurry to get past the prayer station, suddenly they were all smiles, conversing, entering eagerly into the room, baring their very lives and souls, asking us for counsel and prayer, and not even wanting to leave. It was now we who found ourselves having to keep people moving along so the line would not back up. It was truly a miracle. In fact, it was almost as if the bread and water had become sacraments in the way that people gratefully received them and held onto them, eating and drinking with reverence.

Our non-Christian interpreter, Danny, wound up coming to the faith through this experience. The previously chased-away vagabond children were allowed daily through security barriers for bread, water, love, acceptance, and prayer. Many of the hardened soldiers subsequently came to us, asking for prayer or to receive Christ. An orphanage called *Eh'lkirezi* (literally meaning, "Look at God's Precious Pearls of Great Price") for orphaned children has since been birthed out of this outreach. It all started with a simple cup of water and a piece of bread. Sometimes when Jesus says things like "give a cup of cold water," He means exactly what He says—no interpretation needed!

NATHANIEL DUNIGAN
Founder and Director: Aidchild, Uganda
homes, academies, and clinics for orphans with AIDS

the first child brought in to start an orphanage

For Milo

DESPERATION. It hung in the air like a potent, lingering tang. Driven by a series of exposures to hopelessness on previous trips to the area, I had moved to East Africa six weeks before to start an orphanage for children who are HIV positive. But this one was definitely the worst. I could literally smell it.

The little village and the small hut were not in themselves extraordinary. I had been inside dozens just like them and had seen literally hundreds more. But I had entered this small, dark space with such apprehension. *How would I know if the child I was about to meet really needed me? Should I take him in? There are so many needy children here, how could I possibly know where to start?*

But from the first moment I saw little Milo, I knew that he would be my home's first child. He was four years old, but his little body seemed to belong to someone much younger. He had long before passed even the swollen stage of malnutrition and had reached the final, tiny, wasting-away stage of death and misery. He was desperate. As I looked into Milo's eyes and soul, I could see that he wanted out of this body. His sister had died ten days before from AIDS. His mom had died the month before. And he was close, very close!

As my eyes shifted from the spiritual to the physical, they began to look around the room and came to rest on a man seated in the corner. He didn't really look ill, but he had a similar demeanor of desperation, a sense of utter hopelessness. It was easy to tell that, whatever his situation, he had progressed way beyond crying. Or praying. Or consolation.

"Who is that man?" I whispered to my interpreter. After inquiring, the reply came back to me. "He's the father."

The father? I took a deep breath. I have an orphanage. That means I help children who are parentless. Milo has a father? Maybe he wouldn't be my first after all. My eyes went back to Milo's. Another whiff of desperation, I couldn't say no. I couldn't. The father then spoke. He begged me to help. "I feel like I am just sitting by while the last member of my family dies from AIDS. I don't know what to do for him, how to treat him, how to comfort him. Please help me!" There was so much I wanted to say. I wanted to say how sorry I was. I wanted to make sure that he understood that I had no cure, no miracle for him. Instead, I just said, "I will do everything I can." And I took Milo in my arms and carried him to the car.

"Goodbye, Milo," the father said. "Bye, bye, Daddy." I cried

all the way back to the orphanage. Weeks went by. With treatment, Milo did better, then worse, then better, and then worse again. Other children began to come into my home. I watched Milo closely. I could always see that his desperate soul wanted out. He wanted to go home—not to the village but to an eternal home. He was nearly through.

One Wednesday a staff member said to me, "I think he's getting better." "I hope so," I replied. But I knew he wasn't. I knew he had only a few hours at most. The next morning I was up early, trying to go through the morning rituals. I put coffee on. Then Rose, my trusted aide and friend, came running. "Come, you see Milo!" She looked scared.

I ran to his room and quickly put on a pair of gloves. I leaned over his bed and gave him my usual greeting: a gentle touch and a light kiss on the forehead. "Milo?" No response. "Milo?" Still nothing. His eyes were open, but they weren't seeing me. I felt myself take in a deep breath. I had seen this in the dying before. "Nonresponsive," they call it. I then noticed another bad sign: his breathing was regular, too regular. "How long has he been this way, Rose?"

"I don't know. I just came on duty." I told Rose, "Send for a car" and ran back to my room to dress. I had to get him to the hospital. I knew it was too late, but I had to try. I had to. I ran back to Milo's room. "Where is the car?" I was trying not to panic.

"They have gone for it, sir." Milo's breathing was now irregular, a sign that life is quickly ending. "Sing something, Rose." We prayed.

The car came. I scooped him up and ran to it. The hospital is less than five minutes away. About halfway there, his weak little body became limp and perfectly still. My little boy had died in my arms. I cried. Rose cried.

Then I began to notice something. The air was different. Somehow sweet. That dreaded stench of desperation was gone. Milo was no longer desperate.

He was free. He was home. And so was I. This is my work!

young girl in AIDS hospital / Zambia

"In everything I did, I showed you that by this kind of hard work we must help the weak, remembering the words the Lord Jesus himself said: 'It is more blessed to give than to receive.'" Acts 20:35 NIV

NATHANIEL DUNIGAN
Founder and Director: Aidchild, Uganda
homes, academies, and clinics for orphans with AIDS

bedtime in an orphanage

Pray for Bob

As director of an AIDS orphanage in Africa, one of my favorite moments of the day comes at the end: tuck-in time. Not because it means the kids are quiet—well not only for that reason—but because I find them especially sweet as they prepare for sleep. It is a special time for the soul to be alone with thoughts, dreams, and worries. I get to know my kids most at this time.

Every night, my staff and I go through the routine of tucking in the covers and pulling the mosquito nets down over the little beds. Then I go back for individual good-night rituals with each child. With my precious three-year-old girl, Ayine, for example, I stick my head back in and under her net to steal one last kiss. And she always pretends to try and get away from me, but her giggle on contact gives her away every time. And, after I turn out the light in the boys' room, eight-year-old Ronald always says, "Daddy, come back." So I creep back through the darkness to his upper bunk where, every night, I find his lips pressed against the inside of the net. He insists on his good night kiss. They are all different and all wonderful. And I am never more keenly aware of that than I am at bedtime.

One night, after all the little rituals were complete, I turned to leave. Then I heard another voice. It was Ivan's. (We don't know how old he is. No one does, but we guess him to be between eight and ten.) The little voice in the darkness said, "Pray for me, Daddy. And pray for Bob."

"Bob? What about Bob?" I started to ask. We don't have a Bob at the orphanage.

Then I remembered Ivan's small file. One of the few pieces of information it does contain is the name of Ivan's little brother Bob. I wondered where he was that night. I wondered how he was. I wondered how long it had been since these precious little brothers had seen each other.

My heart did a quick rewind to my own bedtime thoughts as a child. My worries. My dreams. I remembered worrying about my little sister, Hannah. And how I would contemplate as best I could the anger I felt for those who had teased her cruelly. Or how I would laugh to myself about my own big brother practical joke of the day. Sometimes, I would dream about her future and hope that it would be wonderful. But never once did I wonder where she was.

My children are so needy. Their bodies are losing a war against a vicious disease, while their hearts are aching because of the horrible losses already suffered at the hands of this killer. Some people say that my willingness to help these children is amazing compassion. If they could be with me at tuck-in time, though, they wouldn't see it that way. They would see it as I do: as a simple, logical response from one heart to another and as an extraordinary blessing from God's hand to my life.

That's what it is. A blessing. A dream come true. So pursue your dreams. Do the work that you know you are meant to do. When the Divine drops a vision into your heart, all you must do is act. I have often said that, in the beginning, the reality of this orphanage was on the opposite side of a river of impossibility. But once I made up my mind to find a way to cross, I easily located the stepping stones that would lead me to my vision. The stones were many, but they were there. All I had to do was move. If I can cross the river, so can you. Do it!

I was never more grateful for those stepping stones than I was that night, now on the other side of the river, standing in the dark room of the orphanage. I breathed a simple thank you before I walked back over to Ivan's bedside and knelt down. As I laid my hand on his little head, I cleared the emotion from my throat, and then quietly said, "Yes, Ivan. I'll pray for you." He opened his nearly blind eyes, and looked directly at me as I added, "and I'll pray for Bob too."

children on the street / Uganda

He comforts us in all our troubles so that we can comfort others... When they are troubled, we will be able to give them the same comfort God has given us. 2 Corinthians 1:4 NLT

once an endangered people group

Twa tribal dance / Burundi

Then we will be able to go and preach the Good News in other places that are far beyond you, where no one else is working. 2 Corinthians 10:16 NLT

DR. ALBU VAN EEDEN
President: Doctors for Life, South Africa
Angola

sharing the Gospel with a very rare and unreached bushmen tribe

Cast your Bread upon the Water

After approximately two weeks of traveling and working in Angola's southern areas, the time came to head back home to South Africa. However, prior to this outreach we had several reports about a certain Bushman camp (one of very few and extremely rare remaining original Bushman tribes in Angola) from a missionary friend, Calvin O'Brian.

Calvin's father was a missionary in Menongue but was chased out a few years after Calvin's birth due to the outbreak and rapidly intensifying war in Angola. They moved to America, but Calvin returned about 30 years later to spread the Gospel in the same area. The Bushman camp was one of the villages he had heard of and wanted to reach with the Gospel. Although his visits were limited and hindered due to the extremely bad roads, he could give us some insight to their physical needs, for example with certain medicines. We were eager to meet them, but finding them was another challenge…an almost impossible one.

When we started packing and headed out of Menongue, we hoped to reach the Bushman camp, as Calvin only vaguely described where he thought they lived. There we planned to have our last medical clinic hopefully by the afternoon. Our instructions were "Approximately 40 kilometers from the bridge on the left-hand side in the forest…" But even with those directions, the chance of meeting them was little to none as Bushman were known for packing up and moving their villages with much frequency.

We left late and saw far more military tank wrecks next to the road than we had on the nighttime drive to Menongue a few weeks before. Land mine warnings were all along the road amid the littered terrain of mangled tanks that had their turrets pointing out of the long grass. Traveling was extremely dangerous with some approximately 10 million land mines still yet to be removed from the roads we were traveling. We could not step or drive off the not so well marked sides of the roads without putting ourselves in extreme danger.

We searched and incredibly found the Bushman camp, but unfortunately we were out of luck as they had recently abandoned the small village and moved on.

It gave witness to their nomadic lifestyle and the simplicity of it all: "Why build something grand if you have to leave it behind in a few days, weeks, or months anyway?" They own as little as possible because they are constantly on the move. Obviously our westernized way of gathering and collecting as many possessions as possible makes much more sense, right?

We found some simple tools left behind that are used for hunting, grinding food, and carrying water. They live simple lives to say the least, and I wondered whether they carried more than their babies, some food, and perhaps a few weapons to their next camp that they would create all over again.

We spent a lot of time and thoughtful moments looking around what was once their recent home. This abandoned site had an eerie silence to it, which called for deep contemplation. The desolation created by people leaving town—not for another job, or a transfer, retirement, or holiday—but just to survive. The thought that we could actually have a chance to run into these nomadic people was almost surreal. What would it be like to meet up with them to communicate with these ancient tribal people? Or more importantly, to have a chance to stand in front of them and share the Gospel! What would it feel like to have the once in a lifetime opportunity to speak to them about God and offer them salvation through His Son, Jesus Christ? When I say once in a lifetime, I mean that they will most likely

>

We felt that we were from two different worlds—ours and theirs—which were shaped by two different time zones: one (theirs) that has stood still since 500 BC; and the other (ours) almost standing on the brink of either destroying itself with its own intelligence and progress or moving into an era that appears to be bordering on science fiction.

not have another opportunity again the rest of their lives to hear the message of the Cross.

So we decided to continue traveling on, driving over the rough roads and through the harsh terrain. Without giving warning to our soon-to-be hosts, we stopped off at another more advanced (in comparison) village of tribal people (the Kanyela). These tribal people were somewhat influenced by Western culture, at least a little in comparison to the Bushman tribes. We held our last medical clinic, thinking we would probably never have the luck to meet up with the extremely rare and scarce Bushmen tribe for which we searched. We could only hope and pray for such a chance encounter. So we made the time and had the medicines left to conduct this unplanned clinic after which we set up camp and showed one more film sharing God's Word for the last time that evening. The time with these people was blessed, and again we could see God's hand in leading us to bring the Gospel to them. Many gave their lives to Jesus Christ that night.

We proceeded to pack up and leave very early the next morning, preparing ourselves for our long journey home to South Africa. All of a sudden we noticed some Bushmen boys standing beside the road, holding long sticks and curiously staring at us. We could hardly control our excitement! Within a few minutes, the whole Bushman village had crowded around our vehicles. Many of them were dressed in very little clothing, mostly animal skins and handmade beads. The men carried roughly made bows and arrows for hunting. They were excitedly speaking in their native tongue, in a flurry of clicking and clucking sounds. Despite their wanderings, we had somehow stumbled across them. God had led us to this exact

moment and time. We knew we must stop and dispense medicine and attempt to share the Gospel with them. This opportunity was too wonderful to let it pass, even though we would not reach the border in time to cross it that day. We felt compelled...and knew deep inside that this was a divine appointment!

Because they live in such a close community, almost all of them had the same diseases. So we de-wormed the entire village and handed out anti-scabies medicine. Special caution was taken in explaining the administration of the cough medicine versus the scabies, as they were in similar shaped bottles. Putting cough medicine on the skin wouldn't be too bad, but drinking scabies ointment would be very dangerous. These people cannot read, and we had to over-emphasize how the medicines work, and God's grace. Translation was from English to Kangela (the local Angolan dialect in that area) and then from Kangela to their very unique language of clicks and clucks. It was quite the undertaking, but we were able to communicate.

One man walked around with a broken leg, which had failed to knit properly after he was shot in the leg and was now dangling loose.

We felt that we were from two different worlds—ours and theirs—which were shaped by two different time zones: one (theirs) that has stood still since 500 BC; and the other (ours) almost standing on the brink of either destroying itself with its own intelligence and progress or moving into an era that appears to be bordering on science fiction. Yet, our interaction with these men and women was perfectly human!

The significance of the moment was overwhelming as we went to share the Gospel with them. It was a remarkable time in which we all felt like we were fulfilling one of the destinies of God's will for our lives. We felt faint and wobbly in our knees as we painstakingly delivered and shared a very simple Gospel message, making as sure as possible that the message was translated correctly into their primitive dialect. It was amazing to watch their faces convey their reactions to what they heard. We were about to pray. From where I stood, I could see many of the group of men and women humbly bowing their heads and closing their eyes. However, afterwards I heard that there was actually quite a commotion going before the prayer was concluded. Some would secretly try and see what the preachers were doing as if to make sure this wasn't a kind of a trick of some sort. Others would also open their eyes and tug at each other to remain silent and close their eyes. This was clearly something new to them, but after a few minutes there was enough silence to pray! The message was delivered, and only God knows how many of them truly asked Jesus into their heart that day. We will only know when we ourselves run across them in heaven.

This was yet another encounter with an unreached people group.

Then I saw another angel flying in midair,
and he had the eternal gospel to proclaim
to those who live on the earth—
to every nation, tribe, language and people.
Revelation 14:6   NIV

✝

orphanage kids / Mozambique

Do not oppress widows, orphans, foreigners, and the poor people. And do not scheme against each other.

Zechariah 7:10 NLT

CLAUDIA RYAN
Mozambique

God leading the start of an orphanage through much turmoil

The Promised Land

I took my first anti-malaria pill in faith. I did not even have a dime towards the airfare. But through a series of unbelievable blessings, less than a week later the entire amount I needed had been raised, and I was soon in Mozambique on my first missions trip.

There were three of us that had recently arrived to lend help at the largest government run orphanage in Mozambique. We were there to help two missionaries who were heading the work at the orphanage. Their primary focus was discipleship and sharing the Gospel, which included providing food, supplies, medicine, and clothing, in addition to church and counseling.

We fell into our work responsibilities quickly without any problems. Some of our jobs included helping in the medical clinic, organizing clothing donations, performing Bible stories for the children, sewing curtains, and putting screens in the dorms. Some of the orphans actually took us cobra hunting in the tall grass surrounding the facility.

It was sad hearing the heart-breaking stories from the kids themselves of where they came from and how they had become orphans. Knowing we were helping them made our work schedule a blessing.

But it wasn't long before we were told that problems were developing with the government. For two years the missionaries had petitioned the government for full contract of the orphanage. Instead the government had responded quite harshly by insisting that all religious activities end immediately—no praying, no church, and no religious teaching. And they demanded the keys be turned over to the old directors of the facilities. These were the directors that had stolen the children's provisions, terribly abused them, and did not seem to have any regard for the their welfare at all. They had deep-seated corruption among them and selfish motives. We were being kicked out!

That Sunday the new regulations were given, and we told the children. There was panic amongst the children, they were genuinely scared of the directors' return. The older ones remembered the years of oppression and abuse they suffered at their hands. We reassured the children that the

directors and government had legal claim on the building but no legal claim on any of them. We could take them with us, but we had absolutely nowhere to go!

It was now apparent that God was leading the missionaries to break away from the government's heavy hand of control and start their own orphanage. For many years it was the missionaries and their ministries that supplied almost all of the finances to buy the materials, medicine, and food to run the orphanage.

From that day forward, we were all praying for a miracle. The packing became frenzied. We had no place to go except to the missionaries' compound in the city. It certainly was not big enough for all of us and all of our supplies! We threw beds, mattresses, and other supplies into large shipping containers. In truth it felt like a funeral— there was a heavy feeling packing up and moving every-thing out. At that moment it all seemed overwhelming as if we were going to die, but we believed the Lord would bear us up on eagles' wings.

In the midst of the packing frenzy, some of the children asked if they could walk a mile down the road to a small patch of land where we held our church services. They wanted to pray to God about our situation and for a place to go (wherever that was). Basically they were praying for a miracle.

Of course we said yes, and twenty children gathered. I led them down the sandy road that was very hot on their bare feet. As I looked at the group of children I was leading along the road, I could see clearly that these children could become the next generation of pastors, teachers, evange-lists, and missionaries, and that through these little lives the nation could truly be changed.

We were then told we had two more days to hand over the keys to the facility. The situation was desperate with the

>

remaining beds, supplies, and personal items still to be taken from the center. By the grace of God, everything did make it into the city. I was assigned the task of going through the center and making sure everything was taken. It was sad and depressing work; we found rooms broken into with fixtures and toys stolen, and other improvements to the facility undone by vandals. With no children playing on the playgrounds or running down the halls, the place was quite depressing when compared to the facility only a few weeks earlier.

While the keys were being handed over, I was to wait down the road with the children that absolutely could not be left—orphans, little ones, and those that had been terribly abused. I started off with two and by the time all was done, I had about twenty-five children hovering around me, scared and not wanting to be left behind.

The day was filled with tension and stress. No one really knew where they were going, but they knew they could not stay. There was fear of the directors and what they may do if they found us leaving with orphans. Even though they did not have legal hold on them, they received money from the government for the number of orphans at the facility. The children were scared to death of them with the horrible stories they shared of the previous directors.

The kids would hide if any car came down the road. Soon the ministry vehicles passed by, and we piled all the children into the backs till overflowing. And we headed off to the city.

The scene in the city was one of true joy. It was as if the back courtyard and garage of the missionaries' apartment had become the Promised Land. There were about fifty children there; they had started arriving that morning in a steady stream. It was like Christmas, the missionaries' children shared their toys. The other thing about the scene was just the safety of it all. There was no longer any fear and uncertainty. The presence of the Lord just wiped out all anxiety.

That night a friend of the missionaries brought food. I think it was just for the staff to eat, but that little pot fed all of us—it was truly yet another miracle of the Lord's provision. After eating, the children gathered for worship and prayer, and there was such unity and harmony that we could have worshiped all night.

During prayer I was blessed by one fifteen-year-old boy's prayer that had been at the orphanage during the really hard, abusive years before the missionaries arrived. He prayed for the salvation of the directors and for the children that remained at the center. He had so much love in a situation that was really hateful, and no resentment or bitterness. Although in a sense he had every reason to hate the directors, he was asking the Lord to bless and to save them. The Lord had replaced all their hurt, anger, and fear with genuine love and forgiveness. The children would share stories of the past and say, "before Jesus was in my heart." Truly these children have had their hearts changed.

There are many more stories to tell and much more to relate about how the presence of the Lord was visible in the children and in the way their Father took care of them. Some of what I experienced is almost beyond words, in that as the children would sing, you could sometimes sense heaven stopping to listen. And there were precious little voices praying to their Father at bedtime, and loud voices commanding the car to start in "the name of Jesus." At a very basic level, God has met these children and was drawing them close to His side.

When I left there were 117 children, many of them had been abandoned children that were picked up off the streets of the city. They were staying in temporary housing at this time. But soon after this, God provided them with the finances and a building for their own facility. In front of my eyes God had become these orphans' Father and Provider, giving them a new home, one certainly filled with milk and honey compared to their old lives on the street and in the old orphanage. And for me it was a beautiful introduction to missions.

orphans field trip to the sea / Mozambique

STEVEN VIOLANO
Doctors for Life
South Africa

from the heart of the AIDS epidemic

People are Dying

It was a sun-filled morning in mid-June when we arrived in Harding. Entering the small town center, only one familiar sight stood out, a KFC restaurant. The smaller shops that lined the downtown area were all foreign to this foreigner who was approaching the edge of "the ends of the earth."

After a brief stop, we headed up a winding road through plantations of gum trees into the mountains to Dee Mount, one of the many villages outside of Harding. After we rounded a bend, a little country store came into sight. Nestled behind this country store, on the same plot of land, was a tin-roofed farmhouse that would be my home for the next two plus months. It all seemed so pleasant that if they isolated themselves, they could forget about the devastation just a few kilometers beyond the gum tree plantations.

I quickly settled in and was welcomed by a host family and the shop employees. My purpose for being in Dee Mount was to assist in converting the residence and commercial buildings into an outpost to reach the surrounding communities with much needed medical help and Home Based AIDS Care training. As I started my work on the grounds, reality began to sink in. One afternoon when I was measuring the dimensions of a storage room in one of the buildings that is being given to DFL (Doctors For Life International), I extended my tape measure and came across something shocking. Before my eyes were stacks of coffins that were for sale—adult coffins, children's coffins, babies' coffins. Over the next three weeks I attended my first two Zulu funerals and saw this little country shop move more coffins than my eyes could believe. "People are dropping like flies," the young Zulu pastor said, with an air of alarm as if the dying had just begun to happen last week. "People are dying," he repeated.

As the children walked to school, laughing and playing, I wondered if it had been like this during the great plagues of Europe. I remember visiting art museums in Europe and seeing the look of dread on the faces of the subjects of the paintings during the time of the Bubonic plague. But this is a different disease. The disease that is killing the people is completely preventable. Sin has lowered the life expectancy here to about forty years. Promiscuity is killing men, women, and children. Married men, who are unfaithful, are bringing the virus home from the city and infecting their wives who unwittingly pass the disease on to their unborn child or nursing infant. The older children will eventually be orphans and left alone to bury their little brothers and sisters.

Adolescents, who refuse to take the road of abstinence, are unwittingly entering into a deadly game of Russian roulette with the condoms that are dumped upon them by those they trust. They are shocked when we tell them that one in five fail. During a conversation with the principle of a high school with some 600 students, I asked about the student that died the previous week. Her response, "Which one, we had three students die last week?" The life expectancy in Kwa Zulu Natal is projected to fall to thirty-five years in the next five years. Latest statistics are between 36 and 40 percent are HIV positive. The high risk group, 20-24 year olds, have a 42 percent infection. In the rest of the country HIV positive people are between 20 and 25 percent of the population.

The statistics are appalling; however, the faces behind the statistics are even more heart wrenching and seemingly unending. Tombe-Zonka is one of those happy smiling seven year olds, despite her skin and bones frame, she enjoys running and playing like a typical child. Unlike children her age, she attends a DFL sponsored day care center because she is often too frail to attend school. Her AIDS test only confirmed what we already knew. It will not be very long before she leaves this earth. Many other toddlers find their way each day to the crèche (day care center) where they get early education, balanced meals, and most importantly love. The orphan day care centers are a welcomed and much needed break for grandmothers and aunties who are raising two to three generations of children that they have inherited.

It can all be so overwhelming and depressing until one remembers that the answer is the same for every human condition found in this world: Jesus. He makes straight the crooked paths, heals the brokenhearted, and binds up the wounded in spirit. His love reaches to all of us who have been pummeled by our own sins, the sins of others, even the sins of our rulers. Like waves crashing on the shore, His love is continually there for us. In Dee Mount the message is simple: there is hope in Jesus Christ. Old, young, healthy or dying—all can open their hearts to the Living Waters found in Him.

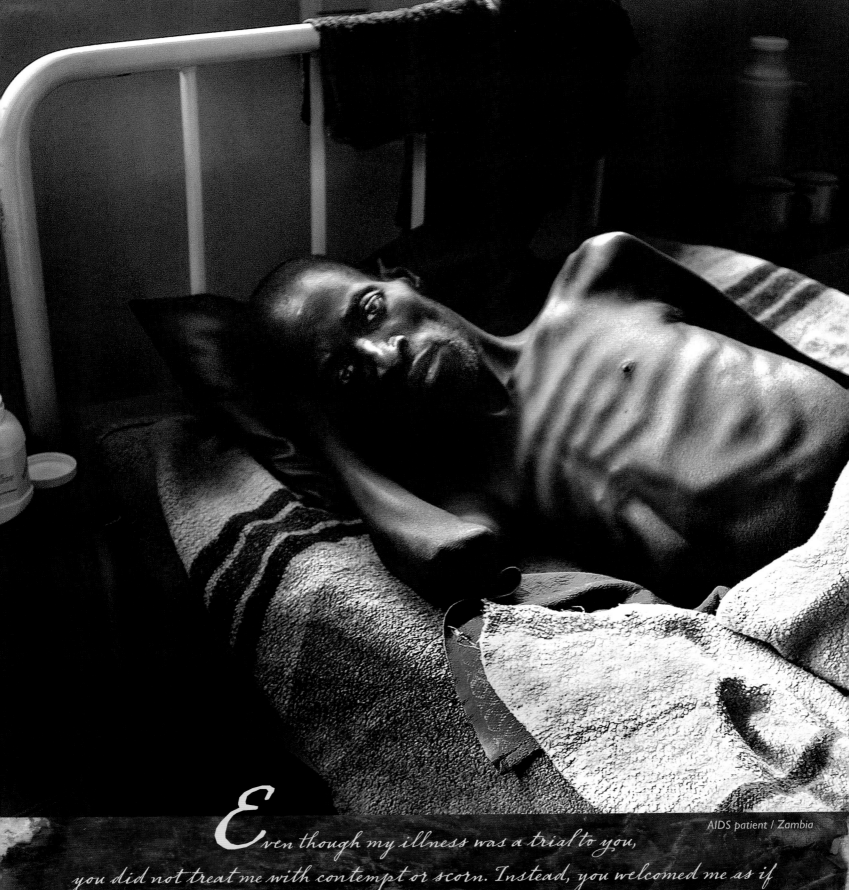

AIDS patient / Zambia

Even though my illness was a trial to you, you did not treat me with contempt or scorn. Instead, you welcomed me as if I were an angel of God or as if I were Christ Jesus, himself. Gal 4:14 NIV

coffin warehouse / Dee Mount, South Africa
coffins sell out every weekend due to the AIDS epidemic

AIDS orphans / South Africa

unlikely missionaries to South Africa's AIDS crisis

Average Joes

Back home my wife and I were average Joes, perhaps even a little less than that. I worked for a major soft drink manufacturer, and my wife worked for a day care center. But here in Africa they call us doctors. Please let me explain.

We always laugh when they call us doctors, and we go on to explain, "No, I am not a doctor! But let me tell you about the power of the cross. It can take a punk, thief, gangster, alcoholic and transform him to fall in love with God, go to Bible college, meet his wife there, and get a Call to the ends of the earth with his wife. (South Africa is the ends of the earth to us.) Oh yeah, and bring them to Africa as newlyweds of six months."

We are missionaries to South Africa, and every day truly is a mission. We both came because of the AIDS epidemic. Africa has the most AIDS in the world, creating an orphan crisis, which makes one just weep. We often cry like babies.

So we came here for the orphans (and they are more precious than we ever imagined). We were heartbroken to think that children had no parents and no family. AIDS—what a destructive crisis in Africa that is killing millions. The province we worked in for our first ten months has the most AIDS in South Africa. The rural areas we worked in, had the most AIDS in the province, so you could say we were in the heart of AIDS.

The needs are so great here that the Lord had me do another type of work while my wife stayed with the orphans. I began to visit huts daily with some medical aid—multi-vitamins, ibuprofen, and prodium, for example, but my favorites are the hope and gift of Jesus. That's the best medicine there is! So that's how I got the name doctor.

What an intense, overwhelming ministry. I've never seen so much death in all my life. To be honest, after awhile I got used to seeing and hearing about people dying. During the first year of being in this country, I've met so many people that are now dead that I've actually had patients die in front of me. One lady died in my vehicle from AIDS. One day a lady came to me and said she needed medicine for her relative. I asked her to take me to the patient. I arrived in her last minute of life when she was gasping for air. I got on my knees and had my Zulu translator tell her, "God sent me here to you. If you die now He wants to take you to be with Him. He wants to forgive you; ask Him into your heart." She looked at me in agreement and then died. Wow, I couldn't believe it. I put on my gloves and closed her eyes. I broke the tragic news to her family, but I felt peace that she was now in heaven. I felt the worst of all when I heard a beautiful little girl weep. I witnessed the beginning of a brand new orphan.

AIDS is killing like crazy in South Africa. You can die within six months of getting HIV there. I actually knew many people like that. We know so many true and awesome stories that we have witnessed or heard firsthand, that they could fill a book. They often start out tragic but almost all of them end up successful and adventurous missions. For example, there was the time I went to a witch doctor's house because he wanted my help. I watched him boil blood and bones. He said he had no control over himself, so he allowed me to pray for deliverance for him.

But overall we came for the sweet beautiful children of South Africa, especially the orphans. They melt my heart. I love hearing their beautiful African voices singing in the morning and evening. They are my alarm clock, and this one I don't want to turn off. They hug us all the time because they love us. They are happy with what little they have.

While we were here, my wife saw a huge need. There were no Christian children books in Zulu. So with God's help, she wrote one and illustrated it, and it was translated into Zulu. We were so privileged to be there. Our lives will never be the same.

We are now being called back to the States for a period of time. We are excited to get involved in ministry back home, but one thing I will think about is the kids. I am sure I will be sipping on Starbucks, shopping in my favorite stores, and I will think of them often. I will be following their examples. You see, it's not bad to sip on a latte or shop in malls, but that's not everything in life. We had a chance to live with these kids, which was far more valuable than any riches. When the person behind the counter gets my coffee order wrong or I stain or rip my favorite shirt, that's fine. So many things have gone wrong in these kids' lives, but they don't complain; they still remain sweet. I can honestly say these kids are my heroes and my wife and I love them!

God is among the orphans, so there is so much joy in their presence because in His presence is fullness of joy, and the joy of the Lord is our strength. It's amazing how God can use average Joes!

old Zulu woman / South Africa

God chose the foolish things of the world to shame the wise;
God chose the weak things of the world to shame the strong...
so that no one may boast before him. 1 Cor 1:27, 29 NIV

older prostitutes are mostly heroin addicts with HIV

old prostitutes in brothel

"If any one of you is without sin,
let him be the first to throw a stone at her."

John 8:7 NIV

PETRA LUNA
Founder: Life Center / House of Life
Durban, South Africa

missionary to prostitutes and pimps

The Church Lady

It was about seventeen years ago that the Lord revealed a vision to me through prayer. He showed me the continent of Africa, and I saw myself ministering to a multitude of people. Since then, the Lord put on my heart to fast and pray three hours every day for the people of Africa.

For many years, I did not understand this vision and how it related to God's plan for my life. I also didn't understand the love that He put in my heart for the lost souls of Africa. It was not until 2003 that the Lord unfolded this vision and opened a door for me to go to Africa. I am now working for Doctors for Life International in Durban, South Africa, in a ministry that did not exist at that time.

Soon after I came to South Africa, the Lord provided a refuge, which today is called Project Life Place. It is primarily a ministry where prostitutes and pimps come for counseling. I minister the word of the Lord to them and pray for them. So far, more than 200 have committed their lives to the Lord Jesus Christ. Life Place is in the heart of the Red Light District in the midst of massage parlors, escort agencies, bars, and drug trafficking; and the corners are flooded with street sex workers.

There is an unprecedented move of God taking place among prostitutes here in Durban. I am witnessing a true revival. The Lord had put in my heart to do outreaches throughout the streets, in escort agencies, and bars, to women, children, and male prostitutes. I believe that the fulfillment of Joel 2:28, "I will pour out my Spirit on all people. Your sons and daughters will prophesy, your old men will dream dreams, your young men will see visions" is taking place as I preach the Gospel on the streets. I share with the male and female prostitutes that Jesus is the only way to a different and better life and that Jesus died for them on the cross of Calvary. Some of them burst into tears and immediately surrender their lives to Jesus. It is obvious that this needy population is hungry for Jesus' love and His compassion.

They call me the Church Lady. To them, I have become their good friend who has opened their eyes to look at themselves as precious and valuable human beings, whereas before they saw themselves as objects to be used by pimps, customers, and family members. The great majority of them come from backgrounds where they have been sexually, physically, psychologically, and emotionally abused by their parents (father) or close family members, customers, and pimps.

Here are some examples of how people's lives have been changed. One time at the beginning of the ministry, I was walking about 1:30 a.m. in a very famous area called Point Road and Smith Street. I saw this beautiful girl laying on the ground, drunk and very high on drugs. I felt the compassion of Christ and I got close to her; I told her that Jesus loves her. She looked at me with a very sad face; her expression said there was no hope for her. However, I said again, "Jesus loves you, and I love you too. I want to help you change your life." Then I took her to Life Place, I helped her clean up, and prepared her something to eat. She sobered up. Then we sat with the Bible, and I showed her the love of Jesus and the sacrifice He made on Calvary for her salvation.

Her maternal uncle sexually abused her when she was five. He continued to abuse her sexually and physically until she was thirteen years old. At that age she became a prostitute, following in her mother's footsteps. This girl was also a thief, giving customers knockout drugs so that she could rob them. She carried a knife and was well-known for fighting with the other girls. Whenever she had an opportunity, she would hurt customers. She was very destructive and angry.

She contracted the HIV virus. Reportedly she had never protected herself and infected more than 10,000 men. However, the Lord has done a wonderful work in this person's life. Today she is faithfully serving the Lord and has been baptized in water and in the Spirit. She says, "Life Place has been a place of heaven to me because through it, I have found my way to Jesus." We praise the Lord for His amazing grace.

Several months ago, I met another young girl in an escort agency. She was raised by her maternal grandmother who

>

was an alcoholic, and consequently, sold alcohol for a living. She was raped at a very early age, and many men that bought alcohol at her granny's place had raped her. She became a prostitute and an alcoholic at the age of twelve. She is a mother of three children who have been placed in foster care. She was seven months pregnant when I first met her and spoke to her about Jesus. She rejected the message.

The next week I went to visit her again, and I brought her maternity clothes. I asked her if I could bring some clothing for the baby. She said no because she was not keeping the baby. I became her friend, and I promised to help her out. I told her that I could bring her to the Pregnancy Crisis Intervention Center for the rest of her pregnancy. She accepted and I did as I promised. However, I was very concerned about the fact that she did not want the baby. I feared that she would abandon the baby when she came out of hospital. I went to the hospital at midnight the day that she delivered. The nurse on duty did not want to let me in until I told her that I was a social worker. She then allowed me to go and see the mother and the baby. I wanted to make sure that the baby was going to be OK before I left the hospital. Today, this young girl is born again. God provided a regular job for her and by the grace of God, she will be baptized in a couple months.

The Bible says, "Go into all the world and preach the gospel to all nations" (Mark 16:3). There was great opposition when I first began the ministry. Pimps used to battle with me because they did not want their girls to be distracted. But after I fervently fasted and prayed for them, the Lord spoke to my spirit, "Pimps too have a soul to be saved." I repented in the presence of God and asked the Lord to give me the love and the boldness to minister His word to them. As I spoke to them, I realized that the harvest is ready, and many of them have accepted the gospel of Christ.

The biggest pimp in Durban was saved this year through this ministry. He had fifty women working for him, including children ranging from the age of eight to eighteen. Because I do a lot of networking with the police, I was informed about a police raid to his business. Some of these fifty women were victims of trafficking from Indonesia and Thailand. He had taken their passports and according to the *Durban Daily Newspaper,* they had a debt with him they were unable to pay. These ladies were tied up in a room and only released when a customer came.

I had the opportunity to briefly talk to him about Jesus, and I gave him my business card with my address and contact details. When he came out of jail, he stepped right into my place while I was having a service and surrendered his life to Jesus! He now comes to Life Place to pray and fast with me. He is a totally changed person and is now working full-time in a legitimate job.

One night I was ministering to the child prostitutes, and they invited me into a bar to sit and talk. At first I thought, *I don't go to bars,* but then I changed my mind. As soon as we walked in, someone said out loud, "The Church Lady is here!" Everyone in the bar put down their drinks and cigarettes. Soon after they turned off the music, and we had church service right there!

I have poured my heart into this ministry, despite the fact that there are constant trials and spiritual warfare. I receive so much joy seeing so many souls saved and on the way to heaven. This is sufficient for me to continue working for the Lord. I thank God for His faithfulness because in the most adverse circumstances I have seen His mighty hands upon this ministry and myself. Praise the Lord!

"*I tell you the truth, the tax collectors and the prostitutes are entering the kingdom of God ahead of you. For John came to you to show you the way to righteousness, and you did not believe him, but the tax collectors and the prostitutes did.*"
Matthew 21:31-32 NIV

old prostitutes in brothel

girl monks Shwedagon Pagoda / Yangon, Myanmar

ASIA

"IF TEN MEN ARE CARRYING A LOG, NINE OF THEM ON THE LITTLE END
AND ONE AT THE HEAVY END, AND YOU WANT TO HELP, WHICH END WILL YOU LIFT ON?"
— William Borden,
SPEAKING ON THE NUMBER OF MISSIONARIES TO THE UNREACHED PEOPLE GROUPS OF CHINA AND ASIA

slum kids / Mumbai, India

If you spend yourselves in behalf of the hungry and satisfy the needs of the oppressed, then your light will rise in the darkness, and your night will become like the noonday. Isaiah 58:10 NIV

GERARD VANDERVEGT
Executive Director: Good Shepherd Homes
Pune, India

the Holy Spirit's leading of a start of an orphanage

Spirit Led

In the few years before I went to India, I was based in Eastern Europe (or what we call now Central Europe), right up to the Polish border in the Czech Republic. I loved that country—the hills, the winding roads, the people—but somehow I felt I was to be there only for a season.

In November '93 I popped my eyes open one morning and the Lord said, "Five days." He was talking about a fast. I was an avid faster in my early Christian days, but the times that God actually led me into fasts were few. And this time I was a bit reluctant. I was in the middle of a busy preaching schedule that involved a lot of travel.

At the close of the fast, I had my favorite foods lined up on the kitchen counter: mackerel, yogurt, and fruit. At 2 a.m. I wolfed my first selection down and rolled into bed.

And the next day, everything had changed. My connection with the Czech Republic, that umbilical chord that you have when God sends you to a place, was gone. And in its place was India. Just like that. From one day to the next. I had never had an interest in India before, but now it was on my heart morning, noon, and night. I felt a slow but certain excitement, a token of promise, the knowledge of appointment. I copied a small map of India and put it over my bed. I wanted God's timing, placement, and direction.

It took a year for me to finally end up on its coasts, but my first impressions of India I shall never forget. Images familiar from newscasts and documentaries were now playing in front of my eyes, accompanied with a whole new set of smells and sensations. On my first days in Hyderabad, I walked the town till my feet hurt, watching the fruit carts being pushed up hill, the puffing brightly colored trucks, the beggars and the roaming cattle. All of it lasered indelible impressions on my mind. I had not come to visit—I had come to live.

The only thing that God had said to me in Europe about what I was to do in India was "Feed the hungry." Well, that didn't mean a whole lot to me. My whole purpose in India was a huge question mark. I prayed, "Lord, where do you want me to go?" "Poona" was the word that had been going round and round in my head for days. I finally looked it up on the map to see where it was, but I

couldn't find it. Someone was helpful enough to tell me that Pune and Poona was the same town. Concluding that a little direction was better than none, I determined to take a night train to this place. "Oh, it's a nice city," I was told. "You'll like it!"

The express train rolled into Pune junction station amidst the customary morning bustle. I was full of expectations. So much so, that as I came outside, I was looking around for someone to recognize me. I had heard stories of God giving people visions of strangers they were supposed to meet. And, would you believe it, after a few seconds a total stranger comes running up to me, grabbed my backpack, and took off with it. Not the hook up I was expecting, but off I was, following the coolie into the rickshaw. Coolies, or luggage carriers, are still around in most stations in India today.

After thirty minutes and a modest shouting match in a hotel lobby about the fare, I was checked into a central Pune hotel room. I opened up the tap for a wash, but the water coming out was black. I stared into the bucket in the corner that was used as a toilet and resolved to postpone. From the window I could see a brown haze draping the horizon from west to east. After observing my neighbors on the opposite balconies in the afternoon lethargy for a few minutes, I lay down on the bed. Here I was, without a contact, without an address, and without knowing where to go. I'd left a prospering ministry in Czech, for what? I said to myself, *I'm going to go out, and I'll speak to the first person I meet. That first person is going to be a spirit-filled Christian. I need some confirmation that I'm in the right place.*

One of the first stores I saw was called Manney's Book Store. I turned into the large jumbled shop and saw a girl standing and reading a magazine. After walking around the shop, I went up to her. "Excuse me," I said. She gave me a puzzled and slightly alarmed look. "Do you know any

>

133

good accommodation in town?" After a moment she said, "Maybe the Bible Centre?" I almost fell over. Christians are a minority of about 3% in India. "Are you a Christian?" I asked. Turned out that she was a spirit-filled Christian, involved in Gospel work in Pune.

Feeling somewhat encouraged that, after all, I was not here in the Orient on a whim, I set out to find out what my mission was. I checked into an ancient (and cheaper!) convent in Pune's Panch Howd (Five Pillar) district. Off and on I would pace the wooden floorboards in my upstairs room to pray. When it came, God's reply did surprise me. This was not the direction my thoughts were headed in when I asked Him about my ministry in India. "Check out the orphanages." Not wanting to waste time, I walked down the narrow, winding stairs, went through the old courtyard and into the street through the tiny gate.

The lady facing me was middle aged, with long grey hair and a dignified look. *Why not?* I thought. *Might as well ask her as anyone else.* "I wonder if you could help me," I began, "I need to find the orphanages in Pune." "You've come to just the right person," she answered. As it turned out, I happened to have come across Sister Filomena, director of St John's Home for Women and Children, an orphanage in the area. We walked into her little office, had some chai, and ten minutes later I was armed with a list of eight children's homes in the city.

Over the next week I was visiting around, quickly establishing that these places had no use for me. Either they taught their children in Hindi or in Marathi, neither of which I knew, or they were Hindu establishments that wanted no Christian input. Fine, so I could move on. I could tick this off my list. *Then why,* I wondered, *was the issue still on my heart?*

I started to think that maybe there was more to this than just visiting a few places. It was around this time that I prayed about a name for the work God wanted me to do.

"Good Shepherd Homes" was the answer that came simply and clearly, as if He had been waiting for me to ask Him. "What? Is this the program?" I was beginning to feel a little uncomfortable. I had been involved in church planting, evangelism, and pastoring, and had loved all of it. Even when we had started a Bible School in the Czech Republic, I had prized every single moment. But now I was hearing about a children's home. This was not my idea of a good time. So far, I had only seen my life in India in the light of what I had done before.

We had seen a move of God in Czech, and more than anything I wanted to see more revival. Now the Lord was asking me to do a u-turn. "What you want to see will happen through the children," He said. "All right Lord, if you say so."

It was time to write my good friend Kofi Banful. Kofi pastored Praise Chapel, my local church in North London. "You are not going to believe this, but I think God is telling me to start a children's home!" The reply came three weeks later. The week before my letter reached him, Kofi had been praying in the church's Tuesday night prayer meeting. As he walked up and down praying, the Lord stopped him in the middle of the floor and said "India-orphanage." God had spoken to both of us at the same time on two different sides of the world.

Once you know, the rest is relatively easy. We assembled a small but zealous staff team, found the right location, and started with a small group of ten street kids. Ten years later, our number of staff and children is over one hundred and fifty. Today we are on the brink of starting a medical clinic, and recently we purchased land in order to build facilities for 400 children in the area. Though I started with just over $100 monthly support, in all these years we have never missed a meal. I have found it to be as they say, "God pays for what He orders."

The wind blows wherever it pleases. You hear its sound, but you cannot tell where it comes from or where it is going. So it is with everyone born of the Spirit.
John 3:8 NIV

slum kids / Mumbai

testimony from a leper colony in India

God's Finger on my Chest

My wife and I work in Central Asia. Before this, we worked in India for twelve years. I was saved in the hippie movement of the seventies out of drugs etc. One day I was invited into this little Pentecostal church near my house with these sweet Pentecostal country people. I had my long hair and a big beard and smelled real bad, but they loved me anyway.

They took me in for six months and taught me about prayer and all about loving Jesus. They were sad to see me leave but released me to go with the Jesus People group called "Christ is the Answer." Two years after I was saved, I was on a bus heading overland into India. I did not know anything about India, and I did not have any formal Bible training. A sister in the Lord from Texas had sent me some memory scriptures on little cards that were what sustained me. My plan was that I was going to turn the world upside down; I was going to be God's mighty man of faith and power.

One day, I had a handful of tracts, and I was handing them out. There was this big pile of garbage with some huts about waist high. The people who lived in them would crawl inside and pull their knees up to their chests and sleep that way. I walked through the field of garbage where there was a lot of human waste. When I arrived at these huts, no one seemed to be there. As I was turning around to leave, I heard a woman cry out, "Help me, help me!" For the first time, I had a human being crawling through garbage to be at my feet. She was a leper; I was standing in the middle of a leper colony in a field of garbage.

I was so afraid, I was sick, and she smelled terrible. One of her hands had no fingers. The other hand had a rag around it, and it was dripping and smelled like rotten meat. I was sick. I was scared, and all I could think about was getting out of there! I was trying to give her a tract, but she had no fingers. She could not take it and even if she did, she could not have read it anyway. So I said a prayer over her and went to walk away. My prayer must have made God sick!

You see, I wanted to be a minister. I wanted to preach the Gospel, and here I was with someone that needed the Gospel, but I didn't want to go that far to meet her. I wanted to stay in my comfort zone. When I turned to walk away from her that day, I met Jesus. Yes, in that leper colony, in that pile of garbage. I did not see Jesus. But I remember as I tried to walk away, I felt His finger on my chest and He said to my heart, "Mike, that's not good enough! You show that woman My love!" I was convicted! I went and got a bowl of warm water and some soap. I took that rag off her hand, and she had such a bad infection that maggots were crawling in her flesh. I cleaned it down to her bone and put on new bandages. All the other lepers came back and when they saw what I was doing, they were crying, and I was able to share the Gospel and the love of Jesus with them.

So the first lesson that God taught me on the mission field was that He is already there! We don't go anywhere; we don't do anything that God isn't already there. Ministry is not about our self-fulfillment, our self-esteem, or our gifts. It is about His heart; it is His character! God is already there waiting for us. He is waiting for someone to come do His work and share His love! God is already there in all the worst places.

The beautiful thing about us is that we were made in God's image. We are made to love; love is the law of our being—to love God more than we love ourselves and to love our fellow man as much as we love ourselves. We are not meant to sit around and live lives focused on ourselves. Jesus said if we try to save our lives we are going to lose them. When we make ourselves the focus, we cannot see what God sees. In the body of Christ, we need to see what God sees. We need to see the things that are breaking His heart. There are so many places where He is, where suffering is, and where we are not. When we focus on ourselves, so many of our problems become so big. After living in the field for so long, I have come to realize that I really don't have any problems.

Don't let your circumstances control you and hold you back from all of the things that God wants you to do for His glory!

A man with leprosy came and knelt before him
and said, "Lord, if you are willing, you can make me clean."
Jesus reached out his hand and touched the man. "I am willing," he said.
"Be clean!" Immediately he was cured of his leprosy.   *Matthew 8:2-3* NIV

leper colony / Pune, India

men waiting in food line / Mumbai, India

the Brothels of Bombay - 60,000 people involved in the sex industry / Mumbai, India

BRAD GUICE
photographer
Mumbai, India

beggar children in India

Hopelessness
becoming a better Beggar!

As a photographer on the mission field I have seen many things, have been many places, and not much really shocks me anymore. But something I heard on this particular day affected me very deeply. Since then, I have prayed and wept about it many times.

On this particular day I was clinging to the back of a motorcycle with my heavy oversized camera bag slung around my shoulders, being driven around by a young man who worked for a local street kid orphanage. His name was Vinny, and he knew the streets very well. He showed me around the city, letting me witness the ministry needs of Mumbai firsthand.

He showed me an incredible amount of drug addicts, many too high to care if I took their pictures. Some of them passed out with the needles still stuck in their arms. We saw many brothels in a city with a sex industry of over 60,000 people (with child prostitution, child slavery, male transvestites, and eunuchs). We visited slums that were basically everywhere (you could not tell when one started and one ended). I saw the devastating effects that AIDS has had on their society through the men and women laying along sides of the road dying of it. We saw street kids as young as three and four years old without a home, and they were everywhere. They were mostly orphans fending for themselves by begging and sniffing glue.

It was a shocking afternoon. We had seen so many devastating things when we pulled up to a rather nice neighborhood. Once again people begging for food and money approached us. This time I noticed yet another young boy without an arm, reaching out and begging with his one good hand. I had seen numerous begging children and adults that day without hands, arms, or legs.

This time I really took notice and finally asked Vinny, my young guide. "Why are there so many people, mostly children, without one limb or another?" His answer was one that I was not expecting. He cleared his voice and said, "Oh, they are all self-inflicted!" I paused and thought a second before responding. "What? What do you mean by self-inflicted?" He answered, "Yes, they go and lie on the railroad tracks and put out their arms so the train will sever them off when it goes by. This way they become better beggars!

This statement took me aback as I thought about it. What was it like to grow up in a society with a caste system in which there was no hope to succeed or become anything greater than a beggar? And even at that, the most you can hope for is becoming the best beggar possible. What kind of life is it to have to fight for any scrap of food or coins to sustain oneself for just another day? What is it like to put your own life in danger and lie down on the railroad tracks to let the train run over your arm, with the thought that losing your arm was the only way to improve your life?

Hopelessness, utter hopelessness!

But we have been given the answer. We have been given hope through Jesus Christ. And God has given us salvation and two arms to reach out with to help others. God only needs us to be His servants, willing to step out and go.

"Praise be to the God and Father of our Lord Jesus Christ! In his great mercy he has given us new birth into a living hope through the resurrection of Jesus Christ from the dead" (1 Peter 1:3 NIV).

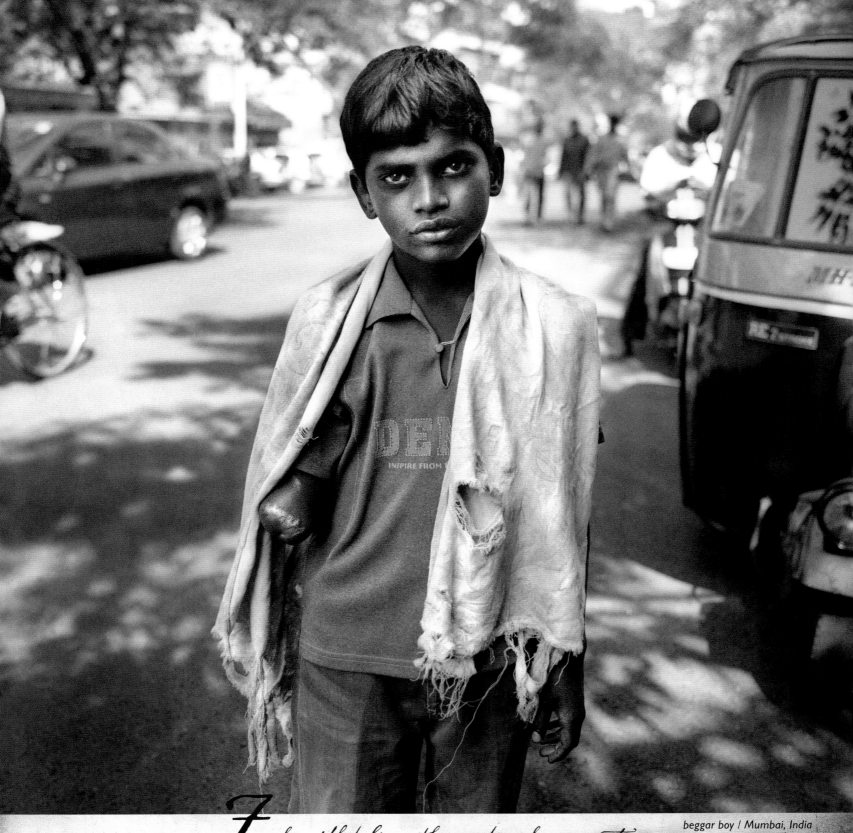

beggar boy / Mumbai, India

For he will deliver the needy who cry out, the afflicted who have no one to help. He will take pity on the weak and the needy and save the needy from death. Psalm 72:12-13. NIV

men in outdoor market place / Afghanistan

*Delight yourself in the Lord
and he will give you the desires of your heart.*

Psalm 37:4 NIV

God fulfilling the desires of the heart

Extreme Calling
Where dreams come true!

In most of the world, it was just an ordinary day. The date on the marriage certificate issued by the Supreme Court of Afghanistan is May 24, 2005. But those who witnessed the wedding ceremony unanimously testify that it was definitely an historic day inside Afghanistan.

Can you imagine meeting and marrying the lady of your dreams while serving in the land of your calling? Can you imagine thousands of Afghans hearing the Gospel for the first time at one of the first open Christian weddings… and you are the groom sharing the Good News? Why such a miraculous moment inside Afghanistan? Why such a divine day? It all boils down to the call of Jesus. And for this testimony, perhaps it is an extreme Call.

God spoke to me back in the early 90s about sharing His love with those who have never heard the Gospel. He further fueled this passion as the Scriptures showed me His heart for His bride from every tribe, nation, and language group. Then as I learned more about unreached people groups, God gave me a specific burden for Muslims. I began crying out to Him for the unreached Muslim people groups in places like Afghanistan, Libya, and Iraq. God really broke my heart for them. At that time God allowed me the privilege of serving Iraqi, Kurdish refugees in the States. What an open door God put before me to share His love with Muslims who had become my neighbors.

In 1997, while on a short-term missions trip to the Philippines, God really confirmed His Call on my life. I had already been involved in ministry and mission work for about seven years. And I had already completely surrendered my life to His Call. On this overseas trip, God put it on my heart to fast. I just wanted to seek God and have extra time to spend in His presence. I wanted Jesus to be my First Love. I was seven days into a fast when God gave me a very vivid dream. What I was doing was not so surprising, but where I was doing it? I was sharing the love of Jesus in a remote, extreme place inside Afghanistan!

After finishing an MA in Intercultural Studies in May 1998, God sent me out to share His love in Central Asia. I had the privilege of serving in Turkmenistan, Uzbekistan, and Tajikistan. All along the way God was up to something, and soon He would send me to the place of my dreams.

In most of the 90s the Taliban were seeking to take over Afghanistan. So it was not the easiest country to enter. However, God opened the way for me from the North, via Tajikistan. He providentially placed me inside Afghanistan in September 2000. It was a long journey to get there. Looking back, I see how each event and experience, every bend in the road and period of waiting, all were part of God's great master plan of preparing me for this extreme Call. What a privilege at one of worst times in Afghan history to be His light inside Afghanistan! It was such a unique time to share the love of God our Father with Afghans. You can read more about this dream come true story in the books I wrote entitled, *Inside Afghanistan* and *A Flame on the Front Line*.

I had been serving the Afghans day and night for about four years as a single missionary before another dream came true. I could have never orchestrated meeting the woman of my dreams in the big city of Kabul, Afghanistan. In fact, I had only been there one time before. When God called me to Afghanistan, He strategically stationed me in the northern part. And in this world of extreme Islam, women completely cover with a burka. I never really saw many women. So the thought of meeting my soulmate inside Afghanistan was the farthest thing from my mind.

On several occasions I made plans to pursue relationships with like-minded ladies back in the States. However, each time I was drawn back to this extreme Call of laying down my life inside Afghanistan. There were times when I gave up completely on marriage. I really didn't want to remain single all my life, but I couldn't reconcile this extreme Call and marriage. I had a burning desire to marry. I wanted to have a wife. I wanted to have kids and to be a family together. I had the privilege of officiating the marriage

>

ceremony of my brother and sister. All the while, I wondered if I would ever "have and hold from this day forward."

The summer of 2004, I just happened to be traveling through Kabul from my place of work in the North. I was sitting in an office foyer talking to an Afghan when I saw the most wonderful woman. I was instantly impressed. Yes I first met Jeanne Louise Bonner in Kabul, the capital of Afghanistan. Was it love at first sight? It was definitely something because we both remember it like yesterday. And no other encounter has affected our lives as much, except this extreme Call to follow the real, true love of our souls, the Lord Jesus Christ.

For us it was an unexpected encounter on that hot, summer day in June 2004. Our meeting was a sovereign surprise, a divine appointment. All those years of dreaming. All those years of wrestling with this extreme Call and the desire to be married. Well, the summer of 2004 our loving heavenly Father led us both to the right place at the right time. Finally at age 34, I met the right one for me inside Afghanistan.

What was Jeanne doing in Afghanistan? Probably not looking for a husband in a land where 99 percent of the men are Muslims. No. Again it was the Call. Strangely enough, Jeanne's journey to Afghanistan began when I was a toddler in Washington, DC. Jeanne was actually born in Kabul back in the early 70s. At this time her parents were on assignment at the American Embassy in Kabul. Their second child, Jeanne Louise Bonner, was born in Kabul early one spring morning in 1972. Jeanne's parents were later reassigned to numerous other countries. As a result, Jeanne grew up all over the world. However, many times Jeanne dreamed of Afghanistan and wondered if God would ever send her back to the place of her birth.

Before God fulfilled this dream, He led Jeanne to New York City via the corporate world of computers. So while I was working in Afghanistan on 9/11, Jeanne was working in New York. After several years in the workplace, God called Jeanne to leave her job and join a ministry to Muslims out of Times Square Church. Then in 2003 God indeed called Jeanne back to Afghanistan to use her skills to serve the Afghan people. For Jeanne the call to return to Afghanistan was indeed like a dream come true. Sometimes the call of Jesus births mysterious destiny.

God allowed us to meet, fall in love, and get engaged while sharing His love with Afghans. Then came the big decision. Where do we get married? God gave us the vision and faith to have our wedding ceremony Afghan style. No English was spoken. None of our family was

able to attend. But we sang, prayed, shared the Good News in the local Afghan language, and united in marriage with hundreds of Afghans watching. Why such an event? It all boils down to the Call. For us the question was more, "Why not?" Why not get married in the land of our calling? Why not abandon it all for the sake of the Call?

Our whole journey to Afghanistan and mutual love story is like a dream come true. When God called us to Afghanistan, we were both single. Before Afghanistan, we lived in some of the same places. Our journeys often intersected, but we never met till that divine day that God ordained in Afghanistan. It was His destiny for us. Neither one of us would have ever dreamed of meeting our future spouse in the land of their calling. And who could have ever conceived of an open Christian wedding in the Islamic State of Afghanistan? There is no way we could have ordained it or orchestrated it. Some of our Muslim friends might say, "Fate allowed it." But we know that May 24, 2005 was a God thing. It was part of His extreme Call on our lives. To God be the glory!

Now we are a Christian couple among our Afghan Muslim friends. Everyday we worship and work, pray and play, teach and train, serve and share, love and live together in the land of our calling. It is a unique privilege to be the salt of the earth and the light of the world in this dark place. Daily we express the love of God in both word and deed. Our hearts' desire is to model the mysterious relationship that Christ has with His Church. And indeed, our continual cry is, "Lord, You are worthy. By Your blood redeem Your bride in Afghanistan."

This extreme call and passion of our Lord has so gripped us that we decided to have our firstborn son in Afghanistan. On a beautiful Friday morning on June 9, 2005, as the sun was rising, John Mack Weaver IV was born at the Cure Hospital in Kabul. Again, another dream came true as God smiled on us. As a result we were able to share again with our Afghan friends about the love of God our Father. Oh, what manner of love the Father has given to us that we should be His children!

As a family we are daily displaying the love of the Triune God. We worship and work together, believing that God has many sons and daughters in Afghanistan. Our family has grown over time, as we have now just had our fourth child. For some this is an extreme Call, but for us it is a dream come true. Afghanistan is indeed the land of our calling, and we consider it a privilege to be in the kingdom for such a time as this.

For all those who have a Calling on their lives and a desire in their hearts to be married, go! Your future spouse may be waiting there for you.

nomads / northern mountains of Afghanistan

crippled man in street market / Afghanistan

snake charmer, street magician performing for crowd / Afghanistan

CINDY EDSON
Central Asia

the start of an orphanage

God, I can't do this! This is Impossible!

When I first flew over this region in Central Asia, I remember looking down at the ground. I thought to myself, *Oh wow, that really is ugly down there! It looks so dry like a desert.* But God had a wonderful plan. He had something so wonderful He wanted to do in my life and in changing my life.

I first went to this orphanage with a sister in the Lord from the local church. We went through the big gates and walked up the stairs into this big building where there were about 250 children. It was the middle of winter. I had my big thick coat on, but the children were just wearing shorts and t-shirts, and they did not have any shoes on, so they were cold. I saw the soup being brought down the corridor; it was bubbling with bacteria and had old moldy bread ripped up inside of it.

I was saddened by what I had seen, and over time, I continued to return to this orphanage with the same sister that had brought me. We continued to come back to the same sections of the big building where we shared the Gospel and prayed with the children.

During Christmas time, I gathered a lot of treats together from the other foreigners in the city, treats such as fruits, breads, cookies, and cakes, thinking that I could take some treats to these kids so that they could taste something really delicious.

It was just before Christmas when I gathered up all of these big bags of treats and went into the orphanage again. I was in the process of handing out all of these gifts, and the kids were ripping the bags open, grabbing and fighting for the food, and stuffing it into their faces. As I was doing this, a young boy came up to me, took me by the hand, and said, "Come and I will take you to a place where they really need these cookies." I thought to myself, *Well maybe he knows something that I don't know.* So he led me down the stairs and walked me across the grounds of the orphanage. I thought, *Wow, he really doesn't know where he is going but I will follow him.* We were heading toward a building where the roof was partially caved in. It appeared to me to be a building that was going to be demolished or torn down. I remembered when I first came to the orphanage for the first time the head director warned me not to go back to this building. I thought at the time it was for safety reasons.

As we got closer to the door of the building, I could hear the screams of the kids, and I could smell some horrible smells. I remember that as I entered the doorway, an incredible oppression and darkness came down on me. The little boy kept pulling my arm, taking me up some stairs where I had to walk through feces and urine to get to the children. I found out later the children themselves called it the "Place of Death." I walked down the hallway to see 35-40 kids in a very tiny room with a bricked up window and a two-slated bench. When the children saw that I had food, they broke past the woman that was supposed to be guarding them at the door. She had a big stick and hoses and started beating them hard as they ran up to me, ripping the food out of my hands. Every one of them was trying desperately to grab as much food as they could and stuff it into their face, not even chewing before they would gulp it down in one swallow.

I was stunned just standing there. The little boy was trying to help me keep the bags closed so that it would be more civilized. Just then an old nurse came down the hallway with tears in her eyes, saying in her local dialect, "Help, Please help!" She grabbed my hand and led me across the hallway as the little boy followed right behind. In this section were all little boys, purple in color from the cold, impacted with roundworms causing their stomachs to be all distended. Many of them were in the advanced stages close to death with roundworms having eaten through their hearts. There was no sewage system at all in this building.

The nurse continued leading me by the hand across to the other side of the hallway. I could see that in this section were all little girls. I really did not want to look inside the room, but I had no choice. I saw once again little girls purple from the cold, many of them naked. I saw them standing naked in their own feces and urine by the two-slated wood benches, but this time I noticed they were eating the wood benches. My heart was just breaking. I had tears forming in my eyes and I thought, *How could this be?*

How could human beings, God's creation, the one's that He loves, be like this?

The nurse reluctantly took me to the next room down the hallway. This door was locked! She unlocked it and inside lay a little girl about thirteen years old. The nurse pulled back the covers and began pointing at her saying, "Help! Can you do something?" When I looked at this little girl, I felt like I was looking into a casket of someone just deteriorating away. Her feet were rotting off, and her bones were sticking through her skin.

The thing that broke my heart was not her body—I have seen a lot of tangled skinny bodies before—but her eyes! I had never seen eyes like that before in my life. Her eyes were so empty and so void. There was hopelessness there. I could tell this little girl had never known love; she had never known even a kind touch or a kind word; she had never known the love of Jesus! I asked the nurse if I could pray for her. She said yes and asked if I would come back the next day. I said I would. I then laid my hands on her and prayed a prayer that I have not prayed since, "God please take this little girl so she could be with You, so she can be in Your presence where there is joy forever more, where there is no pain and she can know what a beautiful life is with You." The Lord took her that night.

The little boy was not yet finished with me. I thought that we had seen the worst. He led me down the stairs and down a long hallway where we had to watch our step or we would fall through the floorboards. You could see the broken sewage pipes beneath the floor. He led me to the bedridden section. There was this incredibly horrible stench of rotting flesh, of death, and infections. I was in shock! When I looked into their beds, I saw two or three children per bed. They had bedsores down to their bones, and they were laying in their own waste, on rotted mattresses with rusted springs. They had not been cleaned up for weeks, maybe months. Again, I noticed the void look in their little eyes.

I got close to them and tried to reach out to comfort them, and they would scream as if they were in pain! They were afraid because they did not know what love is. They did not know a hand could bring comfort or love; they only knew it could bring pain. The little boy then brought me around to the crawling section. Here the little kids were also living in their own waste. These children all had atrophy from being stuck in the same position for so long.

When I left that day, I remember saying, "OK, God, I am going to go back there and make a difference. I am going to get a plan together on how I am going to do things and how I am going to clean up those kids."

Everyday I went back to see those kids, and every week I saw more and more of those kids die. I would lay my hands on the little children and pray for them. I could see a change in them. Some of them could not speak, but they followed me and would speak to me with their eyes.

After a year and a half of going back every day, I was getting very attached to a few of the kids. There was this one little boy that seemed like he was getting better and things were really looking up for him. In my own way, I had attached myself emotionally to him, thinking that he was my hope for this place. I kept believing that something was going to change for him and his circumstances. I came back one day and walked into his room and saw that the sheet was pulled over his head. I wasn't even thinking that he had passed away. Thinking that he must be tied up in the sheet, I pulled it back, but he was dead.

I remember at that point saying, "God this is useless; this is hopeless; this is too dark. There is no way this place is going to change. Kids keep dying. I am not going to do this anymore! There is no reason for me to be here anymore. God, I can't do this! This is impossible!"

I left and I was not coming back again. For a month and a half I prayed, but I could not forget their little faces. I could not get past the fact that I knew God wanted to do something in their lives. I did not know how on earth that was going to happen.

One morning, God spoke gently to my spirit. He said, "Cindy, if you go back and you obey My voice. I will glorify Myself in that place." That is when I realized that I was doing everything wrong. I thought that I was going to make a difference. I said, "Yes, God, I will go back." I went back and let go of all my expectations and thoughts that I was going to accomplish something. "God, you do this, I can't do this! It is impossible anyway!" God began to open doors. It wasn't a miraculous thing or something that happened overnight. But over all the years, I have seen the glory and presence of God. I have seen His infinite beauty, His grace and mercy poured out on these beautiful children. It was new for me to sit back and watch God do what He wanted to do all along. The doors began to open, and God gave me wisdom how to do the work. God then opened the door to start hiring Christian caregivers. Today we now have 76 workers, 16 teachers, 2 massage therapists, and 2 nurses.

God had a wonderful plan. What He does is so beautiful! The enemy comes to steal, kill, and destroy; but God brings life, He brings hope, He brings love! He gave me the privilege, of which I am not worthy, of being a part of 400 little children's lives to bring hope to them. In Ephesians 3:20, Paul says, "Now unto Him that is able to do exceeding abundantly above all that we ask or think, according to the power that He works in us." Eleven years ago I could not have realized what God was going to do in those little children's lives, as well as in government workers, the staff, and me. Now God is being glorified in that place.

orphanage / Myanmar

W hen my father and my mother forsake me,
Then the Lord will take care of me. *Psalm 27:10* NKJV

VIVIAN LI
China

China's orphans

We will be here for you!

"What is the story behind this little one?" I asked Kit Ying Chan. "She is another miracle. One taxi driver, who knows us, brought her in one night. He told us he heard some sounds when he entered a public washroom. Then he realized it was a baby crying."

"However, he looked around and could not find anything. When he decided to give up, the baby's crying started getting louder and louder, leading him to one of the toilets (squat potty). He said to himself, *It can't be… in the toilet?* Soon it became very clear that the crying was coming from the toilet. He placed his hand inside the toilet and touched something soft and pulled it out. There she was; he cleaned her up, put some of his clothes around her, and brought her to our orphanage."

Chan told me this kind of story was very common. Sometimes they will receive several babies during a week. Babies are abandoned all over. Many of them have been left in front of their gate. Some come from state orphanages that can't handle the overflow. And other babies are thrown into rivers, left in garbage dumps, or left in fields where many times they die of overexposure before they are found. The luckier ones are left in railroad stations and police stations, and when found they are eventually sent to the orphanage.

China does not publish reliable statistics on the number of children in its orphanages. It is estimated the country has several thousands of orphanages, many of them with over 400 orphans in each facility with an estimated three million total orphans. As a way to control overpopulation in China, the government created and enforces a "one child per family" policy. Parents can be severely penalized or even punished for having more than one child. In some provinces, would-be parents need a license to have a baby. Compounding the orphan problem is the strong cultural preference for boys. The birth of a boy is often celebrated in a family, while the birth of a girl is usually not acknowledged. Sometimes

they are abandoned, and other times they will be aborted before birth. Great pressure is placed on new mothers to produce a male, since male children are expected to work and support their parents and grandparents. For this reason, tens of thousands of infant girls are abandoned every year with no hope for them to be reclaimed by their family because it is illegal for them to be abandoned in the first place.

Kit Ying is the director of Mother's Love Orphanage in Nanning, Guangxi. Mother's Love started in 1995, and it is the only orphanage that has operated as a co-partnership in China. After 1995, the door was closed for this kind of partnership. Although the door is closed, the love of our Abba Father to those who are fatherless is unchanging. He uses Kit Ying to bring the foster care model to Guangzi, and from Guangzi to other provinces. On the positive side, for the last ten years, the model was well established and adopted by different orphanages throughout China. In the last few years, group homes and foster homes are beginning to bloom in China. Some orphans are benefiting by actually living in a home setting as they grow up or while they are waiting to be adopted.

I praise God for sending different people to care for His children. During my recent trips, I met Christians from different countries who have moved to China and started fostering orphans in their home. Some of them are not just fostering one but rather a few children. Many of them foster those who have special needs like Delphine and Guillaume Gauvain. God called this French couple to serve the blind orphans. Once I asked Guillaume, "How did God call you to start Bethel?"

>

"What if there is never an adopted family for them?" That is a very hard question to ask, but I believe it's even harder for the children to answer. The children's answer was, "It's OK." But you could tell from their faces that they were very sad and heartbroken.

Guillaume replied, "I don't have an exciting story to tell. I heard God's Call when I was washing dishes one night." Yes, sometimes the Call is as simple as it can be, but you know when it is real. What God wants us to do is simply follow His lead and be available.

When Delphine and Guillaume started Bethel in December 2003, they started with three blind orphans. Just a few years later, they have thirty-one blind and visually impaired children. Two were adopted, and they are planning another house that will hold another fifteen children. Originally they would call the state orphanages for children; now the state orphanages are waiting in line to send them their blind and visually impaired orphans. God has been doing a lot of miracles in Bethel. They are growing quickly. They started their own school and opened seven foster care homes. One of the amazing things is that although both of them were not originally specialists in the blind, God sent them people who were specialists in different areas of working with the blind and visually impaired, helping them with both short-term and long-term needs.

I was touched by the love of God through them. Once I sat in a meeting with Delphine and other workers to help two children having trouble with adjusting to the fact that their friends had just gotten adopted. It's not an easy issue to deal with since children in China who are older than thirteen can't be adopted. Also, as the orphans get older, the chances for getting adopted are smaller and smaller. Being blind or visually impaired also adds another level of difficulty for getting adopted.

Throughout the meeting, we tried to help the children express themselves and their feelings about adoption. They felt that their situation was unfair, and they expressed feelings that they wanted to have their own parents all to themselves. At Bethel, the children call Delphine and Guillaume French Mama and French Papa. As the children were sharing with us, it was obvious that they thought that if they were adopted, they would have parents who belonged only to them. I was reminded of some pictures I saw of the adoption families. The orphans they had were not the only children in their family. So Delphine explained to them that in some adoption families, the orphan child would have a lot of siblings. So if these families adopted them, they would need to share the parents with other children. After the explanation, they seem to understand and feel better about it.

Then we moved to a much deeper level of the question. We felt that they should have hope in waiting for an adoption family, but at the same time we have the responsibility to answer their hardest question of all. That hardest question is, "What if there is never a family to adopt them?" That is a very hard question to ask, but I believe it's even harder for the children to answer. The children's answer was "It's OK." But you could tell from their faces that they were very sad and heartbroken with the thought.

Guillaume held one of the two precious orphans on his lap in a fatherly way, and Delphine held the other in her loving arms and said to them, "Don't be sad. As long as you are here, we promise you that we will be here for you." That is a big promise for a child who has been abandoned. God says that He will walk with us and never forsake us. Jesus laid His life down for us. They have laid their lives down for the orphans because of Jesus' love. Praise God for those answering the call and the needs of the orphans!

LORD,
you know the hopes
of the helpless.
Surely you will listen to their cries
and comfort them.
You will bring justice
to the orphans
and the oppressed,
so people can no longer terrify them.

Psalm 10:18 NLT

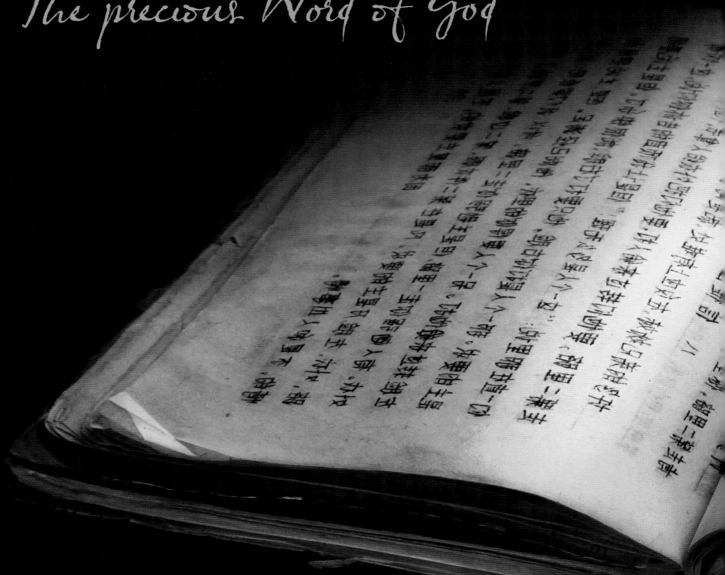

The precious Word of God

In China, underground Christians are often persecuted, imprisoned, and even tortured. The number of underground Christians is estimated to be as high as 100 million. With a mass shortage of Bibles to go around, and smuggling in Bibles very difficult, believers go to extremes to get the word of God. Shown above is an individually hand copied Chinese New Testament.

boy monks Shwedagon Pagoda / Yangon, Myanmar

children at play / Indonesian fishing village

planting rice / Indonesia

The harvest is so great, but the workers are few.
So pray to the Lord who is in charge of the harvest;
ask him to send more workers into his fields. Matthew 9:37-38 NLT

story of an un-reached people group

Begging for the Gospel

On any missions website, the Xai Pheng are listed as an unreached people group (UPG). Their numbers are diminishing as they trade their rice paddy fields for alcohol. They are drunk, diseased, and spiritually lost, with no help from anyone.

Jack and Rolf, two of our staff accidentally discovered the Xai Pheng, one of Vietnam's tribal peoples, as they trekked the highlands near the border with China. When they stumbled into a Xai Pheng village, it was pouring rain. Jack and Rolf remained for three days, trying to communicate with a group of people deeply suspicious of them. After three days, they trekked back to Lao Nong to catch a train to the nation's capital. Their prayers were for God to open the door for them to this UPG.

The following day they called our offices in Malaysia and asked for medical help for the village. My available medical person was Kong Ho, a surgeon, who then made the trip to the Xai Pheng. Kong Ho's assessment was that since there was no clean water or electricity, it was necessary to provide the basics of hygiene before anything else. The people were suffering from diseases that mere soap and water could cure. He also stated that there was one old man in the village who would most likely die if he did not receive immediate medical help from outside the village.

The old man's name was Nu Fah. He had injured himself with a *parang* (machete) while harvesting rice. His leg was rotting away at the knee and it had gangrene. He would die if he wasn't taken from his village for surgery to amputate his leg. He would have to be transported to the nation's capital more than ten hours away by trekking through difficult, mountainous jungle. Nu Fah had never been off the side of his mountain; he had never seen a motorized vehicle other than a helicopter during the war with the Americans. Now we were taking him to Na Hoi, his nation's capital with four million people and a sea of vehicles.

In Na Hoi, Nu Fah would meet Pushpa, a former Malaysian schoolteacher, who now gave her life for the people of Vietnam. Pushpa also spoke more languages than

anyone we had ever met. Beyond her five languages, she also knew several others, at least partially. Still she couldn't speak Nu Fah's dialect, and he did not speak Vietnamese. Slowly, Pushpa communicated to Nu Fah the need to amputate his leg in order to save his life. He trusted Pushpa and agreed to his surgery.

Nu Fah began his rehabilitation in Jack's home with "nurse" Pushpa's help. Within a few days they were somehow communicating. Of course, the language of love spoke loudest. Jack and Pushpa were able to share the Gospel with Nu Fah, and he became the first Xai Pheng ever who believed the Gospel and accepted Jesus Christ as his Lord. Now this previously unreached people group had a believer!

Since Nu Fah and the rest of his village were illiterate, Pushpa had spoken most of the gospel of Mark into a handheld tape recorder and gave it to Nu Fah to take back with him.

He was transported back to his village by Jack, who by now was a familiar figure in the Xai Pheng village. Jack had attracted the attention of the local police, who were committed to eradicating Christianity among the tribal villages. When the police discovered the tape recorder, they confiscated it. Nu Fah and his village needed follow-up, but how?

Over the next two years, Jack constructed a clean water system in the village. Clean water saved lives and attracted the government's attention in a positive way. The government asked Jack if our team could do a similar project in a nearby village.

My wife, Laverne, and I visited Na Hoi often. Our task was both administrative and to be the pastors to our

>

people in the field throughout the region that included several countries. Jack called to tell me of the government's request for another water project. He told them it would be possible, but would require a site visit. Glory to God, we were being invited to visit the Xai Pheng!

The journey to the Xai Pheng is not an easy one. It begins with an eight hour, overnight train ride from Na Hoi to Lao Nong, bordering China. After the train ride is an hour and a half bus ride. The bus adventure ends in Sas Ka. From there the journey requires placing everything on the back of motorbikes and riding for four hours. The good news about the bike ride is there is so much dust, alternating with mud, that you cannot see the road. This prevents you from looking over the sheer drop-off on your right. When the bikes stop, the journey is nearly twenty-four hours from its beginning in Na Hoi. We trekked several more hours to a beautiful verdant rice paddy surrounding a quiet village. The Mai village was our first real resting place, and we spent the night sleeping on the floor of a bamboo home.

The next morning Jack informed me that we were only 3.8 kilometers from the Xai Pheng. I was so excited I was ready to go. I thought, *Hey, 3.8k that's nothing; I'm a jogger.* We left the Mai village at 6:30; six hours later we were two-thirds of the way there. We trekked through jungle that had to be cleared with a machete, crossed bridges that would have frightened Indiana Jones, and waded torrents where we lost bits of equipment. Six hours into our adventure, we encountered our first Xai Pheng— three young women were coming down the mountain we were climbing. They hid behind a large rock as they saw me and especially my wife, Laverne. Laverne is Xa Den (black person). These Xai Pheng women had never seen an African-American. They hid cautiously as they studied her. The girls giggled and ran down the mountain.

Two hours later we entered the Xai Pheng village. It smelled of dead animals. The men were butchering a water buffalo that had been dead for five days. These same brave tribal men all hid as we entered the village. The women cautiously peeked from secure hiding places, but the children ran toward Laverne who had squatted with her arms open. These same children were unafraid, even of a Xa Den. When I surveyed the village, I saw the most primitive conditions I'd ever seen, in spite of the clean water we provided. The children were half-naked and barefoot, their heads were filled with lice and their nostrils with green mucous, and their stomachs were distended from worms. My backpack was filled with lice shampoo, de-worming tablets, vitamins, and soap. I considered how we needed to scrub all the children; then

as I observed Laverne with her arms filled with children, I thought, *We'll also have to scrub Laverne.*

I got such a warm feeling as I observed my wife with the children; she was the appearance of Christ (see I Cor. 15:3-8) with her arms around those kids.

After three days of scrubbing, jabbing, medicating, laughing, and eating with the Xai Peng, Jack asked, "Would you like to meet Nu Fah?" I exclaimed, "Is he here?" Jack replied, "No, but he is nearby." This time the distance was only forty-five minutes up a steep hill. Nu Fah's little village was an elevated suburb to the main village. It was obvious who Nu Fah was because of his amputation; he was sitting on the floor of his small bamboo home weaving a fish net.

When we entered, Nu Fah's wife began to repeatedly place her right hand over her heart. I thought it was an expression of gratitude. But she never ceased beating her heart. I asked Jack to ask Nu Fah to ask his wife why she was doing this. She replied, "How is Pushpa?" I understood her concern for Pushpa; she had been Nu Fah's primary care provider. Nonetheless, I didn't understand Ms. Nu Fah's incessant beating of her breast. I asked Jack once again to find out why she was constantly pounding her chest. Jack asked Nu Fah, Nu Fah asked his wife, she replied to him, then the message went to Jack, and finally Jack, with tears in his eyes said, "She wants to know if Pushpa can come change her heart the way she changed Nu Fah's?" I saw her slip out the door, only to return with her thirty-five-year-old son. She was pounding his heart and saying, "Can Pushpa come change his heart like she did for his daddy?" She was begging for the Gospel!

I wept as I saw a woman literally beg someone to come show her how to get her heart changed. She saw the difference Jesus made in her husband; she wanted that for her son and herself.

The good news is that Jack and Pushpa came and continued to minister among the Xai Pheng. They recruited believers from among the underground church to clandestinely send workers to broadcast the Good News to the Xai Pheng. Today there are more than forty Christians among the Xai Pheng. They are no longer an unreached people group. We experienced firsthand God's help in achieving this goal and His love for the world through these otherwise lost and unreached people.

Never before had I seen anyone beg for the Gospel. Nu Fah is evidence that there is no such thing as a useless old man on the side of a mountain, with his leg rotting off. Everyone is precious in God's sight!

Our hope is that,
as your faith continues to grow,
our area of activity
among you will greatly expand,
so that we can preach the gospel
in the regions beyond you.
For we do not want to boast about work
already done in another man's territory.

2 Corinthians 10:15–16 NIV

Repentance and forgiveness of sins will be preached in his name to all nations.
Luke 24:47 NIV

fish market / Vietnam

incredible circumstances that opened the door for ministry in Vietnam

Are you Spies?

In 1995, we went to visit Ho-Chi Minh City, Vietnam. We arrived at Tan Son Nhat International Airport right before noon. As our plane approached the landing strip, you could see old Russian tanks lined up against the runways, shot down US airplanes, and empty bunkers.

Seeing this made us feel like we were warped back into the 1970s. We took a 45 minute van ride to our hotel in downtown Hanoi. The streets were filled with thousands of pedal bicycles and tri-shaws, weaving in and out of the flow of traffic.

Once we checked into the hotel, we went to scout out the land. Our ministry, Global Ministry Teams, had left operations here back in 1975 when the last of all Western missionaries were forced to leave the country. During that time, the ministry was under Teen Challenge and its facilities were state-of-the-art. When the Vietcong (Communists) conquered the south, they took over the facilities and turned it into one of their operation centers.

Now, years later, we had returned seeking to bring hope back to the nation of Vietnam. Since the war, all trade and access from Western Nations had been restricted. The USA was in deliberations of dropping the embargo with Vietnam and looking towards helping develop the nation through trade and business ventures. We felt the Spirit guiding us to come into the nation and seek the Father's heart for these new ripening fields. We knew God had something in store for this country.

As we began to walk the streets, we saw in the distance a cross above a building. It seemed to be a Catholic church. We asked ourselves, "Could Christianity still be alive in a Communist country?" My three colleagues and I became intrigued to research this building further. We soon realized that we had to cross the Red River to arrive at the church. Walking over to the local ferry, we each paid the equivalent of less than one half a US penny for a 15-minute ride across to the other side of the river.

Upon our arrival, a large gathering of people surrounded us. Many began to point at my colleague's auburn hair,

while others took the liberty to pinch our skin in amazement. It was obvious that they had been limited in their contact with foreigners, and many of them had never seen a westerner in their entire lives. Out of the crowd came a man to our rescue; he stood all of about four and half feet in stature. He exclaimed in perfect English, "Hello, I am Tran! Welcome to Thu Thiem." He must have seen the extreme amazement on our faces to realize how perfect his English was spoken.

Tran continued by saying, "These people have gathered around you because we do not have visitors on this side of our city. This is where all the lepers, prostitutes, and the poorest of the poor people live. Since the government does not want to show these surroundings to the outside world, they restrict any foreigners from visiting here."

Soon, we realized that not only were we in the worst location of the city, we were also in one of the most needy parts of the world. Mr. Tran continued, "I have lived here for many years and I know everyone here. If you are with me, you will be all right." At that moment we realized that God had brought us our own guide and interpreter. With an inquisitive look he asked, "Why are you here?" And without thinking twice, our ministry director, Irvin Rutherford, responded, "We are here to bring hope to your country." "Hope?" Mr. Tran responded. "How can you bring hope to such a poor country?" Irvin's response was, "Because we have come to ask forgiveness, and we have come to bring you Good News!"

At that moment, we pointed to the cross that had brought us to this place. We asked Mr. Tran if he would take us to see the building. He graciously obliged and walked us over to the Catholic church. As we approached, we heard the prayers and singing of a few nuns and clergy inside. The large wide doors of the building were open

>

163

with a full view of the interior. Looking inside we had an awestruck sensation that reminded us of the glory and omnipotence of God. After questioning the origin of the building, we found out that there were only three main legal churches in Vietnam, the Tin Lan being the only recognized above ground church.

Mr. Tran invited us to continue walking with him so that he could introduce us to some of his friends. The road became narrower and less inhabited by people. As far as our eyes could see was the serene landscape of rice paddy fields, creeks, and mountains. Walking through the middle of a rice field for what seemed hours, we finally arrived at a small wooden hut in the center of the vast landscape. As Mr. Tran knocked on the door, a man answered with a cheerful smile and quickly gave us assurance of their friendship. Soon, the man called into the home and invited his relatives to come out and greet us. In rapid succession, the members of his family came out, extending their hands as a greeting. The eldest children quickly climbed a nearby palm tree and began to cut down coconuts. With great speed they chopped them open and distributed them to us as a welcome drink.

Once the excitement settled down, the man spoke to Mr. Tran and asked us to tell them why we had come. Our director took this perfect opportunity to share the story of hope. With Mr. Tran interpreting, we seemed to have had a divine appointment of sharing the Good News. Our team went around taking turns sharing stories of hope for the people of Vietnam. We spoke to them about truth, salvation, forgiveness, and grace. Listening attentively, the family members pondered upon the stories each one of our team members had to share.

While I was sharing, three policemen jumped out of the brush. They had been hiding behind the trees. The message of hope that we had been declaring was too foreign for them to understand. This caused suspicion, and they decided to take action.

They ran up to us and asked us to show proof of our message. At this we were startled! They demanded to see our passports and our airline tickets. As we showed them our profiles, they confiscated all our paperwork, visas, and hotel information. They took us into their custody and to the local police station. As we arrived, they sat us down and interrogated us on our visit to Vietnam. Their interrogations were mean, fierce, and intimidating! After about two hours, they called a vehicle to come and take us away.

The drive was long, hot, and dusty. Along with us was Mr. Tran, who seemed very afraid. After all, we were foreigners, and he was being looked upon as an accomplice. Mr. Tran began to express the years of hurt and pain that he had gone through during the Vietnam War. He mentioned his experiences in Vietnam after having been trained by the US military on Sheppard's base near Dallas, Texas. This brought back memories of misery, hate, and emotional pain. He spoke of the physical torture many went through during their mandatory reeducation camp experiences. Women were abused, children were torn form families, and those who had aligned with the American troops were tortured, abused, and often killed. Their land, homes, and finances were taken away.

As we arrived at the District police station, we were led into a large room decorated with Communist propaganda. At the head of the room was a long red banner that hung from the ceiling to the floor. Centered was a pronounced yellow star with the words declaring, "Vietnam." Right in front was a pinnacle with a large bust of Ho Chi-Minh, or otherwise known as "Uncle Ho" (the father of Vietnam). A very large man then entered the room. His face was angry and his demeanor was intimidating. He sat and interrogated us all over again with questions such as, "Why are you here? Who sent you?"

After reasoning with him for what seemed to be about two hours, without any notice, he stood up and stomped out of the room. We sat in silence. We now were all quite concerned about the circumstances that we had gotten ourselves into. After more than an hour of waiting, a white limousine and two army vehicles pulled up to our building. Two bodyguards led the way for the Deputy Director of Immigration. Dressed in a pin-stripped suit, he calmly made his presence and authority known. He sat directly before us and asked us to give him an explanation for our visit. After hearing our explanation, the Director simply declared, "It is too late for us to do anything right now. I will arrange for you to be escorted to your hotel rooms. You will meet me at 6 a.m. in my office headquarters. We will keep all your documentations."

"And this book you had in you hand; what does it say? Is this a CIA handbook? This must be a CIA book! Are the red letters secret codes? Why do you speak from this book? Are you CIA spies?"

Early the next morning at the Immigration office, we were quickly led into various individual rooms. A supervisor visited each of us separately and gave us a clean sheet of paper and a pencil. His instructions were for us to write in our own words our reason for visiting Vietnam. Without being able to correspond with the rest of our teammates, we just believed the Lord for what needed to happen. Under the influence of the Holy Spirit, we all wrote our testimony, our desire to bring hope to Vietnam, our declaration of faith, and our desire to provide social services and relief work to their country.

After about an hour, they united us all again and led us into a meeting room where the Deputy Director was already present. He had our testimonies in hand and was reading through our words. Beside him, lying on top of the table rested the Bible they had confiscated from us. He look up and said, "Your testimonies sound all the same! Are you lying?" We honestly had no idea that we would have to write anything down, and thus we had no prior preparations of what we were going to declare. With a stern face, he stared at each of us directly in our eyes and said, "Tell me the truth! Why are you here?"

At that moment the Holy Spirit spoke to each of us in the room. We knew the Lord was giving us boldness to speak the Gospel. These were the people who had for years suppressed the opportunity of a new life. Through the power of the Spirit, we each took turns expressing the salvation power of Jesus, the hope for humanity, and an eternal future in heaven. There was no expression in the Director's face. His emotions did not elevate or change throughout our testimonies. After we had all taken a turn to speak, he then asked, "And this book you had in you hand; what does it say? Is this a CIA handbook? This must be a CIA book! Are the red letters secret codes? Why do you speak from this book? Are you CIA spies?"

These questions gave us an opportunity to share the Gospel. We shared about Jesus Christ, His death on the cross, and the hope of redemption that this gave for all mankind. We told him of the stories of Jesus healing and His miracles, and spoke of salvation and hope. We told him the red letters in the book he held marked the actual words Jesus Himself spoke. We all spoke boldly and yet fearfully before God.

Afterwards the Deputy Director simply looked straight down as if staring at the table. He stayed quiet and still for a long period of time. Then, slowly he looked up. With tears running down his face, he said, "This story you have shared about Jesus, I have never heard. Our people have never been given hope. The life we are taught to live is one of fear and oppression. If this Jesus you speak about is the true God, and it is your desire to bring this new life and salvation to the people of Vietnam, then this is the best story I have ever heard." He then continued and said, "I will make you a deal. I will give you back your passports and your airline tickets and allow you to leave the country on one condition…" He then took the small Bible they had confiscated from us and lifted it with his right hand and said, "…if you let me keep this book!"

Flabbergasted by his statement, we all declared in unison, "Yes!"

This wonderful encounter led us to be introduced to the Department of Labor, Invalids, and Social Affairs of the Socialist Republic of Vietnam, and to develop our Five Kingdom Memorandum of Agreement towards bringing hope to the people of Vietnam. Soon after this occurrence, we were invited to sign a Memorandum of Agreement to fund five building projects throughout the North of Vietnam. Currently in operation, we have five facilities that we built and sponsor: Friendship House (an orphanage), a handicapped center, music center, drug rehabilitation center, and an old folks' home.

farmers / Vietnam

Consider it pure joy, my brothers, whenever you face trials of many kinds, because you know that the testing of your faith develops perseverance. James 1:2-3 NIV

RON PEARCE
Executive Director: Empower Ministries, Canada
Vietnam

persecution in Vietnam

The Story of Happy

The meeting was like many others in which I'd participated in various countries around the world. This time I was in Vietnam, in a small, dark hotel room that seemed even smaller when the six national pastors I was meeting with arrived. These pastors resembled a men's choir, all sporting their typical uniforms—black pants and white shirts.

But on this day, one man stood out from the others—a young man with a huge, perpetual smile on his face whom I silently dubbed Happy.

I observed Happy carefully as the meeting progressed, with each pastor taking a turn to share his testimony and give a short ministry report. One by one each shared the story of how he came to know Jesus as Savior and how God had called him to be a church planter. Each shared a few personal details and talked about their wives and children. When prompted, each humbly reported on the number of churches they had planted and the number of people they had led to the Lord. But, they shared more than just the statistics of their lives and ministries; they also shared heartwrenching details. They talked about the times they were arrested for preaching the Gospel or beaten simply because they love Jesus. They talked about enduring hunger and sickness and persecution, along with a host of other experiences.

The room was quiet, each person thoughtful and respectful, as the church planters took their turns quietly sharing their hearts. But throughout the whole process, one man was in constant motion. The man I had dubbed Happy bounced up and down silently in his chair as he listened, like a child waiting to open his gifts on Christmas morning. He didn't make a sound, but his whole body shook, vibrating with anticipation at sharing his story. When each leader completed his report, Happy immediately smiled his huge smile and applauded his co-laborer, cheering him on for the work he had done. Bouncing, smiling, and applauding joyfully, Happy continued this routine throughout the entire process.

Finally, it was Happy's turn, and after witnessing this cheerleader in action, I was eager to hear his story. The physical marks evident on Happy's face and body confirmed that this was the man I had heard about from his ministry leaders. I knew his story was a painful one, but his countenance belied what I had been told about his life.

Showing deep respect for his Savior, Happy told us about the life he lived before he knew Jesus, how he met the Lord, and then explained how God directed him into ministry as a church planter. Continuing his enthusiastic bouncing, he shared humbly but joyfully the incredible number of churches he had started—he couldn't remember if it was thirty or thirty-one churches in his short ministry—and about the hundreds and hundreds of people he had led to the Lord.

Happy told us about his young wife, his partner in life and ministry. This couple's passion for sharing the Gospel with the people of Vietnam and establishing the new believers in churches had driven them into new regions for evangelistic outreach. Their plan was simple: move into a new area with no churches; find the people who were sick and pray for their healing; share their faith and hope in Jesus; lead people to the Lord; start a church.

Happy explained, "When God answers our prayers and heals the sick, the people in the village begin to pay attention and want to know about this God that we serve."

Their system is very effective, and only in heaven will we know how many have come to the Lord through their efforts. But this effective system has also put them on the radar with the less-than-friendly officials who see Christianity as a threat to the way of life that they know. As a result, Happy and his wife have suffered various forms of oppression and persecution.

>

"Once I was hit with a four-by-four log; the side of my face and the bones around my eye were broken, and as a result my eye popped out. When the attack was over, my wife and I went behind one of the huts, put my eye back into its socket, and prayed for it."

"Our house has been burned down seven times. Each time it is burned, we know God wants us to move to a new area and start another church, so we move, build another house, and start church planting again," Happy explained matter-of-factly. "I have received severe beatings many times. Once I was hit with a four-by-four log; the side of my face and the bones around my eye were broken, and as a result my eye popped out. When the attack was over, my wife and I went behind one of the huts, put my eye back into its socket, and prayed for it. And see," he said smiling, as he pointed at his right eye, which aimed off to the right when he faced me. "It works fine!"

"Did you see a doctor to take care of your eye?" I asked him, still amazed at the optimism this man displayed.

Happy shook his head and explained that there was no doctor or hospital in that area, but said, "Our Physician is Jesus." Again he pointed to his face, nodding and said, "It's fine, see."

Then suddenly, Happy stopped bouncing. His perpetual smile faded, and his face took on a serious and pained expression. "The hardest thing I have endured was watching a group of men beat my wife. I couldn't reach her, couldn't help or protect her. The more I fought to get to her, the more I was beaten and restrained." Tears escaped his eyes as he dropped his head, the pain from the encounter still gripping him. "My wife was beaten so badly that she lost our first baby that she was carrying at the time."

My heart broke in that room as I contemplated the hopelessness and agony this man must have experienced at witnessing that beating. Each of us was quiet, waiting patiently while Happy dealt with this deep pain.

A moment later, Happy took a deep breath—a visible sign of his deliberate decision to move on from that memory—and began to share more ministry victories. He talked about those who were healed and those delivered from demons and witchcraft. He talked about showing God's love in tangible ways by sharing what little food he had with the lost. We all knew that to give away his food meant he was going hungry. It is a way of life for many pastors. Story after story he told of God's faithfulness and power. And with each story, Happy's smile grew a little bigger and his bouncing intensified.

He shared the challenges he encounters due to the perpetual lack of Scriptures. "Even when I hear of New Testaments being available somewhere, they are in short supply and difficult to obtain. It is extremely dangerous to transport them." A person caught transporting Scriptures risks having them confiscated, or being arrested, fined, or beaten.

This is reality in Vietnam; the normal life each of these workers face. The normal life each embraces. Their lives are testimonies of victory and remind me of the Scripture in Hebrews 12:1-3 (see facing page).

I looked around at the members of this group. It was clear that they have their eyes firmly fixed on Jesus, enduring the present trials, but not just simply enduring—but enduring with peace and victory. They fully understand the cost they are paying for their obedience in serving their Savior.

Considering the struggles he had faced, Happy was an unlikely name for this man. Through the abuse, persecution, and unbelievable pain and hardship he suffered, he remained a testimony to God's faithfulness and strength, portraying optimism in the face of incredible hardship. While the name Happy spoke to the smile evident on his face, it did not come anywhere close to describing the depth of this individual that could only come from his relationship with Jesus. Though I will always think of him as Happy, now I know his more appropriate name is Joy.

Therefore, since we are surrounded
by such a great cloud of witnesses,
let us throw off everything that hinders
and the sin that so easily entangles,
and let us run with perseverance
the race marked out for us.
Let us fix our eyes on Jesus,
the author and perfecter of our faith,
who for the joy set before him endured the cross,
scorning its shame,
and sat down at the right hand of the throne of God.
Consider him who endured such opposition
from sinful men,
so that you will not grow weary and lose heart.

Hebrews 12:1-3 NIV

testimony of the first day as missionaries

Great Beginnings!

It was our first day as missionaries and our first day in tropical Madang, just a few degrees off the equator in Papua, New Guinea. Brand new missionaries, we were eager to find our way around—so what better place to go to than the local market?

The morning fruit and vegetable market in Madang offered a range of local produce the likes of which we had never seen before. Here we would get to meet some of the people the Lord had sent us to reach with His love, amidst many exotic and inviting smells.

And one of the local people we did meet in a way that confirmed to us we were just where God wanted us to be. A young national lad approached us and asked me if I was a missionary. Just like that!

A little taken aback—this was our first day on the mission field, remember—I paused and then told him I was. He told me his name was Jimmy. He had just had a dream, he said, in which he had been told to go to the marketplace and ask the missionary there about God.

God had spoken to Jimmy, and he obeyed so here he was at the market. What should I do? It all seemed so sudden on our very first day. Was this what missionary life was all about? Countless questions raced through my mind.

I decided to invite Jimmy back to the church. That morning I had been introduced to Yakas, one of the church regulars—a simple lad full of the love of Jesus. And there he was, cycling across the grounds, where he would often help out, cutting the fast-growing grass with a large vicious-looking scythe.

I had just a very basic grasp of the Pidgin language (enough to understand Jimmy, helped by his own very basic English). Yakas was the very person I needed—ordinary, uneducated, not wise by the world's stan-

dards, but with eyes overflowing with the love of God, reflecting a pure and godly heart.

For the very first time, Jimmy heard the Gospel in the local dialect, the language of his heart. And then and there he gave his heart to Jesus. It was a precious moment. Jimmy grew in his newfound faith, committing himself to the local church and later going to Bible college.

What an encouragement on our very first day as missionaries! God was so gracious, showing us in such a clear way that His hand was upon us here in our new home. Jimmy was one of around forty young people who were baptized several months later before we left for a longer term assignment in Indonesia.

Many of these young believers would later be stationed all over Papua, New Guinea—student teachers, health workers, technical workers, most of whom had studied at local colleges. What a privilege to share our lives with them all!

But that encounter with Jimmy was one-of-a-kind. It was a token of what was to come. What a great beginning to our life as missionaries. We learned from the very first day that God has a way to connect us with those in whom His Spirit is at work.

Who indeed knows the mind of God and how He encourages us!

fruit market / Medan, Indonesia

Your beginnings will seem humble,

so prosperous will your future be.

Job 8:7 NIV

KOMP. ± 30 000
KUBURAN
MASSAL
± 30.000

MASS GRAVE

over 30,000 buried here; 230,000+ total dead

tsunami mass grave site / Banda Ache, Indonesia

*W*hen you pass through the waters,
I will be with you; and through the rivers,
they shall not overflow you.   Isaiah 43:2   NKJV

testimony from the tsunami

The protecting hand of God

It was Sunday the 26th of December 2004. It was early, and as usual, my husband and I were preparing for the 9:30 Sunday morning service. The city of Banda Aceh's activities were proceeding as usual, while most people were still at home asleep.

My husband was downstairs on the first floor of the church praying with two of our staff members. During this time, the Lord placed an especially heavy burden on him to not just pray but to intercede for all our church members. It was odd and not his normal procedure, but he continued interceding for each of them, naming one after another. After about an hour, he still felt compelled that they must continue interceding for everyone. Several members were away in a different province for Christmas, while others had stayed behind in the city.

I was upstairs preparing and getting ready for the church service. Suddenly, around 8 a.m., everything around us began to shake, the usual sign of an earthquake. At first we took no notice because earthquakes are quite common in Banda Aceh. But then the shaking became more intense and proceeded to get stronger and continued for quite some time. We hurried outside, fearing the shaking was so strong that the building may collapse.

Crowds of people were gathered, saying that several buildings had in fact collapsed, and one of our congregation member's house was swallowed up so that only one of two stories was left. I went back inside to phone my daughter and my sister to let them know we were fine and to ask for their prayers. But the earthquake had knocked out all telephone communications.

Then the second earthquake struck. It was another long, strong quake that made all of us rush outside again. The atmosphere grew strangely calm as the earthquake came to a stop. Several minutes passed as we were waiting, then suddenly out of the corner of my eye I saw a lot of people running. I was wondering what they were running from when I saw in the distance a fishing boat coming our direction. It was then that I realized the sea was coming!

We were in a state of panic and had no idea what to do because so many people and vehicles were rushing by us.

My husband was knocked over hard by a motorbike and was hurt and stunned. I wanted to run for it, but my husband was not able to run. In the end all four of us decided not to run but to just walk as we joined arms and began praying. Other people ran past us, suggesting we run for it as well. We continued praying out loud as we walked.

The speed of the people and vehicles passing by us was nothing compared to the speed of the water heading for us. We kept walking on the pavement as the water drew near. In a matter of seconds, the four of us were hurled forward by the fierce rushing water. The force of the water was tremendous as we struggled to stay afloat. We were able to reach out and grab a tree. We managed to hold on to the tree for a few moments. We kept praying, while putting ourselves into God's hands and resigning ourselves to His will. I spoke up to the others, "We must put everything in God's hands and let His will be done. So if we are separated and anything happens to us, just believe we will all meet again in heaven." We then forgave and encouraged each other. In the meantime, the rushing current of water mixed with mud, pieces of wood, and metal battered our bodies as it continued to rise higher and higher.

Our two female church workers could not hold on to the tree any longer, the pressure from the flow of water was too great and swept them away. Not long after, my husband was also swept away.

I was still hanging onto the tree as the tsunami kept coming. Water continued smashing against me and rising higher and higher. Wood, tree branches, metal, and other debris pelted me. I kept praying to God and placing my life in His hands. The water was still getting higher, and I closed my eyes as the water covered my head. Then I felt the water stop. With my eyes closed I was unsure what was happening. Why had the water stopped? Then as I

>

got my head above the water I opened my eyes and saw that the water had actually stopped rising and was going down. It was then I realized that praise be to God, I had been saved from this disaster.

The water started to recede. I grabbed a piece of wood and walked slowly back to the church. On the way, I passed a car with the bodies of a woman and a toddler inside. Only a few meters away was a little girl shrieking and crying out, "Help me, Help me!" She saw me and cried out to me for help. But I was powerless and in shock. Just then a man ran up and rescued her.

I made it back to the church. When the tsunami came, it had forced open the door to the church. I went inside as the water left. The building was a mess and in complete chaos. I made my way up to the second floor. It seemed like forever as I waited there, wondering if my husband and our female staff workers were still alive. At long last my husband, Rachel, and Layla walked in. We hugged and cried in each other's arms, praising God that we were all safe and reunited.

My husband told us his story of being carried away by the water as pieces of metal and wood slammed against his body. He got caught on a large heap of debris. A man clinging to the top of the rubbish reached out his hand to him and said," Come on up, boss!" while hauling him up out of the water. My husband sat up to find a huge snake next to him. But praise be to God, he was saved.

Because our church was open and most other homes were closed or destroyed, many strangers came in seeking refuge. There was a father who had lost his family, a mother who had lost her children, a crippled man, and that little girl I mentioned earlier who cried out to me for help was brought in. We all sat together in groups, comforting each other and crying quietly.

It was only after the water receded that the dreadful situation of the town was revealed. The city had been replaced by a sea of corpses sprawled everywhere in sight. A minor apocalypse had hit Aceh. Bodies were scattered right up to the door of our church.

We slowly started hearing from our other congregation members, story after story came in that all of the families were safe and alive. A miracle! God had laid upon my husband's heart a burden to intercede in prayer for each and every member of the church by name before the disaster. None of the families or congregation members died. One six-year-old child was lost for two weeks, but praise to God was found safe. God had protected them all; not one life was lost.

The number of dead and missing is mind-boggling. The province of Aceh was hardest hit by the tsunami with at least 131,338 people dead and another 25,000 missing or never found. The disaster destroyed property, homes, and lives, and displaced multitudes of people. The pain and suffering that people have gone through cannot be comprehended by the normal person. Survivors have struggled to rebuild their lives and communities. In Aceh alone there are 60,000 people still living in tents and makeshift shelters. There are 47,000 people buried in one mass grave near the airport in Banda Aceh.

At the time of the tsunami, through our weakness and God's guidance we decided not to run. Instead we chose to turn our lives completely over to God. We still experienced the disaster firsthand. God showed us His power and protective hand so that it could become a witness to the glory of His name. Now we must admit our weakness once again. We can't possibly help take away the pain and suffering that people have gone through. But God can! We are turning ourselves over to God once again in our weakness so that He can truly use us as His servants to be able to reach out, give, share, encourage, and rebuild many lives through Him.

You are my hiding place;
you will protect me from trouble
and surround me with songs of deliverance.
Psalm 32:7 NIV

a woman who lost her entire family in the tsunami / tent city / Banda Aceh

whole families make their living savaging though trash piled as high as seven stories

Payatas dump children / Manila, Philippines

orphanage / Philippines

men's prison / Philippines

"*The Lord looked down from his heavenly sanctuary. He looked to the earth from heaven to hear the groans of the prisoners, to release those condemned to die.*" Psalm 102:19-20 NIV

JERRY HAMPTON
Elder and Director of Prison Ministry
Times Square Church, NYC

a Philippine prison testimony

An Angel with God's pen

The trip to this particular prison was an unplanned event, at least as far as we knew. When we arrived in the islands of the southern Philippines, we were slated to visit other prisons in the Bocolod City area. We noticed there was a prison right across the street from our hotel, but it was not on our list of scheduled visits.

When we inquired about this facility, we were told the Bocolod City Prison with its 200 inmates was off limits. However, we experienced two significant biblical truths and saw them unfold into reality right before us. The first is that God can and will open doors that no man can open; and second, He will take you to places you don't necessarily plan on going to. Had I known what the living conditions were like beforehand, I can safely say I would not have planned this one. You see, in addition to running the prison ministry for our church, I was also a Wall Street executive whose idea of roughing it was hanging out at the Ritz Carlton.

It did not take long to figure out why this prison was off limits—the warden, whose name was Samson, did not want us there! He was rather definitive about no preaching. When we offered to bring in bread and juices to the men, he relented but "no preaching." I told him we came in peace and only wish to bring Good News to him and his men. He gave in a little more and said yes but "No gospel in Jesus' name as it is not allowed." I then proceeded to tell him there was only one reason why we were there and that was to bring the gospel of Jesus Christ to his men and some food.

A few minutes of negotiating ensued, and Samson was suddenly called away. We proceeded to the cells and began to gather the men into a central area behind the bars of the cell blocks. As the men came out of their cells, they looked and smelled like caged animals. The stench was awful and the sight of open sewage and rotted clothing was revolting. Even more depressing was the look on the men's faces as many were hardened criminals who had committed murder and had nothing to look forward

to except execution. Others were there for various crimes and all were suffering from malnutrition. You see in many Third World prisons like this, the men only eat what the family (if any) brings them. And even then, the ones fortunate enough to get food were often beat up by others and their food stolen.

As we gathered the men, someone brought a small broken speaker and a smelly microphone for our interpreter and me to use. I think my voice was actually louder than the speaker, but they insisted and who was I to deny them this small request. I began to preach the good news of the Gospel and why we were there when suddenly Samson the warden showed up with his pistol strapped on his waist. The scene that unfolded was truly remarkable.

First of all, it was not lost on any of us that the prisoners could have easily stormed and overpowered the warden, taken his gun, and killed all of us, and why not? Many were slated to die for their crimes anyway. As I preached, the warden looked at me very angrily. My interpreter was indeed relating the Gospel message for all to hear in their native tongue, and Samson was fuming. However, he did not move, and I kept on preaching. I kept glancing in his direction and honestly wondered what he planned on doing with that gun as he looked none too pleased with the situation. The room became very quiet when Samson walked directly toward me. I suddenly stopped preaching. He stopped, took the microphone from my interpreter, looked at me, and said, "I will now be your interpreter." My initial thought was that he would twist what I was saying, but he translated word for word. WOW! His prior look of anger was actually conviction from the Lord.

>

179

WOW!! The more I preached, the more animated he became. What I thought was sweat rolling off his face in the stale cell were tears of repentance. In the next ten minutes, thirty men got saved and the warden was healed of a very backslidden heart. Samson had been saved as a teenager but had not walked with God for the past twenty years.

After that day, Samson gave us free access to the prison as we brought in more food, medical teams, and even dentists. Someone fixed the old speaker, and we had daily worship and ministering. As we preached, men were getting saved, were given antibiotics, and had rotted teeth pulled. Samson personally interviewed each new convert to confirm their faith and then handed them a brand new Bible we had brought. He then registered their name and their crime on a list he handed to me. Samson also asked us to pray for the salvation of his wife, and the following night his wife, Joy, gave her heart to Jesus in the sight of many and amidst more tears from her revived husband. What a sight!

By the time our three days were over, we came to know, hug, and hold many new additions to the body of Christ. Special to us all were two brothers who were convicted of the brutal killing of their mother and were sentenced to death. They were wonderfully saved and helped as our security during our time in the prison. They were executed the following week.

Many came to know Jesus, the warden was restored to the Lord, his wife received eternal life, and our team of ordinary men and women witnessed and were instruments of His divine plan. Samson wrote down ninety-three names of the new believers (about half the prison) on his list that day, and we all rejoiced that an angel with God's pen wrote their names in the Lamb's Book of Life! Truly we saw prison doors open and the captives set free.

The Spirit of the Sovereign Lord is on me,
because the Lord has anointed me
to preach good news to the poor.
He has sent me to bind up the brokenhearted,
to proclaim freedom for the captives
and release from darkness for the prisoners,
to proclaim the year of the Lord's favor.
Isaiah 61:1-2 NIV

prisoners giving their hearts to the Lord / Philippines

woman in her kitchen / Essequibo Islands, Guyana

CENTRAL + SOUTH AMERICA

"SOMEONE ASKED WILL THE HEATHEN WHO HAVE NEVER HEARD THE GOSPEL BE SAVED? IT IS MORE A QUESTION WITH ME WHETHER WE WHO HAVE THE GOSPEL AND FAIL TO GIVE IT TO THOSE WHO HAVE NOT — CAN BE SAVED."

— Charles Spurgeon

gauchos in the mountains / Guatemala

Then I heard the voice of the Lord saying,
"Whom shall I send? And who will go for us?"
And I said, "Here am I. Send me!" Isaiah 6:8 NIV

MICHAEL BEENE
Founder and Director: Faith in Action
Guatemala

the start of a ministry in the dangerous mountains of Guatemala

Our Lives are not our Own

A Christian medical team went to the highlands of Guatemala. They were shocked by the over-whelming poverty and sickness. The children were so infested by worms that their little bellies looked like they were going to pop. Their skin and hair showed signs of severe malnutrition.

They also had never seen a dentist before. They looked hopeless. As the team left, they began praying to God for help. They began to ask God to send full-time missionaries to live in this area.

We were invited to visit the area, and my wife and I bought a tent and moved to the top of the mountain in this very remote area of Guatemala. We were in our early 20s. Our first sweet child, Tiffany, was only six months old at that time. In our youthful zeal and love for God, all we cared about was touching lives with the compassionate hand of the Master. We never believed that we would spend the next twenty years serving these precious native people living in tiny villages in the mountains.

It took us years to come to the realization that these people didn't know how to trust us. Having been rejected and shunned by most of the civilized world, they needed more than words to unlock their hearts. After all, not even the government offered law and protection in this remote area. Consequently, they became violent and lawless even within themselves. The question was much more than why should they believe us. It was actually, why should they not kill us?

They lived like scavengers off of the land. The cold, damp bamboo/grass huts made for cold winters were parasite breeding grounds right inside their living areas. They were so isolated; they feared us. They looked at us as intruders who had come from another world. They actually believed we were going to eat their children or make soap out of them. Why have we come?

As I reflect back chronologically over the past two decades, I can see how God brought us to these desper-ate people in the hour of their greatest need. The first three months we cut down trees and began ripping the logs lengthwise to make boards. We were not builders,

but by the grace of God, we erected a wooden cabin with a sheet metal roof that was to be our mission house.

During that time in the initial stages of our pioneer work, we walked for hours to visit a place that someone told us about. This particular time they were having a small family gathering. We walked down the narrow trails, trying to follow the simple instructions of the local by-passers. We would ask, "We are looking for Augustine's house, can you help us?" They would tell us to take a left at the mango tree and then a right by the pine tree and cross the fence at the cedar tree. Get the picture? Can you imagine us trying to find a mango or pine tree in the forest? Yes, we got lost. For hours, we went up and down the mountain until we ran into someone else and ask him or her for directions again.

Upon arrival, we were almost too tired to take upon ourselves the task of passing the enormous mama sow lying in the doorway. After resting a while, hearing the strangely out-of-tune singing, and assessing the extreme amount of energy already invested in this adventure, we decided to press on. We entered the little grass roof lean-to and sat down on a nicely positioned piece of log in the back of the room. We caught our breath as they finished the last song.

A worn and tired looking middle-aged man stood up in front of the small gathering and with quivering lips struggled to share a testimony. "Brothers and sisters," he shared, "I need your prayers. You all know that God has given my wife and me twins. Jeremiah and Isaiah are their names. Well, we know why He gave us twins. We left Jeremiah at home tonight because he is too sick to live. We believe he will be dead by the time we get home tonight."

He seemed dreadfully sad and exhausted, maybe from

>

185

sleepless nights holding their child and praying for healing or an intervention from God. They had finally come to the place of hopelessness, and the smoldering wick of their faith was extinguished. Drifting aimless and alone in a sea of despair and isolation, the only comfort they could find was in the fact that God had given them twins. God was taking Jeremiah home, and Isaiah was left behind to console them.

Our hearts were stirring as we saw the tears running down their faces. How many times did we almost turn back from trying to find this hut? Just when one of us would be ready to give up, the other would say, "No, let's press on! We will find it sooner or later."

Now our hearts were exploding with faith and fear at the same time. We knew by divine order that God had brought us here just for this moment. No matter how hard it may seem, there is no greater feeling than to know that you are exactly in the perfect will of God. At the same time, doubt and unbelief were haunting us with questions like, "What if the baby dies? What if the baby is already dead? Can you save the child?" It seems like the voice of uncertainty screams a thousand times louder than trusting in God's still, small voice.

I moved forward towards the front and asked permission to speak. I acknowledged to them that I understood that we were foreigners and strangers in their mountains. I told them that we were the missionaries living way up on the top of the mountain.

I shared with them, "God brought us to your country from a faraway land. We were led by God to move to your country so we came on an airplane. Then, after being in your country, God supernaturally led us to pitch a tent on top of this mountain and bring the Word of God here. Early this afternoon, we headed

out on an adventure of finding your little church and got lost so many times, we began to lose heart. However, we encouraged one another and continued on until we heard your singing and worshiping the Lord from a distance.

"Now, we stand before you in the name above all names. We believe that God heard your prayers and felt your love and pain for Jeremiah. You may not always understand His ways, but we are here with you by the divine plan of God. We believe with all of our hearts that God gave you Jeremiah and Isaiah to raise for His glory.

"If you will trust us with your child's life, we promise to do all that we can to find him help. We will take him to the city and admit him into a hospital that can hopefully find out what he needs."

The other people were encouraging the parents to give us Jeremiah because they had no option. They said that he might already be dead and that if he wasn't dead, to trust God and give the child to us.

The mother and father ran home to see if he was still alive. They came back to the little meeting with Jeremiah wrapped up in a blanket. We opened the blanket and saw the little malnourished sick child gasping for every breath.

We ascended back to the mission camp and then hurried up to the end of the road where we left our vehicle. It was another two hours of driving off road before we reached the pavement, and another two hours to the city where the hospitals were. I strapped the tiny little baby in Tiffany's car seat to provide the safest journey possible. Many times as I bounced down the rough trails towards civilization, I would hear Jeremiah stop breathing.

I didn't feel like I had time to stop the car, so I reached back and shook the car seat to provoke a response in Jeremiah. The four-hour trip seemed like an eternity, and we prayed all the way.

As I approached the city, I felt a huge relief knowing that Jeremiah had made the long trip and was still alive and that help was near. Little did I know that once again the battle was trying to find a hospital willing to take him in such critical condition. I finally told the head nurse on duty that he could die if she didn't take him. "I don't know what to do for him and he might not make it through the night if you send us away." We were sent away. We went to several hospitals until finally someone accepted the child. The nurse knew exactly what to do to save the baby, and she was willing to take the risk for the baby's life.

Frantically, she took the baby in and began by putting him on an IV with nutrition and antibiotic. She cleaned him and put warm new clothes on him. He was placed in an oxygen tent to ease his breathing. All the other nurses joined in, and I saw that somehow the spirit of death had lost its grip. I knew standing there in the emergency room at 4 a.m. that Jeremiah would be all right.

Six weeks later when the hospital gave us permission to take Jeremiah home, we bought him new pants, a belt, shirt, and little rubber boots. We returned to the village and carried Jeremiah back down the mountain to his parents.

To see the joy on their faces standing there in a state of almost unbelief made it all worth it. Tears running down their cheeks, the words echoed through my mind that the father spoke when we met him for the first time. "God has given us twins because he is going to take Jeremiah home."

This was the very first miracle child that we encountered upon arriving in this region over twenty years ago. Still today, His enduring love continues to reach out and touch their lives using medicine, dental, and physical means to draw them to His Son, Christ Jesus. We are always reminded that our lives are not our own.

Ten years later, we were sitting in a church service with the local men sharing their testimonies. The speaker seemed almost embarrassed to share in front of us, but upon encouragement, he continued speaking to the congregation. "When these missionaries first came," he said, "we didn't trust them. All of us men of the village would get together and plan on killing them before they harmed us! It seemed that every time we came up with a plan, one of our children or wives would get sick. We had no option but to postpone the killing and ask for their help. It took almost three years before we decided that we were not going to kill them and that maybe they really were here to help us. Now," he continued with tears running down his face, "we see them as our parents."

Unless a grain of wheat falls into the ground, it abides alone. There is a mystery that takes place in a life surrendered to God. In the world we are taught to pursue fun, fame, and fortune, but the journey of the Christian pilgrim is different. Success in the Christian's life might well be unseen—in most cases, obscure or immeasurable. However, God reveals His destiny to all those with a hungry heart and thirsty soul looking for a deeper walk with God.

Isaiah 6:8 says, "Then I heard the voice of the Lord say, 'Whom shall I send and who will go before me.' Isaiah said, '"Here I am Lord, send me."'

Remember, our lives are not our own.

mother and child inside their home / Guatemala

Let us therefore come boldly to the throne of grace, that we may obtain mercy and find grace to help in time of need.

Hebrews 4:16 NKJV

ROXANNE BEENE
Faith In Action
Guatemala

a Cholera epidemic on the mountain

In the Time of Need

Michael, my husband, warned me to stay away from the clinic. "They are coming constantly," he said with desperation in his voice. "They are being brought here in hammocks from hours away."

The native mountain people were coming in droves, carrying their sick over treacherous mountain trails and through dense forests to get to our missions clinic. The sickness was so contagious that most of the people who were transporting their sick were themselves getting sick on the way home. Many even died on the trails before they could make the journey back to our clinic.

We diagnosed the sickness as an intestinal bacterium called cholera, which causes severe dehydration by violent diarrhea and vomiting. Because the people feel so bad, they stop drinking water and become skin and bones in a matter of two days; death soon follows. The people brought to us looked like skeletons. The medical treatment for cholera is to find a healthy vein and admit an IV with a rehydration solution. There would only be two and maybe three veins that you could find that were not collapsed that you could put an IV in. Most of the time, if we could get three or four liters of solution back in their body, they would survive.

When a person is infected by cholera, the main danger is that the blood is so thickened by the lack of body fluid that it forms blood clots in the lungs, brain, or heart. These blood clots are dangerous and life-threatening.

Michael clearly told me to stay away from the clinic. We had three small children ranging from three months old to five years old. "You are the mother of my children, and I need you to take care of the kids and be safe and healthy for them. You have to be careful not to contaminate our family."

For the first time a little two-year-old child was brought to the clinic. Trying to find a good vein in a dehydrated adult was very difficult, but to put an IV in a child seems to be almost impossible. This little girl's veins were almost collapsed. Michael was forced to take this child to the nearest hospital hours away to try and save her life. This trip down the mountain would take two or three hours of four-wheeling down the treacherous mountain road.

The rugged road was a narrow path cut through a dense rain forest, hemmed in with jagged mountain cliffs off the sides. In the rains we would pull out the wench cable and pull the truck up the mountain road. We would hook the cable to the nearest tree and go in front of the truck, running from tree to tree to mechanically extract the vehicle out of the mud.

I exclaimed, "Michael, what am I to do if someone comes while you are gone? I have never even seen an IV put into someone's arm. I am not sure of the whole procedure." He told me that I had to change out the IV bottles when they are finished and pray that no one else comes until he returns. He then loaded up the truck and took the tiny sick child and off he went, down the mountain.

Now, alone in the mountains with my children, I soon was startled by an aggressive pounding on the front door. As I opened the door, I saw the desperate cry for help in the eyes of the people who were carrying the hammock. I looked into the hammock and saw what looked like a ninety-year-old man. He was very frail, and his eyes were closed and sunk back into his head. He looked as if he was already dead. I quickly brought them to the clinic.

My heart was full of fear. *This man needs an IV! Oh God, if I don't get an IV into this man, I will be the cause of his death.* I tried to put the IV into the first vein, but I punctured through it and began to draw blood back up the hose. *Oh no, I have to try again,* I thought. But the same thing happened to the second vein. I saw the yearning of hope being extinguished from the eyes of the family. They had carried him up and down the mountainous trails with the hope of arriving at the clinic to save his life only now to watch him die. The father said, "Please, put in the IV and he will live. Please, all he needs is the IV."

>

. . . later I found that ninety-year-old man was really only a sixteen-year-old boy. His cheeks began to fill out and life came to his weak dying body.

Overwhelmed with desperation and at the point of despair, I prayed. My heart was full of hope, but little faith, that I could really accomplish this. I confessed to the family, "I am not a medical person, and I have no ability to do this. But God, my God loves you, and He can do all things; nothing is too difficult for him. Let us pray that I will decrease, and He would increase. That I would disappear, and it would not be my knowledge or ability that would perform this procedure but that God would fill me with Himself, and He would put this IV in and save this man's life." It was the one last chance and the last vein. I put in the needle, and it went in! The IV fluid filled his veins. Three or four liters later, I found that ninety-year-old man was really only a sixteen-year-old boy. His cheeks began to fill out, and life came to his weak dying body. There was great joy in the family.

That day, we all saw the faithfulness of our God. A yielded life is all about God's ability not our own. As missionaries we have repeatedly been put into a places of impossible circumstances, where we have been forced to believe that only God can do it! At these moments it is up to us to believe in Him, and let His supernatural life flow through us.

The Lord is good,
a refuge in times of trouble.
He cares for those who trust in him...
Nahum 1:7 NIV

carrying wood and supplies to market over steep mountain trails / Pinalito, Guatemala

mountain kids / Pinalito, Guatemala

Jesus said, "Let the little children come to me, and do not hinder them, for the kingdom of heaven belongs to such as these." Matthew 19:14 NIV

TIFFANY BEENE
Faith In Action, Guatemala
missionary's daughter

remote mountain children's first visit to the big city

Native's Day Out

It was a sunny day in Pinalito, unusually warm for the early morning hours. An obnoxiously loud rooster could be heard crowing from one of the surrounding bamboo huts. It wouldn't be long before the patter of hands would be heard making the morning batch of tortillas.

Having lived here in Guatemala my entire life, this morning was like most others. As I lay there listening to the morning sounds, I was awakened to the sobering truth: my life was extremely different from most typical American kids. All sixteen years of my crazy life had been hashed out in this primitive village named Pinalito. Here in the mountains, my mother runs the clinic, and my dad, pretty much the rest of the mission. I had spent my days with my two younger sisters exploring the countryside, making friends with the village children, and eating fruit off the native trees.

Growing older and having built true friendships with the local people, this place was never just a village where we helped people. It was home. I had come to love this small, secluded place. It is my world.

I remember one time a couple years back, my parents had decided to take some of the school kids on a trip to Guatemala City, the Big City as they called it. It was December, nearing the holidays, and we thought it would be nice to be able to share some of the outside world with them. As we walked into a mall, I turned and looked with amusement as the kids stopped mid-stride and just stared with jaws open wide.

"Que es eso?" questioned Rigo. Ah! Good-ole Rigo. He's the shortest twelve year old I had ever met; however, his height had never stopped him. Always the leader and clown of the bunch, he was inquisitive about everything. He would make it far in this world if only given an opportunity.

I turned to look at what he pointed at and said, "That's an escalator." Still puzzled we led them over towards the escalator, and after much persuasion, finally got them to ride it. After getting over the initial shock, they actually began to enjoy it and went on it over and over, up and down, to the amusement of all who watched. As the day progressed, we noticed that one of the young men seemed to become more and more tense. It was not long before Antonio approached my dad and in a hushed voice whispered to him, "I don't know what's going on, but I just want to warn you that all day a man has been following us around. I first noticed him in the mall, and he seemed to be everywhere we went. Now he is here in the grocery store." My dad, now curious, questioned, "Where is he?" Antonio glanced quickly behind him and said, "He is wearing a big red coat, a beard, and matching hat to go along with his coat. He is quite big and hard to miss." Turning to look, it suddenly dawned on my dad that this boy was talking about Santa Claus. He quickly explained the story and tried to ease this boy's mind, which was hesitant to believe him. He still kept his guard up the rest of the day.

As we walked through the mall, Mom was shocked to see one of the younger girls with no shoes on. "Where are your shoes?" she asked little Sarah, who looked up with a blank stare. "No tengo," she replied. After buying her some shoes, we continued on to the food court. All the kids' wide-eyed fascination must have been obvious to others in the mall because an elderly lady walked up to my parents and asked if she could speak to the kids for a minute. Mom, slightly worried that this wealthy looking city lady would look down on the kids, was hesitant, but said, "Sure, go ahead." The lady started by sitting the kids down and telling them the history of their country. She then told them how proud she was

>

...compared to the excitement of seeing Tarzan swing through the trees. We watched them in amusement as they ducked and swatted in front of them, thinking that the stuff on the screen was real and coming at them.

---

that they were in school, and ended with buying all twenty of the kids ice cream. Many of them had never had ice cream before and were surprised and delighted when they experienced their first scoop.

The day wasn't complete until we went to see a movie. A simple thing to many, but to children who barely knew what electricity was, it was huge! The shock of seeing such a big screen was quickly forgotten when compared to the excitement of seeing Tarzan swing through the trees. We watched them in amusement as they ducked and swatted in front of them, thinking that the stuff on the screen was real and coming at them. Every second of the movie was devoured by these kids. It was logged in their memory for the rest of their lives. A man on a screen that could fly through the trees, and corn that was soft. Popcorn would make the village news for days.

The following day we returned to the village. The kids scattered and ran to tell to all who would listen of their adventures in the big city. They told of moving stairs that went straight up, the big man dressed in a red coat that stalked them, and soft stuff that was cold. It was a trip that was talked about for weeks and months to come.

It is hard for many to imagine that this kind of lifestyle exists in any part of the world. I have grown up being able to watch as these people experience running water for the first time, a ride in a car, or learn about the outside world. These have all become special moments and memories for me. I realize that I have been presented with a great opportunity to help and give of my life to others. Overall, the trip to the city was a memory I would not soon forget, and neither would they. As a sixteen-year-old American girl, this is my life. It's been a life and an opportunity that I would never want to trade.

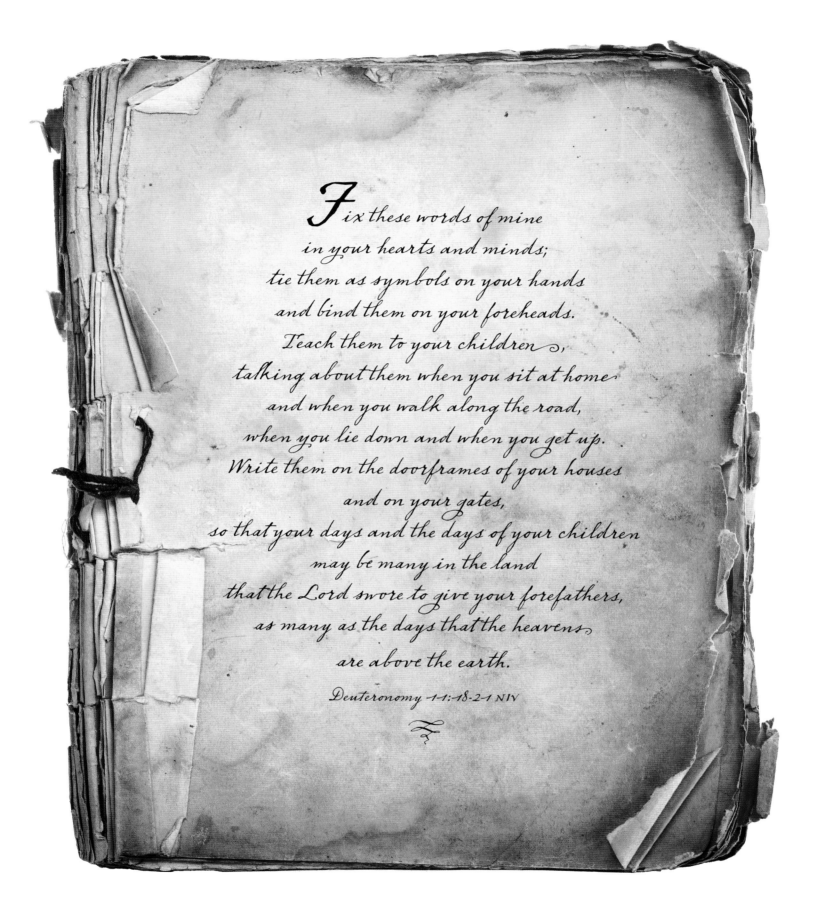

Fix these words of mine
in your hearts and minds;
tie them as symbols on your hands
and bind them on your foreheads.
Teach them to your children,
talking about them when you sit at home
and when you walk along the road,
when you lie down and when you get up.
Write them on the doorframes of your houses
and on your gates,
so that your days and the days of your children
may be many in the land
that the Lord swore to give your forefathers,
as many as the days that the heavens
are above the earth.

Deuteronomy 11:18-21 NIV

DON WOLFRAM
Missionary Ventures International
Ecuador

a colorful message on our higher calling

Yellow Spray Paint

The Bible-training center in a mountainous area of Ecuador was progressing well. The kitchen had been expanded and a dining room added so as to accommodate larger groups. The problem was that the farmer's cows from next door kept trampling the little bit of lawn and the sports field.

The high volume of rain in Ecuador makes it hard to maintain a nice lawn. We had been working so hard to get it level and to conquer the constant problem of mud.

As I arrived at the site early one morning, I saw that the neighbor's cows had left fresh new and deep footprints and even some other piles of surprises all across the sports area. Annoyed to say the least and flustered, I grabbed Jorge the caretaker and headed down the mountain to find the neighbor and his naughty cows. Upon arriving, I forced a very calm greeting and then informed him that once again his cows had made a mess at the training center.

Would he please come and help repair the mess? He agreed to do so. I was very annoyed by the numerous times that this had already occurred. I felt justified in wanting to ensure that this did not happen again, so I just couldn't let it go that easy. I continued, "I'll tell you what, I'll buy some bright yellow enamel paint and when your cows come to visit, I'll just simply paint a spot on them. This way you will know your cows have been visiting me and that you should watch them better. When they are all yellow, we'll just have a big barbecue! Is that fair enough?"

He was confused at the strange gringo suggestion, as was my own caretaker Jorge, but nodded his head in reluctant agreement. I returned with a feeling of glee that I had remained so calm and presented such a witty plan. I was hopeful that the farmer might have actually got the message about looking out after his cows. I thought also that it was harmless enough of an idea. I could just see the poor man trying to explain why his cows had yellow spots all over them. I never expected or wanted to barbecue any of his cows. That pretty much was a harmless threat to make sure my point got across. But I could imagine him frantically scrubbing at the almost

impossible to remove enamel paint as the black and white slowly vanished and the "offering" time drew near.

Needless to say the very next trip in Puyo, I bought a can of bright yellow neon spray paint and set it handy between the front seats of my jeep. Surely I would catch those hole-punching, milk producing beasts at it again and would be able to leave a nice big neon yellow circle on each of them.

A couple of days passed. I had my daughter and her friend in the back seat of my nice clean interior jeep. We stopped to drop off her friend. Impatient with the three-door procedure, she quickly slipped between the front seats and jumped out. I proceeded to push the passenger seat forward for my daughter, but it was jammed so I gave it another forceful push forward. Suddenly and without warning the jeep cab turned yellow as the aerosol can discharged explosively with a loud hiss. The puncture wound received from a sharp corner under the seat instantly released the sticky bright yellow contents. I worked frantically to stop the spray from happening to no avail. My daughter screamed, watching the event unfold as if in slow motion I heard God say, "So what does it feel like to have your stuff spray painted yellow?"

I was instantly convicted of my actions toward the farmer. God made a dramatic statement to me that day. As anticipated, the yellow enamel paint is nearly impossible to remove. I have since quickly let my wonderful idea go but find that everyday I am the one explaining why the inside of my vehicle is neon yellow. It stands as a constant reminder of my poor actions and non-appropriate words to the farmer next door.

You see, I let my guard down for one fleeting moment, letting my flesh rise up in annoyance at the farmer next door and his naughty cows. Not that his cows should not be restrained from coming onto our property, but my actions and words were not how God would have had me handle the situation.

God sees all of our actions, and they are supposed to represent Him. The world and people around us are also viewing them. We are called to a higher place of being ambassadors for Christ. The word of God says, "He has committed to us the message of reconciliation. We are therefore Christ's ambassadors, as though God were making his appeal through us (2 Corinthians 5:19-20 NIV).

Being an ambassador for Christ is a high honor that has been bestowed upon us. An ambassador is an official diplomat or representative sent from one country to another. As Christians we are sent by Christ to represent Him, His love, and His words and give this message of reconciliation to our lost and hurting world. This is an important responsibility that we dare not take lightly. All our actions can and do make a difference in whether people will come to Christ. It is a question that we should ask ourselves, "How well do our actions as His ambassadors represent Christ?"

I have a daily reminder as I stare at the yellow spots covering the interior of my jeep. I have been tempted to paint black stripes in addition to the yellow so as to warn: "Caution! Missionary still in training!"

"And God has given us the task of reconciling people to him.
For God was in Christ,
reconciling the world to himself,
no longer counting people's sins against them.
And he gave us this wonderful message of reconciliation.
So we are Christ's ambassadors;
God is making his appeal through us.
We speak for Christ when we plead, "Come back to God!"
For God made Christ, who never sinned,
to be the offering for our sins,
so that we could be made right with God through Christ."

2 Corinthians 5:-18-2-1 NLT

MONICA WEHRER
Elim Fellowship
Costa Rica

a miracle testimony from a nursing home

The Book of Acts

After catching the "missions bug," I would sign up for any trips I could go on. The Lord was establishing a foreign missions department at our church, and it was exciting. One night in my private time I remember praying, "Lord, I sure would like to see the power of Your name."

We use it in prayer, and sing about it, I sure would like to know and see the power in the name of Jesus. It was just one of those things that comes out of your mouth, then you file it away in your brain somewhere, but the Lord hears every utterance.

I signed up to go to Costa Rica. What a beautiful country with beautiful people! They were so friendly and welcoming. We set up a medical clinic and had services for the kids, and of course prayer with anyone that wanted it. I was playing a game with the kids while the clinic was taking place. I was teaching them "Ring around the Rosie" because I had run out of games, when our team leader asked me to come with her and others to pray for a teenage boy.

Several of us went into a tiny office room in the school where we were ministering. The national pastor put his hand on this boy to pray and immediately the boy fell to the ground and began writhing—he was demon possessed! We all began to pray and intercede like we had never done before. The whole experience was surreal. I felt the warfare in the room; it was like you could touch it. I kept praying for strength for us because we were all getting tired. I don't even remember how long we were in there, but it sure felt like a long time. Finally, after much travail the boy began to have a peaceful look on his face. He stood up and declared Jesus Christ as Lord! He had been delivered. So I went from Ring around the Rosie to spiritual warfare in probably one hour! Who says the Christian life is boring?

The same day, we all jumped into a van and went to minister at a nursing home. When we arrived, we teamed up and began to talk with the patients. My partner and I went to talk to one particular woman. As we approached her, a nurse who worked there told us not to bother because the elderly woman was blind and almost deaf. We figured we could at least pray for her. As we prayed for her, the elderly woman began to cry and say, "Hallelujah! I can hear! I can hear what she is saying." The Lord had opened her ears. She said, "Pray for eyes, pray for my eyes! We prayed and again she began to praise the Lord. She grabbed a tract out of my hands and began to read the tract on how Jesus loves her and died for her sins! Reading with her new healed eyes. God be praised!

The whole time this was going on, the nurse who told us to leave her alone, was watching this event. She was a backslidden Christian. She started crying and asking for prayer. She wanted to give her life back to the Lord!

What a day! What a trip! As I was leaving Costa Rica, the Lord reminded me of the prayer I had prayed, "Lord, I would like to see the power of Your name." It was the name of Jesus in which the boy was delivered! It was the name of Jesus that healed the blind and almost deaf woman in the nursing home! It was the power in the name above all names—JESUS! I remember thinking, *This is real, this is like the Book of Acts! God You are so powerful; You really are!*

How I thank God for the awesome privilege to serve Him and see Him move in the nations! It was and is life changing!

nursing home

These signs will accompany those who believe: In my name they will drive out demons; they will speak in new tongues... they will place their hands on sick people, and they will get well.

Mark 16:17-18 NIV

in line for food and a place to sleep, homeless shelter / Medellin, Colombia

I will give them an undivided heart and put a new spirit in them;
I will remove from them their heart of stone
and give them a heart of flesh. Ezekiel 11:19 NIV

DOUGLAS CALVANO
Founder and Director: Ciudad Refugio
Medellin, Colombia

the start of a homeless shelter

Burnt bricks

It was a life-changing Saturday night in 1994, a very critical time of great violence in Colombia. I was on a one-year commitment as a young missionary to Medellin, Colombia. The church where we labored was located in one of the most dangerous and dark sectors of the city.

The youth at our church there met every Saturday night for fun and fellowship, and their meeting had just come to an end. It was one of those days when everything seems to click, and it's exciting and productive. But it was also a day of great labor, so intense at times that it felt like a marathon run. In fact, we often called our weekends the Great Marathon because we had to prepare five messages and also do street evangelism. By the end of the weekend we were exhausted but also fulfilled, knowing we had made a difference in people's lives. Come Monday, a new week would begin with a new heavy workload.

I was just 25 years old in 1994 and single, a status I would painfully come to know as a difficult one to endure in times of great loneliness. As if all that was not enough, I was suffering from insomnia. But soon I would know that even my insomnia would be part of God's plan. The insomnia offered me special times of prayer with God.

One sleepless night without giving anyone notice, I did something many would consider crazy. With the burden of depression and insomnia already weighing heavy on my shoulders, I added an extra load. In my hands I took a stack of tracts, and I was off to the dangerous streets of Medellin.

After only a half hour of journeying in the streets of Medellin, as the clock stroke midnight, I found myself with twenty indigents. They were not wandering aimlessly in the streets; the streets were their home. The homeless population of Medellin is quite large composed of alcoholics, drug addicts, men kicked out of their homes, and even abused children who had run to the streets and become glue addicts. Gangs, male and female prostitutes, displaced transients from other countries looking for

work—they almost all ended up addicts and on the streets!

As I approached the dark stairwell where these men laid asleep, it was clear to me that their burden was far heavier than my own. Many of them were sleeping right on the hard, filthy concrete. A few had laid out cardboard boxes to make a bed for themselves. Others had found pieces of plastic to pull over themselves in an attempt to keep warm. The whole area had a stale smell of rotten trash and urine. Their clothes were mostly old, ripped, and very dirty from living on the streets.

They were all asleep with the exception of one. This man was surprised by my presence. You see no one ever paid them any attention, especially not in such an unexpected hour. Mostly these men were feared, ignored, rejected outcasts of society. I started to converse with this one homeless man as he partially sat up from his makeshift bed. We talked about many things and finally our conversation led us to speak about the Lord. I could see the years of pain, despair, and loneliness on his face as tears filled both of our eyes, and together we prayed.

I will never forget what happened next. As we prayed, I heard a strange noise. Suddenly I was aware that I stood in the middle of a violent war zone completely alone. Fear captivated my senses, and I remember thinking my time on earth had come to an end. I tried desperately to hide my fear, but as I opened my eyes I prepared for the worst. But what I saw next, words couldn't describe. The sight before me was indescribable. The ones that slept were beginning to rise, and those that were fully awake had their eyes fixed on me. One of the men approached and spoke for all the others. "We want you to pray for us!" In

>

201

Jesus instructs us to be the voice for those whom no one listens to. He emphasized that love be reflected in concrete works. He charges us to feed the hungry, cloth the naked, and visit the sick. God spoke and I listened. That night a ministry was born, but I didn't come to know this until years later.

---

his voice I could hear that it wasn't as much a request as it was an order. Unexpectedly, the meeting was transformed into a small service. I shared with them about the peace and the joy that only our Lord and Savior gives. As I ministered to these children of God my own burden, the weight of depression, was lifted up from me.

Together we prayed and in a corner of that violence stricken city, they all accepted the Lord Jesus as their personal Savior. There wasn't a dry eye in that place. The presence of God was so real! I was overwhelmed with joy.

I returned to the church where I stayed, but when I arrived I couldn't sleep so I prayed and read. When I opened my Bible, it opened precisely in Matthew 25. This scripture speaks to us about the judgment of the nations. Jesus instructs us to be the voice for those to whom no one listens. He emphasized that love be reflected in concrete works. He charges us to feed the hungry, cloth the naked, and visit the sick. God spoke and I listened. That night a ministry was born, but I didn't come to know this until years later.

I could never have imagined what the Lord had given birth to that night and how it would impact my life and that of many others.

There are specific defining moments in our lives that we never forget. One of these moments came to me years later while I was at a worship service at my church in New York. The sermon was about the opposition we suffer because of the call of God on our lives and the importance to persevere and continue at any price. And God spoke to me like He had not done in a long time and said, "Finish what you have begun!" I accepted the conditions and made plans to go back to Medellin.

I have been told countless stories of missionaries who have brought suitcases full of bottled water and toilet paper rolls. But I believe each missionary brings a suitcase full of fears and uncertainties each time he

steps onto the mission field—especially if you are going to a country like Colombia—and I was no exception. Things like abductions, selective murders, institutional instability, and a general dislike towards the American people do not necessarily make Colombia an attractive destination. But the day arrived, and I was on a flight to Colombia. My heart was racing as if it were trying to run away from itself. In Medellin, my calling awaited me. I was going to be challenged, and fear embodied me.

It has been many years now since arriving in there, and through all the fears, uncertainties, struggles, severe depression, extreme doubts, and with many tears, God has been doing something wonderful. He has changed that young man in me that was once very insistent and hasty. He made me drop all my pride to give way to a meeker and more patient man who stands on a firm foundation of faith. He has made me a servant to those that have been forgotten and who desperately need Him.

Pay careful attention to this story. God asked a man to push the stone; the man obediently began to remove the stone. Time went by—hours, days, then the days turned into years—and the stone never moved. The man began to question the fruitfulness of such effort. In an almost defiant manner he tried to comprehend the impossible task the Lord had given him to do. The stone in front of him symbolized his failure. He had dedicated his life to the impossible. God knew his thoughts, and so He asked the man what was troubling him. The angered man replied that in spite of his efforts the stone had not moved even an inch. God surprised the man and reminded him that He had not asked him to move the stone but to simply push the stone. The man, bewildered by His answer, asked the Lord, "Then why did I push this for so many years?" The Lord pointed to the man's body. He told the man to take a look at himself. The man lowered his eyes to see that his body was not the same. His body that once had delicate white skin now was coarse, resistant to the cold, to heat, and to wounds, and his body no longer housed weak bones but was a strong body.

Finally the man understood. God wanted to change him before the stone was removed.

For Moses the stone was the forty years in the desert, and for Joseph, it was years in prison. For Paul it was thirty years of waiting before beginning His ministry.

Colombia was my stone. I have pushed it for many years, and the stone did not move. Today I am no longer the same man. The young man that was once very insistent and hasty has begun to give way to a meeker and more patient man that stands on a firm foundation built through faith. Now each time God tells me to push the stone and the stone does not move, I continue pushing, and I do it without questioning.

In construction they say that the tiles and old bricks exposed to the elements are more resistant and lasting. These characteristics many times convert them into materials far more exclusive and valuable than the new. Those who don't know their value reject them without a second thought. But those who have walked through this path know that their quality is indisputable, and its service is guaranteed.

The book of Nehemiah narrates the story of the rebuilding of what at one time had been an insurmountable fortification but later had become a pile of semi-burnt and weak bricks of a wall. The wall represented a silent testimony. It spoke of the decadence of a people, their fallen arms, and their forgetfulness of a promise made to God. What once was a great city became a public shame. This man, in the midst of his generation, received a tremendous call of God. Nehemiah was raised up to reconstruct the city, and the materials that he sought to use were semi-burnt bricks. The story tells that Nehemiah found the bricks on the outskirts of the ruins, and he did not give it a second thought to put the bricks to use. I doubt that the reason Nehemiah decided to use these old semi-burnt bricks found on the outskirts of the ruins was because he lacked new ones. I believe there is a message in the story for you and for me, and that this message repeats itself throughout the pages of the scripture.

God used and continues to use burnt bricks to raise up a powerful testimony. Fallen men can be raised again. Men and women from broken marriages can be restored, after healing, for service in God's army. And even those elderly men and woman who wasted their best years in the darkness can still become vessels in which the light of the Lord shines through. If you are a burnt brick and you read this, then I invite you to reconstruct the testimony of God in the land. God wants to use you! God often even prefers burnt bricks, to show His glory, mercy, and unconditional love.

Here in Colombia, God is restoring and using burnt bricks. He is restoring the whole person. He is restoring homeless men and women who had their lives ruined by an enemy that came to steal, kill, and destroy. God has seen a beauty in these men and women that only He could—after all, He is their all-loving Creator.

Through all the years of pushing, God has and is establishing a wonderful ministry here in Colombia. He has made a homeless shelter that sleeps and feeds between seventy to eighty men a night. He has raised up a home for single mothers and their children when they have nowhere else to turn. He has also built a drug rehab facility for the addicts on the street, to give them a foundation in the Lord, and through His strength, the ability to rebuild their lives. And yes, we still go to the streets with feeding programs to bring God's restoring hand to reach out to those yet to be restored burnt bricks that can still be used for God's glory.

Therefore, if anyone is in Christ,
he is a new creation;
the old has gone, the new has come!
2 Corinthians 5:17 NIV

Yanomami tribal women / Venezuelan rainforest

For even the Son of Man did not come to be served,

but to serve, and to give his life as a ransom for many.

Mark 10:45 NIV

Indigenous tribes in the rainforests of Venezuela

Someone sent me

My ministry is in the rainforests of Venezuela. I travel as much as ten hours at a time, up the Caura River in a hollowed out log canoe with an outboard motor. Sometimes I must maneuver through rocks and rapids to get to the many indigenous tribes along the river's banks and also to those that live inland.

The river is the home of piranha fish and anaconda snakes while the jungles are teaming with monkeys and beautiful species of birds.

The tribes here are hunters, fishermen, and gatherers. Many of them have tribal painted faces, bows and arrows, and blow guns with poison darts. They are in desperate need of humanitarian aid and medical attention. Their physical needs are great with many deaths attributed to malaria, parasites, and worms. The infant mortality rate is 72 percent. Young girls get married and pregnant as early as eleven years of age to ensure the continuance of their tribe.

There are tribes like the Pemon, Jimi, Sanema, Yanomami, Pio Poco, and Yequna, to name a few. Their spiritual needs are even greater, being heavily influenced by the shaman (witch doctors). Many people have died in their hands because the shaman say they have the medicine but mainly they rely on calling on the spirits.

God called me at a young age. My father was a missionary for forty-seven years. I grew up as a child, watching my father serve the people of Venezuela. When I was eleven years old, something significant happened that changed my life forever. A woman came running up to my father after hiking through the jungle for three hours. Her husband had been bitten by a snake and wanted my father's help.

We traveled by boat to pick him up and then we put him in our canoe to take him to get help. He had been bitten by a snake that we call the "Four Noses" snake. Its poison causes the victim to bleed out of its eyes, ears, nose, and mouth. Sitting in the front of the canoe that day, I saw this man die as my father did everything he could to help him. I remember hanging my head down and saying to God, "If you give me the opportunity to get a medical education

and college degree, I will come back to serve these tribal people.

Years later God reminded me of that moment after receiving my education at Auburn University in Alabama. It was then that God called me back to Venezuela.

How do you reach out to the spiritual needs of these tribes when they have so many people dying and sick? Do you do it by telling them God loves them? They don't understand this, for if God loves them so much, why are so many of them dying? I would pray and ask God about this. God then led me early on in my ministry to be a living testimony of Him. He led me not to go in to their villages and change their culture but instead to just show them His love.

For years I went supplying medical aid and other needs just to gain their trust. One particular time after spending two days with the Yanomami tribe teaching them how to grow large fish in ponds for harvesting, they called me to gather together with the entire village for a special meal.

They sat me down and brought before me Casabas bread and a large pot full of boiled worms. They then prepared a sandwich for me with the Casabas and worms. All eyes were on me that day as I stared at the specially prepared meal for me. I slowly proceeded to eat it. There was an overall excitement and a cheer of acceptance as I finished that meal. The Yanomami declared that I was now accepted by them and considered one of them. News quickly spread up and down the river to many of the tribes that I was now one of them!

Over the years I continued to wait on the Lord and be a living testimony for Him by serving these people. I would sit off to the side of the village in plain view and read my Bible. They would come up to me and ask, "Why do you

>

> "Time continued to pass by and I became depressed and wondered if any of my efforts would ever pay off in reaching them spiritually."

---

do all these nice things for us?" I would tell them, "Because, Someone sent me." I was always trying to pique their curiosity until they would ask.

I continued to bring medicine and other necessary aid to the villages. I set up radio units for communication so the villages could call for help in case of emergencies. I built small medical clinics and even supplied a few outboard motors for their canoes. The people would come to me and say that too many of their children had died at the hands of the shaman, but my medicine is good.

I continually asked God over and over, "When, Lord, will I have a breakthrough with them?" Again they would ask, "Why have you come; why do you do these things for us?" My answer again was, "Someone sent me!" Then they finally asked, "Who is this person that sent you?" My reply, "My God sent me. His name is Jesus!"

Time continued to pass by, and I became depressed and wondered if any of my efforts would ever pay off in reaching them spiritually. Then one day in the Sulupire tribe, I was asked one evening to join in a big feast for a special occasion. The whole village came together. They sat and asked me to sit in a place of honor, while they passed around big baskets of food. It was the tradition that everyone would share from the same baskets; each basket would have a different food in it. Exotic fruits, plantains, coconuts, fish, jukka, and casabas, along with other cooked items were all part of the feast that evening.

In the middle of the feast, they stopped to make an announcement. "We thank you so much for the things that you do for us." I was stunned as they continued; "We want you to teach us about Jesus, your God, the One who sent you! We would like you to build a church here." I was overwhelmed with emotions and started to cry. I could not believe it. The breakthrough I had awaited for so long had finally happened!

Soon afterwards, many of the villages came to the Lord, now eleven of fourteen villages have been reached. Some of them have turned into entire Christian communities. Many have come to ask me to build places for them to worship the Lord. The witch doctors made it difficult for me in the beginning, but now in at least three of the communities they are helping us.

Jesus Himself was a living testimony to us. Jesus taught us to love our neighbor by being a servant, but He also took action and did it Himself. Jesus took on the form of a servant at the Passover Feast. He got up from the table, took off his outer clothing, and wrapped a towel around his waist, poured water into a basin, and proceeded to wash His disciples' feet. He truly showed His disciples the full extent of His love by showing them how He expected them to serve others by putting His love into action.

Our faith would have no limits in reaching people with Jesus' love, if we would become more of a servant like He showed us. We all need to learn to live and act as Jesus taught. Unselfish service to each other and to those less fortunate has become a distinctive trait of Jesus' true disciples.

"For even the Son of Man did not come to be served, but to serve, and to give his life as a ransom for many" (Mark 10:45 NKJV).

Yanomami mother with child; parrot was freshly killed for dinner by a dart from a blow gun / Venezuelan rainforest

indigenous rainforest family living along the Caura River / Venezuela

"*I tell you the truth, unless a kernel of wheat falls to the ground and dies, it remains only a single seed. But if it dies, it produces many seeds.*" John 12:24

BRENT HIGGINS
Awe Star Ministries
Vice President International Operations

a son's legacy

A Kernel of Wheat

What does surrender look like, if the life given is your child's? Our children are a gift from God, no doubt about it. As believers, we sought to train our children to pursue Christ with their whole hearts. When that resulted in one of them giving his or her life serving Him, we were overwhelmed—not just by grief, but by His love!

Our son BJ was a young man who pursued God's heart from the age of six. He was a prolific writer and did a lot of journaling. Those journals would one day impact the world. He was small in stature but known for his belief in Christ. He gave speeches in his public school, and the Bible was his text. When he wrote book reports as class assignments, they were from the Word of God. He witnessed to others as often as he encountered them. He grew up watching his two older sisters, his mother, and I go to the mission field with our church. He could not wait for his turn. When he was fourteen (and then again at fifteen), God called him to serve in Peru for the summer. He did not want to return to Peru the second year, as he wanted to minister in Thailand. He sensed a great need there. He had become wise well beyond his years.

Ultimately, he would follow God's heart to Peru that summer, and it would cost him his life. His journey is chronicled in the book entitled, *I Would Die for You, One Student's Story of Passion, Service and Faith.* His life was laid down five days shy of his sixteenth birthday. The book title carries the same title as the MercyMe song inspired by BJ's surrender. Much of the book is assembled from the journals he filled with wisdom and passion.

No parent expects their child to precede them in death. When it happens, what is our response to be? My wife, Deanna, and I pressed hard into our Savior. We knew the promises from His Word to be true. We clung to Him, as we grieved and sought to take next steps. His love continues to amaze us.

Conventional wisdom teaches us not to make any major decisions after a life-altering event like this. However, God revealed to us that we needed to go in a new direction, and the timing was His not ours. Six months after he died, we moved from Indianapolis to Tulsa where I joined the staff of the mission organization with which BJ had traveled. My wife and I began to lead mission teams around the world to proclaim the love of Christ to every nation we could enter. With the Lord's help, we raise up students and leaders to staff each team and have seen God bless these efforts and receive the glory!

The last country my son was called to was in North Africa. He told his oldest sister, "You are going with me you just don't know it yet." Shortly after, he would pass away. In the coming months, the Lord would reveal to my wife and I and our two daughters that we were to take our son's place ministering in this country. We took his ashes and placed them high atop a mountain, overlooking several Muslim villages. We did so out of obedience to the Lord, and as a symbol of hope for Christ to come into this land.

The view from this mountain is amazing. Our host city was below. No believers were in this village. The man who acted as our guide heard the Truth from us over the course of the next month on several occasions. He was not ready to make a decision at that point in his life. Seeds were sown. Jesus said, *"I tell you the truth, unless a kernel of wheat falls to the ground and dies, it remains only a single seed. But if it dies, it produces many seeds"* (John 12:24).

Three years later, our guide has not only surrendered his life to Christ but pastors three house churches in the city below the symbol of hope we left. That symbol is a piece of our hearts and a kernel of wheat for his Savior.

A surrendered life produces a ripple effect that changes generations. The promise of eternity is brought about by our example if we live according to His truth. He is worth our surrender, our all.

The loss we experienced was deep and searing. We miss our son every day. We do not wish him back, though at times we desire to. As he lay down his life, Christ has produced many new seeds.

We are called to obedience every day. I must keep on surrendering myself to His will, and allow Him to work through my weakness.

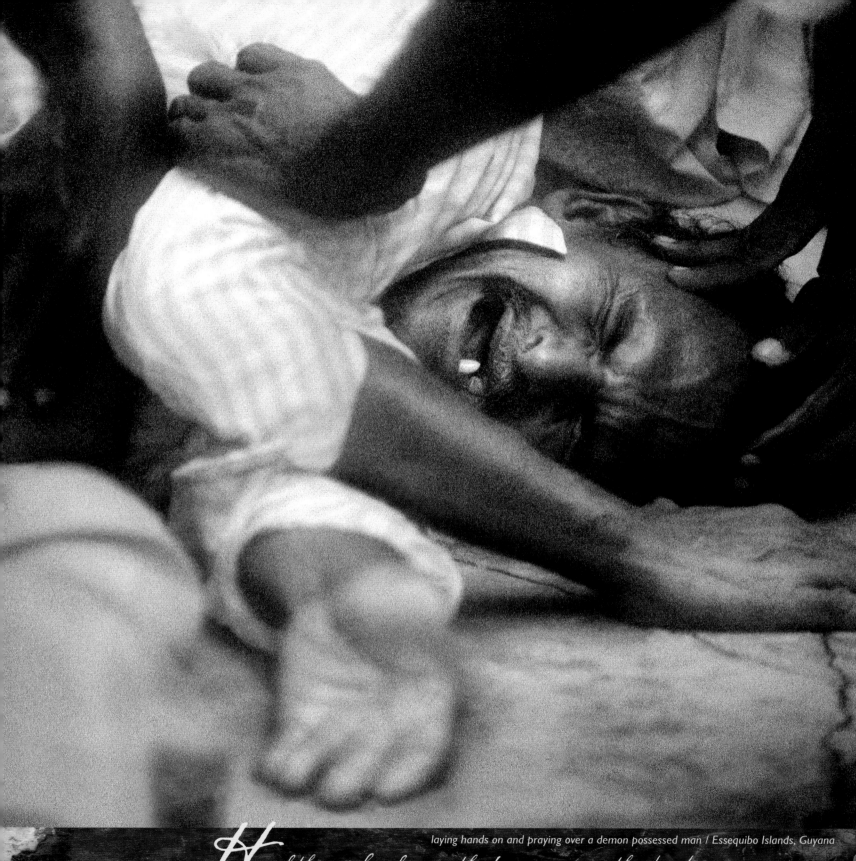

laying hands on and praying over a demon possessed man / Essequibo Islands, Guyana

Heal the sick, cleanse the lepers, raise the dead, cast out demons. Freely you have received, freely give.

Matthew 10:8 NKJV

BRAD GUICE
Photographer
British Guyana

a demon possessed man

In the name of Jesus, Demons must flee!

It was my second missions trip. There were about twenty-five of us who had come to Guyana on a two-week medical/dental missions trip—surgeons, doctors, interns, dentists, nurses, our missions director, myself (the photographer), and a few others to lend a hand in any way they could.

Many of the medical team had flown in from different parts of the United States to join the team.

When we arrived in Guyana, we split our team into two groups. One group stayed on the mainland in an area that was extremely impoverished, and the other group positioned itself on a small tropical island off the coast. This island was part of a cluster of many islands.

The island was purely tropical. There were about 250 people total living there. We stayed in grass huts owned by members of the local church. We had mosquito nets over our sleeping bags, no electricity, bats flying through the outhouse, and the only way for us to bathe was by using a bucket and cup filled with water from a local stream.

But it was a tropical paradise with monkeys swinging in the trees, parrots everywhere, mangos you could reach out and pick, coconuts and other exotic fruits gathered and cut by the local people for our enjoyment. Each morning our group would pack up our medical and dental supplies and put them on a boat and then travel to one of the nearby islands. Occasionally we had to battle with the low tide causing us to have to push the boat full of our medical supplies through waist high thick mud to get out of our harbor.

On such a day we traveled to an island with a population of about 500 people. We carried our supplies to a little Pentecostal church where we set up our clinic for the day. The news had gotten out to the island's inhabitants that doctors from America were coming to conduct a free medical clinic. People were already crowding around the church seeking medical care.

Patrick, an emergency ward physician, enlisted my help in conducting crowd control. We asked the people to form a long line and handed them numbers as they entered the church. It seemed as if the whole island had shown up.

After we spent a couple hours leading people into the church and directing them to the right medical staff, a man entered who had a very strange presence about him. I just thought he was odd as I clicked a few pictures of him with a long lens from across the room. Time went by as he sat in the pews waiting. Then Patrick, who was dressed in his hospital scrubs, called me over to him. He leaned over to me and whispered, "Brad, that guy over there wrote on the back of his number that he is demon possessed and would like help! What do we do?" I quickly responded, "You're asking me? I don't know!" You see at that time I was only a year old in the Lord and new to the mission field. Even though I had already had some incredible experiences with God, my reaction inside was, "What? Demon possession! Are you crazy? You mean to tell me this stuff is really true?"

Both Patrick and I looked around the crowded room and caught the attention of our missions director and asked her opinion on what we should do. She instructed us to take him outside and pray for him and be as quiet as possible.

So we approached the strange man as he looked up at us with his very intense eyes and asked, "Sir, can we pray for you? Would you mind coming outside with us?" He nodded as to indicate yes. He walked hesitantly, almost like a Zombie, as he followed us.

Once outside, Patrick and I both laid our hands on him and bowed our heads. Having never done this before, we prayed out loud, slowly at first and then powerfully, "In the name of Jesus, Satan, you must flee!" The instant that we mentioned the name of Jesus, the man started screaming and convulsing. We had led him outside quietly, not trying to draw any attention to ourselves. But that changed quickly when everyone waiting for medical attention came around the corner of the church to see what on earth was happening. People hung out of the

>

windows of the church. The doctors even paused to see who was causing all the screaming. It was truly amazing!

I remember thinking that this was unbelievable, so unbelievable that I took a reality check and looked around. This was really happening! We continued praying, and every time the name of Jesus was spoken he screamed. You could really feel the power come down from heaven. There really is power in the name of Jesus!

More people started joining in by laying their hands on him and praying. His rib cage would do this incredible ripple movement as he opened his mouth and did this burping like convulsing action upward. You could almost see with spiritual eyes the demons leaving him. We all agreed that he must have a legion of demons as it speaks about in the Bible in Mark 5:9. He just kept repeating the same movement over and over again for hours. We traded turns praying over him as the doctors tried to continue their work.

It was almost five hours later, at the end of the day, when he was finally set free! The crowd cheered as he stood to his feet. He had the most peaceful look on his face. Wow, what a difference!

We stood around him as he shared his experience with us. He told us his story of how he had walked away from the Lord and gotten involved in witchcraft and the occult. He thanked all of us with tears of joy in his eyes. He hugged us and waved goodbye as our boat pulled away from the island. It was sunset, and our boat ride back to our island was awesome! The bright golden glow of the sun shimmered off the surface of the water. We worshiped and praised the Lord, singing, clapping, and dancing. We even sang the song, "Higher, Higher. Lift Jesus Higher; Lower, Lower. Stomp Satan Lower." I remember the worship was as if all heaven was joining in with us. The joy was incredible. We truly had witnessed a miracle and the victory of a soul being freed from the grips of the enemy. (By the way, of course I got it all on film!)

That little island was certainly changed that day because no one could deny what they had seen and experienced. I know I was changed…forever!

That was my second missions trip. I did not know that that would be the first of hundreds of incredible experiences that I would have on the mission field.

In the synagogue there was a man possessed by a demon, an evil spirit. He cried out at the top of his voice, "Ha! What do you want with us, Jesus of Nazareth? Have you come to destroy us? I know who you are—the Holy One of God!" "Be quiet!" Jesus said sternly. "Come out of him!" Then the demon threw the man down before them all and came out without injuring him. All the people were amazed and said to each other, "What is this teaching? With authority and power he gives orders to evil spirits and they come out!" And the news about him spread throughout the surrounding area.
Luke 4:33-37 NIV

Leguan Island, Guyana

"Believe in the Lord Jesus, and you will be saved - you and your household."
Then they spoke the word of the Lord to him and to all the others in his house.
Acts 16:31-32 NIV

EVELYN ORTIZ HERNANDEZ
Argentina

amazing testimony of one family finding God

You and your whole household

We arrived in Rosario, Argentina, about a week before our scheduled international outreach dates. Our church had long been planning for the three-night Gospel event to be held in a local soccer stadium. Over two hundred people had traveled from the United States to participate.

During the days before the major outreach, teams led by our missions department went out visiting *barrios* (a term used to define poor Spanish neighborhoods) around the city, inviting people to the event while also encouraging the small local churches to participate.

It was on a Friday that our missions team of eight people went to visit a local church in a very impoverished barrio. We decided to walk around the neighborhood in groups of two or three, handing out flyers and inviting people to the three-night event. We also shared the Gospel with as many people as we could.

This particular barrio was extremely poor. Many of the homes were run down with tall overgrown weeds, trash and broken items tossed about the yards. Old car parts and abandoned cars littered the streets. We even saw many chickens running to and fro. The houses were more like poorly constructed shacks at best. Most of the yards had gates and fences out toward the street's edge as an entrance. It is customary in this case to stand at the gate and clap your hands to see if someone is home and will come out to talk. This was their unique substitute for not having a doorbell. We proceeded walking throughout the neighborhood, clapping our hands and speaking to as many of the local people as we could.

My friend Thomas and I were paired together to walk around the neighborhood. We were ministering to everyone on the street we came in contact with and those that would answer to our clapping. Just then we turned the corner to see a small storefront. Many homes in the barrio are turned into small businesses. This one sold refreshments, fruit and vegetables, and package goods.

As we approached the store, there was a doorway in the middle with an older man to the right and a younger man to the left. I started to share with these two men the love of Christ. The older man was engulfed in the conversation and was listening to me intently, but the younger man was laughing at me under his breath.

Thomas had been off to the side speaking to a third man who seemed as if he wanted nothing to do with the Lord. Just then as I was talking to the two men, this third man Thomas was talking with came walking out and stood in the doorway. My attention immediately went to him as my eyes met his. The Lord at that moment strongly impressed upon my heart to share with him my testimony.

I said, "Sir, I came to Argentina all the way from the United States. I don't know who you are, but the Lord has told me to share with you my testimony. You see, my husband and I were on drugs and alcohol for almost eighteen years, and God has set us free!" At that moment the man started weeping and weeping, facing toward the ground. As I was speaking, the Holy Spirit's presence was so strong. I said, "I don't know why God wanted you to know that." Just then he turned his slumped head upward and looked at me through his tears and said, "That is what I am struggling with. I so desperately want to stop."

Looking into his eyes filled with tears, I saw a man that was broken and had no more hope left. He knew at that moment that God was speaking into his life. I simply said to him, "If you are struggling with this, you don't have to struggle anymore, because God has come this day to set you free!" He was sobbing uncontrollably, and he prayed the sinner's prayer with me and asked God to deliver him from his addictions. The other two men were so deeply moved by this that they joined in and prayed too. We all felt an amazing movement of God.

After that wonderful moment, Thomas and I continued on our way, walking around the neighborhood evangelizing. About an hour later, we came up to a house and clapped our hands to see if anyone was home. We saw a woman at the side of her house next to an old wooden shed, washing clothes by hand and hanging them up to dry. We clapped our hands, and she came to the gate. We started talking to her and asked if we could enter. She invited us in through the gate.

>

Once again we strongly felt the presence of the Lord. After speaking to this woman for a few minutes, we asked if she would like to accept the Lord into her life. She answered yes. Just then her young daughter of about eleven or twelve years walked up to her mother's side and said, "Mom, you are going to become a Christian now!" We stopped and asked her daughter also if she wanted to become a Christian also. She answered in an excited manner, "Yes, I do!" As we were starting to huddle together in a circle to pray, yet another one of the woman's daughters about four years of age stood in between us and started to cry. I looked down at her. This little girl had an amazing resemblance to the man who had accepted the Lord earlier. We finished our prayer. I was hesitant to ask the mother but felt compelled to do so. I said, "'Does your daughter look like her father?" She replied in a very positive manner and said, "Yes, she is the splitting image of him; she has the same face as her father!"

I was amazed and then asked, "I think I just met your husband. I believe he accepted the Lord earlier." She responded with a wonderful smile on her face, "Yes you did, he came home earlier and shared that something amazing had taken place. He proclaimed that he was delivered and was changed by the Lord Jesus!" We were all so excited as the Lord's presence was upon us, and we were amazed by this set of circumstances. We realized that she and her two daughters were saved within an hour and a half after their father.

The next day our missions team went to another barrio on the opposite end of the city. We were nowhere close to where we were the day before. Again we walked around evangelizing and inviting people to the international outreach. Just then I saw the same four-year-old little girl running by us! I was amazed at this and thought I was seeing things, but there she was. I said, "Come here! Did I not see you yesterday on the other side of the city?" She answered, "Yes, you did!" but she was playing with her friends and quickly ran away. I did not think much more about it but thought it was odd.

We continued walking around the neighborhood. We came up to a house without a gate and knocked on the door. A woman answered the door that had the same face as the man from the day before who accepted the Lord. I asked her, "Are you related to the man we met yesterday?" The woman immediately responded and realized who we must be. She had been told of her brother. As we were talking, the man's mother (the grandmother of the children) came walking out with her other sister. I saw inside the house—there was the man's wife from the day before, and this time his son also was there. So his whole family was there—his mother, his sisters, his wife, his daughters, and son.

All of a sudden the man himself walked out, but this time his face was completely changed! It was much softer than the day before. He now had a peaceful countenance and a smile that completely overwhelmed his face. He was so happy to see us and excited to share with us how God had truly touched him and healed him the day before. The Lord had amazingly transformed him into a totally new creation in Christ. The whole family gathered together with us in a circle, each one believed and accepted Christ into their lives, as we led them in the sinner's prayer. The joy overflowed in that house that day as the whole family came to know Christ as their Lord and Savior.

It was amazing how Christ brought together the man's whole entire family—the grandmother was there, his two sisters, his wife, the man and his three children! And they were all from different parts of the city. It reminded me of the jailer in the book of Acts that asked Paul and Silas what he needed to do in order to be saved.

"Sirs, what must I do to be saved?" They replied, "Believe in the Lord Jesus and you will be saved—you and your household." Then they spoke the word of the Lord to him and to all the others in his house…He was filled with joy because he had come to believe in God—he and his whole family (Acts 16:30-32, 34 NIV).

You see each member of this man's family needed to believe in Jesus. And all of his entire family did believe and were saved. God orchestrated everything perfectly, healing the man of his addictions and bringing his entire family together to be reconciled to each other and to Him. God did all this for one family to enjoy a spectacular moment of belief, salvation, healing, and reconciliation. There was so much joy in that household that day! So, believe on the Lord Jesus and present Jesus to your entire family and to others so they may also believe!

He was filled with joy because he had come to believe in God — he and his whole family. Acts 16:34 NIV

mother and child / Medellin, Colombia

children living in one of hundreds of tent cities after the earthquake / Port-au-Prince, Haiti

NORTH AMERICA + THE CARIBBEAN

"THE BEST REMEDY FOR A SICK CHURCH IS TO PUT IT ON A MISSIONARY DIET."

ANONYMOUS AUTHOR

300,000 dead from earthquake

one and a half million people living in tents / Port-au-Prince, Haiti

"And who knows but that you have come to royal position for such a time as this?"

Esther 4:14 NIV

ANDRE & SYLVIE DRISDELLE
Executive Directors: A.S.A.M.
Haiti

brought to Haiti in God's divine timing

For Such a Time as this

When I was eight years old, missionaries came and spoke at our church in Canada. That is when I first felt the Call upon my heart to be a missionary. For years my wife and I heard about the needs in Haiti. We had the chance to go with mission teams but because of finances and children we put it off.

I was finally able to go on a two-week missions trip to Haiti. I brought home photographs of the children at a mission house being fed. The photographs stirred my wife's heart. So we started to pray and ask ourselves what we could do. Giving and sending money is always good, but we had a deep desire to do more.

We spoke to the missionary about returning to Haiti to help for a three-month period. He accepted us; we quit our jobs and put everything in our lives aside. After the three months, we returned home only to discover God had placed a deep burning desire in our hearts to return. That is when we knew that we were being called to Haiti.

September 2009 we returned and settled into ministry in Haiti. We started a work program for the impoverished women living in the ravine. We showed them how to start and manage a small business so they could create a livelihood for their needy families. On the afternoon of January 12th, we were waiting for the women to gather at our house to pick up their supplies.

It was about 3:30 in the afternoon, and we still had time before they arrived. Sylvie, my wife, said, "I have to go to the grocery store, why don't you stay home and take a short nap?" I had been very tired from the work I had been doing, but I felt deeply compelled at that moment to take a walk with my wife. This was unlike me to go to the grocery store with her.

We were shopping when I glanced down at the time. I said, "We must go right now, the ladies will be gathering outside our house waiting for us." We hurried to pay. Within three minutes of our leaving, the earthquake hit. We knew immediately it was big. I pulled Sylvie to the middle of the street for protection. Things were falling down everywhere. The grocery store behind us that we

were just in, completely collapsed, killing 150 people left inside. People were screaming and crying at the top of their lungs; there was complete panic.

We got to our house, and it was completely collapsed. We were struck with panic! It seemed like we were in a movie; it all seemed impossible and nothing seemed real.

One lady that was living with us was left in the house. We heard screaming at the top of her lungs and praying from inside the ruble. We called to her and asked if she was OK. She was stuck under three floors of concrete. We started digging and tried to find tools and get people to help. But it was chaos, with people running everywhere screaming. There were more earthquakes every ten to fifteen minutes throughout the night. Every time we had to stop our digging and run into the street for protection. Her brother came to help. We dug all night, praying the whole time that she would come out alive. The next morning at 9 a.m., we were finally able to get her out. She came out safe since she had been wedged perfectly in between two floors of concrete with her head inches from being crushed.

We felt God's hand of protection had been upon us as my wife never goes to the grocery store at that time of day. In an effort to find our passports, we dug through the rubble of our house. When we got to my bed I realized God had saved my life. We should have been dead but God decided otherwise. I would normally have taken a nap, and my bed was completely crushed under concrete!

Immediately following the quake, aid organizations were desperately trying to get into the country to bring much needed help. We found refuge at the local orphanage where they gave us a place to sleep. It was chaos on the streets. It was two days before we could make contact

>

221

People were carrying dead children in their arms screaming. Dead bodies were being lined up on street corners with sheets thrown over them. The stench was horrible.

---

with home, and they told us to go to the Canadian Embassy. The Canadian Embassy said, "We can give you emergency passports and you can leave today." I looked at my wife Sylvie and said, "No, we came here to Haiti to help; I don't want to go home now. What do you want to do?" It was then that we said to each other, "We can't go home now! We need to stay here; they need us now!"

We had nothing; we had lost everything in the quake but we could not leave. Our families did not understand. "Andre and Sylvie," they pleaded, "that is enough now, come home!" We felt that God had prepared us through all the years of sitting in church. We were just regular people in the congregation. We were not pastors, but over the years God had lit a fire in our hearts to do more, to step out, to help for "such a time as this"!

Our mission was now clear. We spent the first week at the orphanage, which had a 24-hour medical center where we worked endlessly to help them out. They had great needs, not enough workers, and supplies were limited.

During the days following the quake, people were just lost, walking aimlessly in the streets; many looking for lost loved ones. People were carrying dead children in their arms screaming. Dead bodies were being lined up on street corners with sheets thrown over them. The stench was horrible. Many people had injured arms and legs, needing extreme medical attention and even amputation. There were cries of hopelessness from everywhere. Many people would come up to us asking for a glass of water; they had lost everything and needed the basics to live.

Humanitarian aid in the beginning was very slow to arrive. Nothing started up for weeks. My wife and I were walking in the streets about a week after the

earthquake, and three teenagers came up to saying, "We are hungry. We have no food and we have no water!" It broke our hearts.

We were staying in the orphanage; they were feeding us, and we had no access to money. All the banks were closed. I had maybe $70 US dollars on us total. We started going out with what little we had, buying fruits and vegetables were we could find them. We took them to this small group of twenty-five people sleeping outside with nothing over their heads. So we started feeding them, but after a few days we were broke. One of the ladies from the orphanage gave us $100 to keep feeding the people on the streets. A woman journalist went around with us, saw what we were doing, and gave us $150, which was everything she had.

Then it was God that hooked us up with an organization called Convoy of Hope. They gave us ready to hand out food. So in a matter of days, we started to feed 1,500 people a day in the streets. We would drive around in our 1985 blue Mazda truck, handing out the boxed food. Convoy of Hope would give us fifty boxes at a time; one packet would feed six to seven people. We drove around to the different tent cites, handing them out. For more than a week Convoy of Hope gave us enough food that we were able to feed up to 4000 people a day. They helped us tremendously.

Looking back, it was amazing how when we first opened our wallet and gave everything we had, other people and journalists would give us all their money to help also. Then Convoy of Hope came and helped us. The more we gave, God gave us more to give.

We still did not know where we were going or what more we were supposed to do. We were brought out to another orphanage where God just opened the door for us in a miraculous way, in an area that we knew nothing about and never had been to before. A house came open for us. My thoughts were that it would be great if we had a guesthouse so that we could host missions teams that could come and help out.

The first week we were in the house, people were knocking on our door from the local tent cities saying, "You're our neighbors; can you help us?" We soon had 393 families—some 1500 people. We made lists of their needs at each tent city. We sent the lists off to Oxfam USA and Canada. They sent tarps and plastics to make tents. Many people before this slept under bedsheets. They also started putting in toilets and drinking water.

In those first days we had more and more people from different tent cities coming to us for help. They would say, "We heard you are helping this area, would you please help us too?" We ended up helping twelve more cities with 4000-5000 people. I was embarrassed to go to Oxfam USA to ask for more help, but they helped tremendously by sending us a couple forty foot trucks filled with supplies.

We now have lists of more than 18 tent cities and 15,500 people we are trying to help. God gave us that guesthouse to host missions teams on a steady basis. Medical teams, construction teams, etc. started coming, and people began raising funds for us in support.

We work with mostly forgotten people off the beaten track. The big organizations came in and helped many people, but now many organizations have left. The people's needs continue to grow. The temporary tent cities made out of tarps have now become permanent housing. The tarps are now falling apart, not providing the protection needed in the hot sun and pouring

rainstorms. The people have nowhere to go, and many have no way to make money to buy food. Malnutrition is setting in throughout the camps. Babies are the worst affected. In five years people will still be living in tents because they have no way to help themselves.

We are still normal people that just stepped up to serve God. It is a challenge, and we need His strength. In the process we have discovered what we can live without—so many things don't matter in our lives— and we now know what is really important. We now know what love is through God's eyes, and how giving a hug can bring so much hope into people's lives.

Jesus said in Matthew 25, "I was hungry and you fed me, I was thirsty and you gave me drink, I was naked and you clothed me." For us the basics of Christianity are those actions. This part we can do! In the process of showing His love for the least of these, the doors open up for sharing His word. And we have found that if you give your life in servanthood to Him, He may just use you, "for such a time as this"!

canal family / U.S. - Mexico border

All they asked was that we should continue to remember the poor, the very thing I was eager to do. The Apostle Paul - Galatians 2:-10 NIV

RICK HAGANS
Executive Director: Harvest Evangelism
Mexico

testimony from a US - Mexico border town - Reynosa, Mexico

Dig or Pray

In 1980, while a Bible school student, I went on my first short-term mission trip. We visited an inner-city church in San Antonio, Texas. It was love at first sight for me. Love for the Mexican people I met there and love for missions as part of my spiritual journey.

After Bible school, I founded a ministry back home in East Alabama called Harvest Evangelism. We have a men's home called His Place and a ladies' home called Hosanna Home. Our homes provide a place of hope and healing for men and women with life-controlling problems. I also travel all across America as a preacher. Short-term mission trips have become an integral part of both our re-hab work and church ministry. It has been my experience for more than twenty-five years now, that nothing so moves men and women towards Christ than seeing His love in action. In fact, that has become the motto of our ministry, "Putting God's love in action…where the action is at!"

Let me give you just one vivid example of how love works—first *in* folks, then *through* them, ultimately touching them and molding them as no mere sermon or song ever could do.

It was the summer of 1997, and I was leading a youth group on a short-term mission trip on the streets of Reynosa, Mexico. Like most border towns, Reynosa is full of brokenhearted people looking for a job, a home, a life worth living. What these people most often end up with is a shack made of pallets and cardboard, with no water, no electricity, and no hope of things ever getting better. Such border town ghettos (or barrios, if you're Hispanic) are sad, hot, dry, dirty places full of pimps, poverty, and broken promises. They are what I call, "refugee camps of the soul." They are also the type of place where Jesus loves to show up. He did in His earthly ministry some 2000 years ago, and He did that one hot summer in 1997.

I can still remember the frantic call of teenagers from our group that let me know something was wrong. What I found when I reached them was a picture indeed "all wrong." Some of our kids were standing around a little

girl, who was probably no more than five or six years old. Her clothes were tattered rags, her feet bare, but beyond the pains of normal poverty (if poverty was ever meant to be normal), this little girl appeared to have leprosy. Her face was a hideous mass of sores and scars. Skin hung from her cheekbones. There were only patches of hair on her head. Flies were swarming around the silent hole that was once her mouth. She looked like all the pictures I had seen depicting leprosy's ravages, but she was no picture—she was a little girl. Nonetheless, I picked her up and took her to our team's nurse. Even sick children need a hug, especially sick children.

Surprisingly, our nurse told us that the child didn't have leprosy but rather the worst case of chicken pox she had ever seen. A severe infection, probably from washing in the filthy waters there, had not only disfigured her face, but, the nurse told us, had also entered her sinus cavity and even the lining of her brain. In such a condition, in that location, her prognosis was death. In fact, our nurse told us, once an infection, as this child now suffered with, had entered the sinuses and brain, the best that could be hoped for would be that the child would be deaf, blind, and severely retarded. Death was the more likely prognosis and seemingly the more humane. But try to tell that to a bunch of teenage Christians, no more than children themselves. Neither death nor deformity seemed an option to those kids. They wanted a miracle.

Our group of middle-class American teenagers stood blank faced or else weeping for this little ragamuffin angel. "What can we do, Pastor Rick?" they asked me earnestly. I told them, "You found her—you pray for her." All she had left was a prayer. The kids there with me said, "We can't pray. We're not preachers. We've never prayed for anything like this before."

>

Then I saw her face, or a least I saw a girl that looked like her, but this girl was laughing and leaping as she received a Christmas doll.

"Well," I said, " if you won't pray, at least go find a shovel and dig her a decent grave." I walked away, leaving those kids with a choice—either dig or pray. They prayed!

I watched them from a distance and listened to their prayer. It was the earnest, humble prayer of a child, praying for a child. Such did Jesus pray and such does He hear and answer.

Nothing happened immediately that day. In fact, the trip ended, and we returned home with nothing happening.

Five months later, I returned to Mexico for a Christmas mission and found myself in that same barrio. To be perfectly honest, that little girl wasn't even on my mind as I was seeing to the distribution of thousands of Christmas gifts there. Then I saw her face, or a least I saw a girl that looked like her, but this girl was laughing and leaping in the air as she received a Christmas doll. This girl was definitely not sick or dying. My interest was so piqued that I went over to this little picture of Christmas joy and found her mother.

"Is this the little girl we prayed for in July?" I asked the mother. "The one with the chicken pox that had infected her brain?" Her mother smiled and said, "Yes." I asked, "But is she OK now? I mean, is she deaf, or blind, or retarded?" (like our nurse had said would be her best outcome). "No, look at her," her mother beamed, "Just look at her!"

A miracle obviously changed that little girl's life. Likewise, her mother and all who knew her had to have been touched by the love of God that changes a little girl's pain into praise. But I can tell you, I think the biggest change of all may have been that little Baptist youth group once I told them the end of her story. For it's one thing to hear about God's power, but it's altogether something different, something more, to see His love in action…where the action is at!

Come on a mission trip, and see for yourself!

mother with child / U.S.-Mexico border

dump / Reynosa, Mexico

"I now realize how true it is that God does not show favoritism but accepts men from every nation who fear Him and do what is right."

Acts 10:34-35 NIV

GARY DENNIS
In His Steps Ministry
Mexico

a foot washing

The Church in the Dump

Perhaps the most profound experience of God's presence I have ever known was not in a church building but near a garbage dump in Mexico.

For several years we had gone into the dump to bring food, shoes, clothes, and the Gospel of hope to more than 200 people who live in the dump and the hundreds who live near it. A mansion sat on the hill, overlooking the dump. Its high fence, manicured lawn, and beautiful, irrigated garden stood in stark contrast with the shanties made of wooden pallets, sticks, plastic, tin, and discarded carpet across the road. I was reminded of the story of the rich man and Lazarus. The pigs in the dump were in much better shape than the people.

On the opposite side of the dump, our mission team had been working hard to prepare a lot for the construction of their future church building. The whole community was excited and thrilled that they would soon have their own church. The church was to be named Golgotha, but the local people called it the Church in the Dump.

Each night after working all day, we fed the people and preached the Gospel. The last night of the mission trip, we decided to forgo an outreach and meet with just the church members for prayer and edification. Pastor Filiberto gathered the members and we prayed together for about forty-five minutes.

Our mission team was ready to say their goodbyes and get back on the bus, when one of the ladies in our group came to me and said, "Pastor, I really feel that the Lord told me that, before we drive off, we need to wash Pastor Filiberto's feet." With some degree of hesitation, I thought to myself, *That's strange, I didn't hear the Lord say this.* It was already later than we planned on leaving and feeling very responsible to get our group back to their destination, I was about to say no. Just then the youth minister of our group came up to me and said the same thing, that the Lord had also spoken to him about washing Pastor Filiberto's feet.

I reluctantly agreed to ask Pastor Filiberto if it would be OK if we could have a foot washing. He thought it was a great idea and then asked through his translator: "Just two or three or the whole group?" I was surprised that he would actually expect our whole group to wash his feet, once we offered to wash them. Still feeling a little pressed for time, I replied politely, "Just a few but not the whole group."

He sent for warm water, soap, and a chair, and very humbly with his head hung down as a servant, he pointed to the chair and said to me in his best broken English: "Sit here." I suddenly realized he had actually assumed that we had asked him to wash our feet. I said, "No, brother, not us—you. You sit, we want to wash *your* feet!"

Big tears formed in his eyes and began to roll down his face as he started to weep loudly. Always the servant, he was prepared to wash the feet of our entire group of thirty-seven. As he sat down, some of our group removed his shoes and began to wash his feet. A river of tears gushed from his face, and he wept uncontrollably. Those washing his feet also began weeping, their tears splashing into the pail of water and onto the bare dirt beneath them.

The Holy Spirit was not finished yet. Pastor Filiberto's river of tears soon turned into a flood of tears as all thirty-seven members of our group joined him in the godly act of "weeping with those who weep." The members of the tiny church began to weep and cry out. One elderly lady began to wail uncontrollably. She could have been heard two blocks away. One sister fell on the ground praying and crying out to God. His Presence was so overpowering that the entire group continued to weep and pray for quite some time. I was so overwhelmed that I don't even remember how long this

>

lasted, but I do remember that not a single soul present had any desire to leave this awesome fellowship.

I have never experienced anything this wonderful before or since. The Lord gave me an understanding of what had taken place. The people of this church and indeed the whole area were very poor and considered themselves beneath the "rich" American Christians who brought money and supplies in abundance. A deep sense of inferiority, dependence, and shame hindered them from understanding their true worth and value to God. They expected to serve us but never thought of themselves worthy of being served. When we began to wash this pastor's feet, God began to show them how valuable they are to Christ. He broke the power of Satan to keep them beaten down and feeling shame. The presence of Christ began to heal their wounds and wash away their pain. He also worked in our group to break down pride and feelings of superiority.

What a great deliverance was wrought that night because ordinary people dared to obey the voice of the Holy Spirit and humble themselves before God and man. God values broken hearts and contrite spirits far above religious rituals and majestic buildings. I find that God often uses mission trips to bring believers face to face with their need of humility and teaches humble believers to have a profound awareness of their own unique value to our mighty Creator.

God has made it possible for this wonderful event, happening in the humble setting of a garbage dump, to be shared with you. There is a powerful effect that church mission trips can have on people around the world and even more so on themselves, discovering the power of the Holy Spirit while becoming acutely aware of the joy of serving Him and others.

The result is revival and glory to God in His church.

It was just before the Passover Feast.
Jesus knew that the time had come for him to leave
this world and go to the Father.
Having loved his own who were in the world,
he now showed them the full extent of His love...
so he got up from the meal, took off his outer clothing,
and wrapped a towel around his waist.
After that, he poured water into a basin
and began to wash his disciples' feet,
drying them with the towel
that was wrapped around him.
John 13:1, 4-5 NIV

blind woman with family / Reynosa, Mexico

Yup'ik Eskimo children / Alaska

"However, I consider my life worth nothing to me, if only I may finish the race and complete the task the Lord Jesus has given me—the task of testifying to the gospel of God's grace." *Acts 20:24 NIV*

DON & YVONNE SLEDGE
Harvest Evangelism / F.R.O.M.M.
Alaska

Eskimos in the far reaches of Alaska

Arrow through my Heart
You are never too old!

My wife, Yvonne, and I are way past retirement age. Originally from Alabama, we retired many years ago from our professional careers. As time went on, we came to realize God was calling us to full-time service for Him out of our retirement.

We are missionaries to the "Land of the Midnight Sun." The aurora borealis or northern lights are a common sight here. Yes, I am talking about Alaska, the largest state in the U.S., most of which is uninhabited. During the summer solstice, we can get as much as twenty to twenty-one hours of sunlight a day; and in the cold, dark winter, as little as four hours. During winter we have seen it get as cold as -65°. It is a land of extremes and provides for Third World missions without the need of a passport.

We reach out to the native Bush population of Eskimos and Indians. We travel to villages on the western frontier of Alaska; these villages are reachable only by small Bush planes and are predominantly Yup'ik Eskimo. We have even driven up the frozen rivers in the cold winter to reach some of them. A few of these are truly unreached people. There are about 7,000 indigenous people in some fifty-six villages across the Yulon-Kuskokwim Delta. Many of the villages are small, with as few as fifty Eskimos per village.

There is a great need to rebuild the hearts and lives of many people lost to drugs, alcoholism, sexual abuse, and physical abuse, which have all become rampant throughout the state, but especially among the native population.

The Eskimos have lost their identity; they don't know who they are anymore. Fifty years ago they lived like 2,000 years ago. It is as if the Stone Age is in collision with the 21st century, with all of the ill affects dumped on these poor natives. Suicide is the highest in the nation right here among the Eskimos. Many of them develop

S.A.D.D. (seasonal affected depression disorder), sadness, or deep depression. You can almost feel the spirit of depression hovering over some of the villages. Most of the suicides happen right at the very end of the long winter nights.

Today we are back in Nunapitchuk. This is where our present call to service began. It was while on a summer mission trip to Alaska that God placed on our hearts the Call to full-time mission work in this great land. I remember the morning in July as we loaded our gear on the boat for the return trip to Anchorage. That was when a little Eskimo girl named April said, "please don't go; if you leave, who will teach us the Bible?" At that moment God shot an arrow through my heart!

My wife had left the day before, bringing one of our fellow missionaries with a heart problem back to Anchorage. Unbeknownst to me, God placed the Call on Yvonne's heart at the same time to come to Alaska for full-time ministry. Over the next several months, as we prayed and talked about what we knew to be our destiny, we came to full agreement that God was calling us to this ministry. Here we are back in Nunapitchuk. There have been many other Bush villages over time, but this is where it all began. The feeling of returning is overwhelming.

After unloading the boat and walking to the church where we sleep, eat, hold VBS, preach, teach, and counsel, an Eskimo boy walked up to me and said, "I remember you!" Wow what a greeting! He grasped my pants leg and from that moment on, for the entire stay Wassillie never left my side. You see, to the Eskimos if

>

you come back to see them again, that means you love them because no one comes back.

Each day we had around fifty in Bible school. Fifteen prayed the last day and gave their hearts to Jesus. But I am always reminded that numbers are people and they have names: Wassillie, April, Nickolai and Sadie. It's always about the individual, the one. One of the most memorable moments was with two teenage boys. They are twins and had been separated at birth, living in two different villages but who come together each summer in Nunapitchuk. I became their father figure, and they worked with me for four days. I led both these young men to Jesus.

I don't know if you understand this, but our hearts belong to the Eskimos. Their needs overwhelm us, but not God. Their drug usage, pot smoking, alcoholism, suicide, rape, incest, and depression need Jesus. Jesus said, "The fields are white unto harvest, pray the Lord of the Harvest to send workers into the fields."

How can we leave them? Geraldine, a Yup'ik Eskimo said to us, "You know my people don't like or trust whites, but you love us and you are accepted." I was humbled and wept. My prayer continues to be, "Lord, let me see as You see and love as You love."

A few months ago I was asked by a fellow missionary, "Don, what do you and Yvonne plan on doing when you retire?" My answer was, "We are doing it, and we are retired." When God called us to this ministry I asked Him, "God, do you know how old I am?" Well, of course God knew, and He knows what He is doing also. You see, it is ironic that the Eskimos have great respect for their elders. God was bringing us here in His perfect timing and put us in a place where we are immediately respected due to our age.

I see so many people as they get older drop out of ministry. How many retired individuals and couples are out there with the resources and even the talents to still serve the Lord! There's retired doctors, nurses, and other skilled people who are missing the most fulfilling and productive time of their lives. There are so many needs on the mission field, and God can use you. If we can do it, anyone can do it. We love what we are doing, and God has given us an incredible love for the Eskimos.

Remember you are never too old!

Even in old age they will still produce fruit;
they will remain vital and green.
Psalm 92:14 NLT

Yup'ik Eskimo tending to his sled dogs / Alaska

RICK HAGANS
Executive Director: Harvest Evangelism
USA

A homegrown testimony from the byways of America

Church in a Bar

Once a year I take a month off and go on a pilgrimage, not to holy sites to find relics but to the highways and byways of America to find Jesus. My preacher friends think I'm crazy to leave the stained glass sanctuary of the church and spend thirty days walking across back roads and down alleys,

hitchhiking back to my truck each evening to spend the night sleeping on the floorboard, parked on the side of the road. That's what I do—walk and simply trust God to see what happens. I don't know why such behavior seems so unusual; it's pretty much how Jesus lived His life.

A few years back, my annual pilgrimage took me across the state of Virginia. I walked the Shenandoah Valley from the West Virginia line to North Carolina. It was early fall, and the scenery was beautiful, the trees all painted by God in reds and yellows. The air was crisp and clear as if God had breathed it anew from heaven itself. I can still close my eyes and remember most every step of that 380 mile trek. I don't have to close my eyes to remember what God did on that journey. It has changed every step I've taken since…

After walking 20-25 miles, all I ever want to do is find a place to sit and take a load off my feet, maybe get a bite to eat. There are places in rural Virginia, in the Shenandoah Valley where that's not necessarily easy to do. There are simply not many places to eat in some spots. So when the sun started sinking low that day, with not another building in sight, I decided to walk into "Ma's Bar and Grill" and call it a day. Ma's Bar and Grill was a ramshackle collection of cement block and peeling paint. The gravel parking lot held a few pick-up trucks, not the new fixed-up types, but work trucks, hunting trucks, and 18-wheelers loaded and idling. This was not a Hollywood movie set type of place; this was real life America.

I'm a Baptist preacher. I don't normally go to bars, but Ma's said it was a Bar and Grill. Baptists have nothing against Grills, so I went inside and took a seat on the "grill" side. As I ate my Country Fried Steak and drank about half a dozen glasses of iced tea, I noticed I could see right through the kitchen to the "bar" side of Ma's establishment. There was a television set high above the bar with a baseball game playing. I like baseball. There were people scattered through the bar shooting pool, talking to each

other, and listening to sad country music from a jukebox. I like people and to tell you the truth, I was lonely. I didn't feel like climbing in the back of my pickup truck to face another evening apart from my own wife and kids. So, I crossed the divide, from the grill side to the bar…

As I was sitting there in Ma's bar watching the ballgame, drinking a coke, I heard two men begin to argue loudly behind me. An argument in a bar probably isn't an unusual occurrence. What was unusual was what they were arguing about.

A loud, definitely drunk voice proclaimed in a slurred shout, "I'm telling you, salvation is a work of grace by faith. You can't do it on your own. It's not what you've done or ever can do that'll save you. It's what Jesus did on the cross…"

That voice was answered by an even louder voice, which I had now turned to see coming from a huge man with jet black, long hair in a ponytail, crying out, "What do I have to do to really be saved?"

The big man was crying. He wasn't buying the truth his drunken buddy was telling him. They seemed poised to actually fight. The drunk evangelist of sorts was determined that his big buddy listen to him. The big man wasn't buying it.

I thought to myself, *I've been a preacher for over twenty years, and I've never had an opening like this.* So, I stepped over to the bar and said, "Hey y'all, I couldn't help overhearing your discussion about Jesus and what does it take to really be saved. You may not believe this, but I'm a preacher and I think God has put me right here tonight to answer your questions."

Their first question was why, if I was really a preacher, was I sitting at a bar on Friday night? Fair question, so I told them about how I was walking across Virginia raising shoes for orphans in Mexico. They were a little skeptical—who wouldn't be seeing a preacher at their bar? My walking attire, complete with a t-shirt that said "Rick Hagans' Pilgrimage of a Promise," finally convinced them I was indeed a preacher, even if I was the first ever they'd seen in a bar.

After I had further introduced and explained myself, I found out the big guy was named Larry. His wife had come to join us, as well as another cowboy, but the little drunk, preachy fellow slunk off. Religion never wants to share its stage, or even its barstool in this case, with Truth.

Larry really did want to know what it took to be saved. He was miserable in the life he was living and terrified of dying and facing something even worse. Like the Ethiopian eunuch that Phillip shared with in Acts 8:27-38, all I had to do was share the simple truth of the Gospel. Larry was ready to respond.

What a joy it was to ask Larry, there at that bar, the same question I've asked at hundreds of church altars, "Would you like to ask Jesus into your life? Would you be willing to repent of the life you're now living in exchange for the life Jesus wants to give you?" Larry was more than willing. His answer was an emphatic "Yes!" So we prayed, right there at a bar with a jukebox invitational. We prayed.

I opened my eyes from praying with Larry, his wife, and the cowboy to find a lady staring at me. A short skirt, plunging neckline, and make-up like a Las Vegas dancer told me this was no ordinary lady. This was the legendary face of many a country song—a "honky-tonk angel." And this was no ordinary honky-tonk angel either. An introduction from Larry informed me that this was Ma, the owner of the Bar and Grill.

Ma wanted to know what in the name of the bad place preachers talk about, was going on? Before I could even try to explain, Larry blurted out, "This here's a preacher who's done come in here and saved us."

I was going to try and explain that salvation was by grace, through faith, and all the biblical truths associated with it, but Ma would have none of that. She grabbed me by the arm and said, "You're coming with me." I figured this would end my time in her bar with a swift kick out the door. Instead she took me to a quiet table in the back where she brought over another honky-tonk angel—her sister and co-owner of the bar. Sitting there in the dim light with a sad country song blaring in the background, they told me an even sadder story—the story of their lives.

It seems that both Ma, whose real name was Lucy, and her sister, whose name I don't recall, had both recently ended miserable marriages. They had parlayed all their life's savings and alimony allotments to buy the bar—an excuse they said to stay drunk all the time, so as to hide the pain in their hearts. After time, it turns out there wasn't enough alcohol to numb the deep ache in their souls. Not even the dim light of a late night club could hide the despair in them.

I listened to their stories, sad ones indeed. Then I very simply told them about Jesus. About how He had met a woman very much like them, by another drinking spot—a well. I assured them, He felt their pain and would like nothing better than to touch them, to heal and fulfill them. Then and there with little leading, Ma and her sister both asked Jesus to forgive their sins, come into their hearts, and change their lives.

I opened my eyes to see tears streaming down those two ladies' faces. Mascara mixed with tears streaked their cheeks. There was even the glint of something holy happening in their honky-tonk eyes. I just couldn't help thinking that God was up to something really special here. This wasn't your normal dry-eyed, hurry-up and get home altar call. This was the stuff legends are made of, and God wasn't even finished yet.

Before I could even hug the ladies' necks and welcome them into the family of God, I heard a loud commotion back in the bar. Tables were crashing, chairs were being shoved across the barroom floor. Pool balls were flying

>

237

"I'm dying of cirrhosis of the liver. I shouldn't be drinking, but I'm dying; so what's it matter? What does anything matter?" He looked at me with as honest a plea as I've ever seen and said, "Do I need a prayer? Boy, do I ever!"

---

and people were shouting. Above the fray, the loudest sound of all someone who was herding everyone up into some sort of a line. He was yelling, "Joe, you owe me for pulling your truck out of the ditch. Billy, you owe me for that game of 8-ball." On and on he bellowed out their debts. It seemed like most everyone in that bar owed Larry for something. Tonight he was calling in his payments.

As I walked over to where Larry had everyone herded up, I heard him explain. "You all owe me, and all those debts will be paid up if you let this preacher who saved me (pointing now at me) pray for you."

They were shocked. I was beyond shock. I figured I won't try to explain things to them one at a time. So I told Billy, the first in line, that I really was a preacher, but this prayer wasn't my idea. It was Larry's, who had only moments before prayed the first prayer in his life, for God to save him. I assured Billy this was no scam and if he had a prayer request, I would indeed pray for him.

"Preacher," he said, "We've all got things we need prayer for. I, for one am dying of cirrhosis of the liver. I shouldn't be drinking, but I'm dying; so what's it matter? What does anything matter?" He looked at me with as honest a plea as I've ever seen and said, "Do I need a prayer? Boy, do I ever!"

Every man and woman in that dance hall prayer line had a prayer request—lost children, broken marriages, bounty hunters chasing them, fears, pain and suffering, honest prayer requests from deep in dying men and women's hearts. And I know God heard my prayers because He's always loved desperate lives.

After I prayed, everyone stayed gathered around me. I didn't know exactly what to do. It was pushing midnight, and I had to walk again in the morning. I figured these folks would have to do whatever it was they did every day too. So I told them the next step was for all of them to find a church come Sunday morning where

they could go and learn more about Jesus and what that really means.

I will never forget their faces as they thought over my advice. It wasn't apathy or anger or even a lack of interest I saw in their eyes as they answered me. It was pain—a deep, dark, sad confusion. Larry, the big biker, looked at his tattooed knuckles, Ma and her sister pulled self-consciously at their hem lines. Others wiped smudged mascara while others stood still with a faraway wistful look on their faces. Finally, Ma spoke out, spoke for each of them all and said, "Preacher… the church don't want us."

The Baptist preacher in me wanted to tell this crowd that the church would love and accept them, but the Christian in me rose up to demand the truth. The truth is, the church has not always done the Christ-like thing in welcoming strangers into their congregations. This group would definitely qualify as "strange" should they leave their bar to enter most any church. Religion has never handled reality very well. The reality of tattoos, pony tails, mini-skirts, and hangovers stood little chance of being welcomed by the local religion where polyester suits rule. Less, a chance of being loved.

So I shared with my barroom congregants as much as I could in the time I had, what they needed to do next. I told them they needed to pray and believe God would answer their prayers. I told them to read their Bible, to start with the Gospels, and every time they read something about Jesus to mark it, remember it, emulate it.

I even got all my Christian tapes, CDs, and preaching tapes out of my truck and gave them away. Everyone started fighting over who was going to get which tape. Never has Dallas Holm and Andre Crouch been so popular in a honky tonk. We finally made sign-up sheets and taped them to the bar so folks could check the tapes out.

Finally it was time to go. I didn't want to go, but I had twenty miles to walk the next day, and the sun comes up early when you don't get to bed before 2 a.m. It was already past midnight.

Larry and his wife, Ma and her sister and the cowboy all walked out on the porch with me to say goodbye. I think there were tears in everyone's eyes. I couldn't tell for sure because there sure were tears in mine. I gave everyone a big hug and reminded them of how much Jesus loved them. As I walked off that porch toward my truck I looked back at five of the most unlikely converts I'd ever seen, silhouetted against the neon light of a bar. Unbelievable! But should it be?

The last thing I heard as I walked away was Ma shouting out to me, "Preacher, I sure wish we could have church in this bar every night."

"So does Jesus, so does Jesus." I murmured as I walked away.

Rick Hagans continues to walk across America on his annual fall pilgrimages. To date, he has walked over 7,500 miles, across 33 states, raising money for over 100,000 pair of shoes for the impoverished needy people of Mexico.

Now the tax collectors and "sinners"
were all gathering around to hear him.
But the Pharisees and the teachers of the law muttered,
"This man welcomes sinners and eats with them."
Then Jesus told them this parable:
"Suppose one of you has a hundred sheep and loses one of them.
Does he not leave the ninety-nine in the open country
and go after the lost sheep until he finds it?
And when he finds it,
he joyfully puts it on his shoulders and goes home.
Then he calls his friends and neighbors together and says,
'Rejoice with me; I have found my lost sheep.'
I tell you that in the same way there will be more rejoicing in heaven
over one sinner who repents than over ninety-nine
righteous persons who do not need to repent."
Luke 15:1-7 NIV

Conclusion

LIVING THE BOOK OF ACTS

How, then, can they call on the one
they have not believed in?
And how can they believe
in the one of whom they have not heard?
And how can they hear
without someone preaching to them?
And how can they preach
unless they are sent?
As it is written,
"How beautiful are the feet
of those who bring good news!"
Romans 10:14–15 NIV

✝

Kutchi nomadic tribe, an un-reached people group
northern Afghanistan

The Call to Closure

7/29/14

IRVIN E. RUTHERFORD
Executive Director
Global Ministry Teams

The use of terms in missions and the kingdom of God are important. If our definitions are correct, our direction will be correct and thus we will fulfill our destiny. In fulfilling the destiny of the church of Jesus Christ, closure is an important definition.

God's redemptive plan is to establish His kingdom (the rule and reign of Christ in each individual heart) to the ends of the earth.

Matthew 24:14 clearly defines this objective: "And this gospel of the kingdom will be preached in the whole world as a testimony to all nations (ethnic groups), and then the end will come." This is the essence of closure as presented by Jesus himself.

The Call to closure is the most significant part of the Great Commission because it defines a timeline that God Himself honors. It allows the church to learn to give strategically rather than just sentimentally. Roughly 60 percent of all unreached peoples live in countries closed to Western missionaries. Thus the Call is for us to go to the regions beyond our own comfort zones. We need in our minds and hearts the pictures of peoples that are off our radar screen, as it were, for us to obey the words of Jesus to get this Gospel to all people.

The mandate to bring closure to the Great Commission creates a passion for being a pioneer even today. The pioneer spirit of missions is greater than ever when we get beyond a non-Western view of the Great Commission. Many Christians want Jesus to come quickly because they are bored with daily life, or their mortgage is due and they do not have the money for it, or they are tired of church activities. Jesus is returning when His objective of the glory of God covers the earth, and all peoples are in reverence and awe of Him.

Outside of our over-churched, Western environment is that significant block that represents 90 percent of all the unreached peoples in five major cultural blocks:

3,300 unreached Muslim groups.

2,550 unreached Tribal groups.

1,660 unreached Hindu groups.

830 unreached Han Chinese groups.

830 unreached Buddhist groups.

Bringing closure by sharing the Good News with these peoples is the real challenge of the Great Commission. An unreached people group is one with no indigenous community of believing Christians with adequate numbers and resources to evangelize their own people. This is where we find 1.5 to 2.5 billion people today.

This all may sound like an impossible task with impossible numbers to reach. But God is reaching these people groups right now, through His servants like you and me, and native believers who are making up a larger and larger percentage of missionaries around the world.

These numbers can be reached in our lifetime. That is why God's Call upon each and every heart is important. A Call upon your heart and your obedience can and will make a difference. He placed it there for a reason.

The Hebrew people knew in their understanding of God's global heart and our global mandate in the church, that it was God's desire to bless the nations when they sang the global song recorded in Psalms 67:

"May God be gracious to us and bless us and make his face shine upon, Selah,

that your ways may be known on earth, your salvation among all nations.

May the peoples praise you, O God; may all the peoples praise you.

May the nations be glad and sing for joy, for you rule the peoples justly and guide the nations of the earth. Selah.

May the peoples praise you, O God; may all the peoples praise you.

Then the land will yield its harvest, and God, our God, will bless us.

God will bless us, and all the ends of the earth will fear him."

Bringing closure to the Great Commission is our Call. It is only satisfied when God's global cause becomes our daily Call to obedience.

A Journey of the Heart ♥

My mission's journey began in the year 1992 with a single desire: I simply wanted to give back. Little did I know a career in missions would catapult me into the most challenging, most heartrending, and most exciting time of my life.

Today I thumb through old passports with stamps from nearly 100 countries, and memories flash through my mind—seeing thousands come to Christ…witnessing the blind regaining their sight, the deaf hearing, the demon-possessed set free…meeting valiant servants of the cross laboring in obscure, forgotten places…sitting across the table from heads of state one day and kneeling next to the poor in the filthiest slums the next.

I recall sleeping in tents with snakes crawling about us in Mozambique, bats flying around us in our bathrooms in Guyana, and our van being confiscated by the police in Russia. I remember bombs and land mines exploding nearby in Kosovo and riding on tanks through war torn villages gutted by the fighting. I will never forget the horror of 40,000 skulls on display in Rwandan churches.

Then there were the kids sniffing glue in Medellin, Colombia…the cries of urine-soaked orphan babies in Romanian hospitals…Russian inmates confined to tiny, filthy prison cells where twenty men had to share ten beds.

I think of the huge crowds and the bright lights in giant stadiums as I accompanied David and Gary Wilkerson on international speaking engagements as God revived and restored the lives of pastors and their wives the world over.

Life on the front lines has been a whirlwind, to say the very least. But today I have a new appreciation for missions—a more personal understanding.

What I have learned is that the mission field is not just a place to go or a people to evangelize. Rather, it is a journey of the heart, as God slowly captures more and more of each of us until we are His and His alone. A quote from David Wilkerson says it best as he recalled what God had spoken to him: "David, I don't want you to win the whole world for me—I want to win all of you."

So here I am. Still on the go, but my mission is different. It is no longer a question of what is bigger or better or more exciting. It is a quiet place. An obedient place. A humble place.

It is taking a towel, giving a cup of cold water, caring for the sick, reaching out to a neighbor. It is rest, it is joy, it is bearing the burden of a friend in tears.

Yes, we need more missionaries to the nations to proclaim the salvation message, to faithfully carry the Light into dark places, and to fulfill the Great Commission. But may we never forget God's greatest desire is that we give Him what He treasures most—our whole heart. It is in this way that He can fully use us.

BETTINA MARAYAG
Director: Please Pass The Bread
International Conference Director
World Challenge Inc.
www.pleasepassthebread.org

Toba Indian child—tribe living in extreme poverty
Argentina

shepherds in the northern mountains
Afghanistan

Counting the Cost

There is a cost to serving and following Jesus.

Jesus said, *"Anyone who loves his father or mother more than me is not worthy of me; anyone who loves his son or daughter more than me is not worthy of me; and anyone who does not take his cross and follow me is not worthy of me"* (Matt. 10:37-38 NIV).

We can all find reasons in this world to hold us back from a life of truly serving and following Christ. But Jesus wants our love and loyalty to Him. He wants us to drop our self-serving ambitions and to pick up our own cross and follow Him.

What does this mean? The Romans knew what it meant to take up your cross. It meant going to your death! For all Christians it means at the minimum denying self and seeking God's will for our lives. For some it may mean death! Yes, this sounds harsh! In a new world of headlines of religious martyrdom, this may even sound crazy and scary. But as Christians on the mission field, this means something extremely opposite of those headlines.

We as Christians are being sent by our Lord to share His message of love in words and in actions. Are we truly willing to go all the way to share God's love, the Good News of the Gospel with this world, wherever that may take us? Into any place or situation, whether this takes us into harm's way or not? Are we willing to fully trust Him with our lives?

In many places around the world, Christians are persecuted, beaten, imprisoned, and even killed because of their faith. The mission field is potentially a dangerous place with wars, famine, disease, and many other extreme situations. But those are the same reasons why we are called to begin with—to show God's love to this hurting world. Whether it is to an AIDS orphan living in the gutter or in war torn or disease stricken areas of the world, we are called to share God's love through our actions and in our words. This is our Call! Was not Christ's death on the cross for each and every soul on this earth?

When I first started being involved with missions, I have to admit I just believed that God would protect us no matter what, and He does for the most part. I have witnessed many miracles concerning God's guidance and protection. He takes a very active part in our obedience to His Call. But I have also met a missionary dedicated to helping the plight of Sudanese refugees, who lost his life and become a martyr because of his faith. I also traveled into the Amazon rainforest to visit the Auca Indians, the same Indians that are world famous for killing five missionaries back in 1956. They are now a totally Christian community as a result of those five missionaries faithfulness, and indirectly through them, some thirty-seven indigenous communities inside the Amazon are now being reached. So what is my point? We need to trust our Lord and Savior to give us an abundantly full life, serving Him in the Call He has placed upon our lives!

I have seen many people that have answered this Call, living the most exciting, fulfilling lives, in some of the most exotic places of the world. They would not trade their lives for anything. The average Christian reading this may not fathom the blessings that await them if only they could or would seek out and follow God's Call.

In Jesus' own words the Bible says, *"I assure you that everyone who has given up house or brothers or sisters or mother or father or children or property, for my sake and for the Good News, will receive now in return, a hundred times as many houses, brothers, sisters, mothers, children, and property—along with persecutions. And in the world to come that person will have eternal life"* (Mark 10:29-30 NLT)

What do you really have to lose anyway, especially if you are someone who has picked up your cross already; you are already dead to self! God promises to give you a wonderful and fulfilling life of doing the one most important thing to do on this earth. That one thing is a life of showing, sharing, and spreading God's love both through our actions and the sharing of His Word!

BRAD GUICE
author and photographer

LIVING THE BOOK OF ACTS

Luke, the author of the book of Acts never completed writing it. Why? The ending is still being written today by us, His disciples, and will continue being written until the Gospel reaches all the way to the ends of the earth and Christ returns.

Most people think that this work is for someone else to accomplish. But it is for all of us as His disciples to act upon.

Acts 1:8 states, "But you will receive power when the Holy Spirit comes on you; and you will be my witnesses in Jerusalem, and in all Judea and Samaria, and to the ends of the earth" (NIV). The book of Acts is the working through of Jesus' last words. The Great Commission is for each and every one of His disciples to be witnesses—witnesses unto Jesus, to share the Good News of who He is and all He has done! Christ's death on the cross was a love letter from our almighty God to each and every person on this earth, and we are commissioned to share this message of love with the entire world.

"How can I possibly make a difference?" you ask. "I have no special skills…this must not be for me to answer…it must be for someone else to answer this Call. I could not possibly go to the ends of the earth!"

By reading this book, *The Call to Missions*, you have read a collection of testimonies from a limited number of individuals and ministries. You can easily see the impact of a single individual life and how it can make a profound difference in the lives of others with God's help. Think of the thousands of ministries spread out across this country and the world, and the impact God is making through the combined efforts of each individual. This is the Call to missions—each and every individual's participation matters, and this is how He will ultimately fulfill His Great Commission.

So what is our part? Jesus gave us an outline of how we can accomplish this task in Acts 1:8. He says, "You will be my witnesses in Jerusalem, and in all Judea and Samaria, and to the ends of the earth." Jerusalem was the disciple's home. For all of us who cannot go to the ends of the earth, we need to start right at home and work our way outward. Pray for our unsaved family members and share the Gospel with the boldness and power of the Holy Spirit. And more importantly, live a life as an example of Christ to all those around us on a daily basis.

We next need to get involved with our own churches and see what community outreaches we can participate in helping our churches to be positive influences on the needs of the community around us. Then we need to work our way outward to eventually go to the ends of the earth…to become involved with missions work around the world, supporting missionaries, praying for their needs and praying for the nations…to seek out and give to charities and mission programs that are close to your heart.

All of this, we do, not just to share the Gospel but also to show Christ's love to the poor, the lost, the sick, and the needy. We should always be willing to share Christ's love with the least of these of this world. Always remembering the importance of one soul! So many people and ministers these days want a huge ministry, to preach to the masses, and to be part of mega churches. There is nothing ultimately wrong with the desire to reach masses of people. But we have to be careful not to lose sight of the true heart of God. Jesus' heart is and will always be for

the one lost soul, and the humility that it may take for us to reach that soul. He would leave the ninety-nine sheep to go after the one lost lamb. Jesus would have gone all the way to the cross for just one of us. We too need to be willing to go the distance that it takes to reach a single person's life, even if it means to lower ourselves onto our knees and into a gutter to help a homeless orphan. This is what true religion is!

Our lives and ministries will truly be blessed by God and ultimately be of the greatest service to Him when He sees that our good works are not done for the accolades and praises of the world around us, but through our truly laid down lives they are done as pure offerings for His glory and advancement of His kingdom!

The Call to Missions is to be involved in the world around us, putting our faith in action, being active in working through His Great Commission. It is an exciting life when we live the book of Acts!

— BRAD GUICE

Mission Quotes

"God isn't looking for people of great faith, but for individuals ready to follow Him" - *Hudson Taylor*

"If God has fit you to be a missionary, I would not have you shrivel down to be a king." - *Charles Spurgeon*

"There is more hunger in the world for love and appreciation than for bread." - *Mother Teresa*

"He must increase, but I must decrease" (John 3:30) - *John the Baptist*

"This generation of Christians is responsible for this generation of souls on the earth!" - *Keith Green*

"Christ alone can save the world, but Christ cannot save the world alone." - *David Livingstone*

"I have but one candle of life to burn, and I would rather burn it out in a land filled with darkness than in a land flooded with light" - *John Keith Falconer*

"You have one business on Earth - to save souls." - *John Wesley*

When *James Calvert* went as a missionary to the cannibals of the Fiji Islands, the ship captain tried to turn him back, saying, "You will lose your life and the lives of those with you if you go among such savages." To that, Calvert replied, "We died before we came here."

"Let my heart be broken with the things that break God's heart" - *Bob Pierce,* (founder of World Vision)

"Here am I. Send me" (Isaiah 6:8) - *The Prophet Isaiah*

"The Great Commission is not an option to be considered; it is a command to be obeyed" - *Hudson Taylor*

"We must be global Christians with a global vision because our God is a global God." - *John Stott*

"Had I cared for the comments of people, I should never have been a missionary." - *C.T. Stud*

"If you can't feed a hundred people, then feed just one." - *Mother Teresa*

"Sympathy is no substitute for action." - *David Livingstone*

"Here is a test to find whether your mission on earth is finished: If you are alive, it isn't." - *Richard Bach*

"Today Christians spend more money on dog food than missions" - *Leonard Ravenhill*

"You can give without loving. But you cannot love without giving." - *Amy Carmichael*

"The opposite of love is not hate, it's indifference." - *C.S. Lewis*

"Expect great things from God; attempt great things for God" - *William Carey*

"If you found a cure for cancer, wouldn't it be inconceivable to hide it from the rest of mankind? How much more inconceivable to keep silent the cure from the eternal wages of death." - *Dave Davidson*

"Become the change you want to see in the world." - *Mother Teresa*

"If Jesus Christ be God and died for me, then no sacrifice can be too great for me to make for Him."
- *C.T. Studd*

"I will place no value on anything I possess or anything I may do, except in relation to the Kingdom of Christ." - *David Livingstone*

The great evangelist *D.L. Moody* was asked, "What would you do today if you knew Jesus Christ was coming tomorrow?" His answer came, "I would plant a tree."

"Is not the commission of our Lord still binding upon us? Can we not do more than now we are doing?"
- *William Carey*

"We talk of the 'Second Coming'; half the world has never heard of the first." - *Oswald J. Smith*

"If a commission by an earthly king is considered a honor, how can a commission by a Heavenly King be considered a sacrifice?" - *David Livingstone*

"The true greatness of any church in not how many it seats but how many it sends!" - *Unknown*

"Good works are links that form a chain of love." - *Mother Teresa*

"'Not called!' did you say? 'Not heard the call,' I think you should say. Put your ear down to the Bible, and hear Him bid you go and pull sinners out of the fire of sin. Put your ear down to the burdened, agonized heart of humanity, and listen to its pitiful wail for help. Go stand by the gates of hell and hear the damned entreat you to go to their father's house and bid their brothers and sisters and servants and masters not to come there. Then look Christ in the face—whose mercy you have professed to obey—and tell Him whether you will join heart and soul and body and circumstances in the march to publish His mercy to the world." - *William Booth* (founder of the Salvation Army)

"I want to be an influencer, a light! If I help to show one person the way to God, if I can make one person question the meaning of life and find it, I will have fulfilled my goal and part of my purpose for living."
- *B J Higgins* (*15 year-old boy who died as a result of going on the missions field*)

"To know the will of God, we need an open Bible and an open map." - *William Carey*

"Some wish to live within the sound of a chapel bell; I wish to run a rescue mission within a yard of hell."
- *C.T. Studd*

"Never pity missionaries; envy them. They are where the real action is—where life and death, sin and grace, Heaven and Hell converge." - *Robert C. Shannon*

"God had only one Son and he made that Son a missionary." - *David Livingstone*

Testimonial Contributors
MINISTRY CONTACT INFORMATION

Aidchild
P.O. Box 26100
Christiansted, VI 00824-2100
www.aidchild.org
Email: director@aidchild.org

African Prison Ministries, Inc.
48 Wall Street, 27th Floor
New York, NY 10005
www.apmin.org
Tel: 212-346-9009

A.S.A.M. enr.
Delmas 75 Cassagniole Prolonge #5
haiti-asam.blogspot.com
Email: asam.ministries@hotmail.com
Tel: 509 3 667 9580

Awe Star Ministries
P.O. Box 470265
Tulsa, OK 74147
www.awestar.org
Email: awestar@awestar.org
Tel: 1-800-Awe Star (293-7827)

Bethel China
40 Highland Ave.
Barrington, RI 02806 USA
www.bethelchina.org
Email: info@bethelchina.org
Tel: 830-625-4527

Children-N-Christ
http://geocities.com/childrennchrist/

City of Refuge
www.ciudadrefugio.org
Email: ciudadrefugio@une.net.co

Doctors for Life International – USA
333 West 57th Street – Suite 810
New York, NY 10019
www.doctorsforlifeinternational.com
Email: mail@dfl.org.za

Elim Fellowship
1703 Dalton Road
Lima, NY 14485-9516
www.elimfellowship.org

Elisabeth Elliot
www.elisabethelliot.org

Emma's Kids
Church of God World Missions
2490 Keith Street - P. O. Box 8016
Cleveland, TN 37320-8016
www.cogwm.org   Project #715-0116
Email: emmaskids@gmail.com
Tel: 800-345-7492

Empower Ministries International
6000 Fairview Road, Suite 1200
Charlotte, NC 28210
www.emintl.org
Email: office@emintl.org
Tel: 800-575-1863

Faith in Action, Inc.
P.O. Box 451346
Kissimmee, FL 34745-1346
www.FIAministries.org
Email: michaelandrocky@mac.com
Tel: 407-574-6253

F.R.O.M. Ministries, Inc.
P.O. Box 210644 Anchorage, Alaska 99521-0644
www.fromministries.org
Tel: 907-569-7000

Global Community Development Ministries, Inc.
1262 Alabama Highway 77
LaFayette, AL 36862
Email: gcdmharmon@charter.net
Tel: 334-459-0071

GlobeLink Foundation
706 N. Lindenwood Drive, Suite 100
Olathe, KS 66062
www.globelinkfoundation.org
Tel: 512-772-1751 Skype International

Global Ministry Teams
a training & facilitating agency
P.O. Box 19434
Shreveport, LA 71149
www.globalministryteams.org
Email: irvingmt@me.com
Tel: 318-671-7100

Good Shepherd Homes
PO Box 17527
Pittsburgh, PA 15235, USA
www.gsh.org.in

Harvest Evangelism, Inc.
P.O. Box 2888
Opelika, AL 36803
www.harvestevangelism.org
Email: missions@harvestevangelism.org
Tel: 334-332-3932

House of Life
45 Pickering Street, Durban 4001 South Africa
http://houseoflifeministries4jesus.blogspot.com/
Email: luna_petra@yahoo.com

Missionary Ventures International
P.O. Box 593550
Orlando, FL 32859-3550
www.missionaryventures.org
Email: info@mvi.org
Tel: 407-859-7322

Pro-Health International - USA
6003B Landmark Drive
Charlotte, NC 28270
www.prohealthinternational.org
Email: info@prohealthinternational.org
Tel: 704-804-4436

Regions Beyond Evangelism, Inc.
P.O. Box 700513 Tulsa, OK 74170
Email: RegionsBe@aol.com
Tel: 918-254-7253

Steve Parsons Music Ministries
www.steveparsons.net
Email: info@steveparsons.net

Times Square Church
TSC Missions
1657 Broadway, 4th Floor
New York, NY 10019
www.tscnyc.org
Tel: 212-541-6300

John Weaver
books available on Amazon.com
Inside Afghanistan
A Flame on the Front Line

World Aid New York
1657 Broadway, 4th Floor
New York, NY 10019
www.worldaidnewyork.org
Tel: 800-709-2771

World Challenge, Inc.
P.O. Box 260 Lindale, TX 75771-0260
www.worldchallenge.org
Tel: 903-963-8626

World Challenge Missions
1775 Jet Stream Drive, #105
Colorado Springs, CO 80921
www.worldchallenge.org
Tel: 719-487-7888

The Call on Your Heart

An Invitation

If you have been reading this book, and you find that there has been a stirring in your own heart, and you find yourself wanting to know God the way these individuals know Him who have contributed to this book. You too can have your own personal relationship with Jesus Christ. Would you like to receive Jesus as your personal Lord and Savior? If so, it is simple and life changing!

Pray with me

"God, I confess with my mouth and believe with my heart that Jesus Christ is your Son, and that He died on the cross, and He rose from the dead so that I might be forgiven and have eternal life in heaven. Jesus, I ask you this day to become my Lord and Savior and to forgive me of my sins as I repent from them. I invite you, Lord, to change my life, and to rule and reign in my heart from this day forward. In Jesus' name Amen."

I believe that if you prayed this prayer that you are now saved, for the Bible says:

"If you confess with your mouth that Jesus is Lord and believe in your heart that God raised him from the dead, you will be saved. For it is by believing in your heart that you are made right with God, and it is by confessing with your mouth that you are saved" (Romans 10:9,10 NLT).

"For God so loved the world that he gave his one and only Son, so that everyone who believes in him will not perish but have eternal life" (John 3:16 NLT).

Proceeds from this book

A significant portion of the proceeds from this book
will be donated to the following charities:

Please Pass the Bread
www.pleasepassthebread.org

Child Cry
www.childcrynyc.org

World Aid New York
www.worldaidnewyork.org

Additional donations will be made to various
missions programs and missionaries around the world

Jesus said,

"Peace be with you!

As the Father has sent me,

I am sending you."

John 20: 21 NIV

✝